MEMOIRS OF THE AMERICAN FOLKLORE SOCIETY • VOLUME 48 • 1957

MYTHOLOGY AND VALUES

An Analysis of
Navaho Chantway Myths

BY KATHERINE SPENCER

PHILADELPHIA   •   AMERICAN FOLKLORE SOCIETY   •   1957

International Standard Book Number 0–292–73528–6
Library of Congress Catalog Card Number 57–13891
Printed in the United States of America

Third Printing, 1975

Distributed by the University of Texas Press, Austin, Texas 78712

PREFACE

This analysis of Navaho chantway myths was carried out in connection with the Comparative Study of Values of the Laboratory of Social Relations, Harvard University. The multi-faceted approach to the investigation of cultural values embodied in the Values Study opened up some useful perspectives on the analysis of mythology. Among those associated with the Values Study, I am particularly indebted to Clyde Kluckhohn for his generous encouragement and support during my earlier work on Navaho materials and for his care in making critical comments at several stages of the work on mythology. I am also grateful to Evon Z. Vogt for his professional and administrative support and to Ethel Albert for the benefit of her critical discussion of a number of theoretical problems.

The manuscript was completed in 1952 and submitted in substantially its present form to the Department of Anthropology of the University of Chicago as a doctoral dissertation. It was prepared for publication in 1954, with some slight revision and the addition, principally in footnotes, of new materials that had appeared in the literature up to that time. My initial interest in mythology as a graduate student was stimulated by Manuel Andrade and A. R. Radcliffe-Brown, and I am grateful to Robert Redfield and Fred Eggan for their advice and guidance in completing the dissertation. The Department of Anthropology, University of Chicago, kindly made available microfilms of the unpublished collection of mythological texts and translations by Father Berard Haile.

For financial support in the preparation and publication of the manuscript I am indebted to the Values Study for funds supplied under their grant from the Rockefeller Foundation. Publication has been made possible by the support of the Values Study, the American Folklore Society, and the generous assistance of the Bollingen Fund.

Cambridge, Massachusetts   Katherine Spencer
August, 1956

CONTENTS

		Page
	PREFACE	v
I.	INTRODUCTION	1
II.	NAVAHO CHANTWAY MYTHS	11
III.	PLOT CONSTRUCTION AND VALUE THEMES	18
	The Pattern of Plot Construction	19
	A. The Hero's Predicament	21
	B. The Hero's Rescue and Acquisition of Power.	23
	C. The Hero's Family and Affinal Relations.	26
	Value Themes.	30
	A. Health and Illness	31
	B. Power and Knowledge	33
	C. Family Relationships	35
	D. Self-Assertion and Responsibility.	37
IV.	EXPLANATORY ELEMENTS	41
	Health, Fertility, Ritual Observance, Sex and Family Relations, Aggression, Irresponsibility, Property, Animal Origins, Miscellaneous	
V.	SANCTIONS AND STANDARDS	51
	Introduction.	51
	Subsistence and Property.	54
	A. Subsistence	54
	B. Poverty.	55
	C. Responsibility	58
	Sex and Marriage	60
	Family and Kin	65
	A. Parents and Children	66
	B. Siblings	69
	Some Aspects of Interpersonal Relations	73
	A. Companionship and Hospitality	74
	B. Aggression	77
VI.	CONCLUSIONS.	86
	Review of Findings	86
	Discussion of Theoretical Problems.	95
VII.	ABSTRACTS OF CHANTWAY MYTHS	100
	Hail Way	100
	Water Way	107
	Male Shooting Way	116
	Big Star Way	122
	Mountaintop Way	126

Prostitution Way 134
Moth Way 148
Beauty Way 150
Night Way 155
    The Visionary 156
    The Stricken Twins 162
Plume Way 164
Navaho Wind Way 176
Chiricahua Wind Way 184
Eagle Way 189
Bead Way 194
Flint Way 202
Ghostway Ritual of Male Shooting Way 208
Enemy Way 211

VIII.   REFERENCES 219
    Notes 219
    Bibliography 235

I. INTRODUCTION

The present study proposes to explore a portion of Navaho mythology to see what light it throws on the life view and values of the people whose literature it represents. This is primarily an anthropological investigation and as such has precedent in anthropological studies of cultural reflection in myth. These studies have been concerned with establishing the fact of cultural reflection and with exploring the extent of this reflection. Boas' analysis of Tsimshian and Kwakiutl mythologies provided the impetus to and classic example of such cultural analysis,[1] and later workers have pursued some of the implications of this approach with reference to other bodies of mythology.[2] The fact of cultural reflection has been amply documented by these studies. In the functionalist tradition cultural reflection in mythology has been accepted as a premise rather than raised as a question for investigation; it has formed a basis, implicit or explicit, for analyzing the manner in which a specific body of mythology contributes to the operation of the socio-cultural system in which it participates.[3]

In presenting descriptive material, many of these studies have indicated the mythological reflection of the native life view and values — by the use of such terms as native values, motivations, mental life, mode of life and thoughts of the people — but they have not systematically pursued this particular type of data nor some of the problems involved in its analysis. Working in the Boas tradition but with a greater interest in the psychological correlates of cultural phenomena, Benedict has developed this facet of cultural analysis in her study of Zuni mythology and in her use of Japanese literature as a means of understanding the Japanese way of life.[4]

Use of literary and imaginative productions of a people as an avenue for better understanding their motivations and values has precedent also in the work of literary critics and social historians. Implicit in such studies is the assumption that these imaginative works have some significant relationship to the life view of their authors and, by extension, to the life view current in the cultural setting and period in which they were produced. For the most part such literary or historical interpretations are content with this assumption and do not concern themselves with the psychological and socio-cultural processes involved in this relationship. The analogous anthropological use of the myths and folklore of nonliterate peoples has had to be more explicit about the processes operating in the relationship of such imaginative productions to the socio-cultural forms with which they are associated. At the same time some of the particular properties of myth and folklore, as contrasted with the literature of complex civilizations, offer a clearer field for investigating these relationships. We have in mind here both the more homogeneous character of nonliterate societies and

1

also such characteristics of myth and folklore as their "communal authorship" and their intimate connection with ritual forms. On the anthropological side, the work already referred to — of Boas and his followers and of the functionalists — has been concerned with some of these basic problems in the relationship of folklore to its cultural context.

From another direction, the development of a psychology of personality which stresses the operation of unconscious mental processes has given impetus to the study of the psychological mechanisms operating in the creation and perpetuation of popular imaginative productions. Again, the particular properties of myth, which freely utilizes symbolic expression and abounds in representations of fantasied fears and wish fulfilments, offer a fruitful ground for psychological investigation. Tendencies that are not freely accessible to consciousness seem to come to clearer expression here than in the more realistic literature of civilization. The reason why this should be so is not entirely clear, but, given this kind of data, it should be possible to utilize some of the psychological principles which have elsewhere proved useful in the interpretation of fantasy to supplement the anthropological approach to mythological materials.

In the present analysis the narrowing of focus from the wide range of cultural reflection to deal more intensively with values provides a second reason for introducing psychological principles. Values clearly have a psychological as well as a cultural dimension. They are linked on the one hand with motivations to action within the individual and on the other with cultural standards which form the external societal reference against which these individual and personal motivations are measured and judged. Thus, both the subject matter (values) and the expressive vehicle (myth) of our study have important psychological connections which provide an opportunity, and even an obligation, to cut across the traditional lines of academic disciplines.

Values [5]

What we broadly term a people's life view includes their beliefs and ideas about the nature of man, of the universe, and of man's relations to this universe and to his fellow men. Within this comprehensive area of the life view we may distinguish two classes of ideas: first, those that are existential, that explain the what and how of existence; and second, those that are normative, that are concerned with what "should be," with norms of taste, propriety and ethical rightness. In the expression of a people's life view existential and normative elements are not always, nor even usually, held clearly separate; they interpenetrate and blend together. However, in establishing a working definition of value for the present analysis, it becomes important to distinguish between these two elements and to indicate our area of interest with reference to them. It is on the normative elements in the Navaho life view that our interest will center.

In Kluckhohn's analysis of the notion of value, three essential elements are specified — the affective, the cognitive, and the conative.
His definition of value will be utilized in this study: "a conception, explicit or implicit, distinctive of an individual or characteristic of a
group, of the desirable which influences the selection between available
modes, means, and ends of action."[6] The cognitive and conative aspects of value phenomena appear in the processes of judgment, apprais-
al, and selection indicated in this definition. The affective element
centers on the key word "desirable," which implies wish and motivation
within the individual actor but also a normative standard against which
these wishes are measured and in accordance with which their expression in action may be modified. Kluckhohn emphasizes the fact that
the "desired" and the "desirable" may not be identical, that motivation and value are not synonymous. In accordance with this definition
we may think of values as ideas which are held as normative standards. As a shorthand formulation we may think of the operation of
values as the influence of "oughts" on action.

The present study will be concerned with the operation of normative
ideas in Navaho culture as they are expressed in mythology. Attention
will focus on those standards that carry a feeling of obligation and
have a compelling influence on behavior, insofar as they can be identified, rather than on those that seem to reflect simple preference. In
other words, the principal interest will be in the area of what would
popularly be understood as Navaho ethics.

We have noted how both existential and normative ideas enter into
the total life view of a people. Cultural practice or custom, in the
sense of ideal pattern, may be thought of as action that is congruent
with underlying cultural beliefs or ideas. In the case of normative
ideas, such cultural practice accords with native aesthetic or ethical
standards, that is, an act is felt to be right and proper in a formal or
moral sense; in the case of existential ideas, it is congruent with the
native conception of reality, that is, an act is felt to be effective in an
instrumental or causal sense. When practice and belief are thus
viewed in conjunction, the theoretical distinction between existential
and normative ideas may become blurred; in actual life both causal and
moral considerations may participate in varying degrees, or may even
be felt to coincide, in the explanation for a given course of action.
Thus, for example, in the mythological data standards of hospitality, of
honesty, and of appropriate or inappropriate sexual behavior clearly
contain a large normative element. But even in these areas, and more
clearly so in judgments and actions relating to health and illness, existential elements also enter the picture. The Navaho rule against
brother-sister incest, whose origin is traced to a mythological incident,
states at the same time the consequences of its infringement, i.e., that
the participants will "go crazy." In the mythological incident to which
this rule is referred the offenders "go crazy" and rush into the fire
like moths. The belief that this particular kind of insanity is caused
by incestuous activity is existential in nature and at the same time

normative in its effect. The numerous etiological explanations which
attribute illness to violation of ritual taboos likewise have a prominent
existential element.

In much of the mythological material we shall find this blending of
normative and existential ideas. For value notions which are generalized and organized and which include definite existential ideas, Kluckhohn uses the term value-orientations. He refers to a value-orienta-
tion as "a set of linked propositions embracing both value and existential elements," and then goes on to elaborate the relations between these
elements: [7]

> ... Such a "definition of the life situation" for the group contains more than
> normative and aesthetic propositions; it contains also existential propositions
> as to the nature of "what is." The relationship between existential and nor-
> mative propositions may be thought of as two-way: on the one hand, the nor-
> mative judgments must be based on the group's notion of what in fact exists:
> on the other hand, the group's conception of the universe (of "what *is*" — "what
> is natural or obvious") will presumably be based partly on prior normative
> orientations and on interests. What "must be done" is usually closely re-
> lated to what is believed to be the "nature of things"; contrariwise, beliefs
> about "what is" are often disguised assumptions of "what ought to be."

Although we wish to deal principally with normative elements, their
occurrence in these mixed expressions will necessitate considering a
broader range of phenomena in which the normative elements are often
embedded. In the myths we find evidence of certain generalized notions
which form an important part of the Navaho life view and which contain
both normative and existential components. Because of its literary
character, the mythological material lends itself to a thematic analysis.
These generalized notions can be identified as themes which recur in
different forms and contexts throughout the stories, and we shall refer
to them as "value themes." The connotations of the term "theme,"
understood as a "subject of discourse" which lends itself to variation
or development, make it appropriate to this use of literary material.

The "value themes" are in their mixed character similar to what
Kluckhohn has termed value-orientations and we might also have used
this term. However, they do not answer all of the requirements set by
the definition of value-orientations. Although the major themes here
identified have some logical interconnections, they do not form a fin-
ished system, a complete and organized totality which represents the
Navaho life view.[8] For this reason a term with more general connotations has been retained, and the value themes here identified are
viewed as important elements which enter into such an overall description of Navaho value-orientations.

The value phenomena with which this investigation will be concerned
are, then, of two orders. Such normative ideas as are contained in
ethical or moral principles will be sought in the mythological material.
In addition, the plot construction and form of the stories will be examined for more general value themes which combine existential and
normative elements. For convenience of exposition we shall deal first

with the value themes (see III), since description and analysis of the plot types will provide a background and familiarity with the story content whereby the ethical principles can better be perceived in their appropriate context.

Method and Procedure

Except in distributional and historical studies, in functional interpretations, and to a lesser degree in literary studies, the use of folklore in cultural analysis does not seem to have received the attention that the rich body of available data would warrant. Anthropological methods for utilizing this data have by and large not been systematically developed. The studies of cultural reflection by Boas and his followers represent one type of cultural analysis, but they do not seem to have been fruitful in opening paths and problems for investigation beyond the fact of cultural reflection. Perhaps their most immediate usefulness is in presenting a body of data suitable for historical and distributional analysis. For the most part the resultant picture of correspondences between myth and custom in this type of analysis has a certain flatness; the living connections of the material are lost. There would seem to be two directions in which these connections may be profitably established: one is in the functional relation with socio-cultural forms, and the other is in the dynamic relation to individual psychological processes. The former is the field of interest of the anthropological functionalists; the latter reaches over into personality psychology and the more recently developed area of "personality and culture."

In its anthropological aspects, the present analysis will follow the precedent of studies of cultural reflection, but it will also attempt to establish functional connections between the mythological value data and certain aspects of the Navaho socio-cultural system. This process will entail identifying correspondences between values in the mythological picture and in ethnological observation, but when possible it will go further than this to indicate the possible functional relationships of the value data to the pattern of life experience. For example, the mythological picture of the youthful hero's separation from his family in a series of self-assertive acts will be viewed in relation to the circumstances and pressures of Navaho family life. This approach, then, involves a double examination of relationships — first, the correspondence of the mythological and ethnological representations of value data; and, second, the relationship of the value data as it appears in the myths to other aspects of culture.

In its psychological aspects, the mythological analysis will utilize pertinent principles from personality psychology, and the rationale for their use warrants some preliminary discussion.[9] It is of interest that the original impetus to studies of cultural reflection was in part a reaction against an overly narrow psychological interpretation of the symbolic content of myth. In undertaking the Tsimshian analysis Boas

was partially interested in refuting the then-current theory, typified in
Ehrenreich's work, that folklore originated from the contemplation of
natural phenomena. He concluded, by contrast, that the origin of folklore must rather be sought in the "ordinary play of imagination" on the
social life of the people concerned.[10] Elsewhere he emphasized the
role of human wish fulfilment tendencies, as expressed for example in
myths about the return of the dead: "When we are filled with an ardent
desire, imagination lets us see the desire fulfilled." He saw the ultimate origin of folklore in the play of imagination on life experiences,
the specific form of the resulting product being influenced both by the
particular cultural phrasing of life experience and by the type of literary material that comes to hand through dissemination.[11] What he
terms the "ordinary play of imagination" is a psychological datum
which he, quite properly in his framework, accepted as given. In the
light of developing knowledge about the operation of imaginative processes and because of the close linkage of our particular subject matter
with motivation, it becomes both possible and desirable to examine
further the psychological basis of mythological phenomena.

In individual psychology imaginative processes are related to human
need satisfactions. These needs may be felt as positive or negative, as
a reaching out for something desired or as an avoidance of something
feared. The need may be experienced consciously or, due to repression, the basic impulse may be unconscious and become experienced
only in an altered form. The inner need, whether conscious or not,
evokes images which are connected with it in past experience.[12] In the
unimpeded process of need satisfaction, these images help to set in
motion activity that will answer the need. Thus, in practical planning
one "imagines" the steps necessary for the successful completion of
future activity. For various reasons, both within the individual and
inherent in the outer reality with which he deals, it is often not possible
to proceed to actual satisfaction of needs. Interference with this satisfaction does not, however, eliminate either the need itself or the
imaginative processes connected with it. We shall use the term "fantasy" to designate the elaboration of these imaginative processes. In
some circumstances, when external deprivation or internal conflict
prevent satisfaction, the mechanism of projection may come into play;
the images may be projected and assume for the subject the aspect of
reality, as in the extreme cases of dreams and hallucinations. In certain types of myths and folklore the fantasied objects and events are
felt as a "reality" which happened sometime in the remote past.

In its symbolic qualities mythological fantasy is akin to dreams.
According to the principles of Freudian psychology, unconscious impulses may come to expression in various symbolic forms. The original reason for repression of these impulses and their exclusion from
consciousness is the anxiety and conflict aroused by their recognition.
They are allowed expression only in a disguised form acceptable to the
conscious parts of the personality. The symbolism of dreams is one
such expression. Although symbolic activity is a general characteristic

of human mental processes, the exaggerated and bizarre quality of some dream symbolism seems to indicate areas of special conflict held in uneasy equilibrium by the other forces of the personality. In their very exaggeration there seems to be at the same time a need for a deeper disguise and a warning signal of danger.

Similar processes are assumed to be operating in the production of myths and in the appeal which these fantasy products have for their audience. In individual psychology both the extent of indulgence in fantasy and the content of the fantasy are related to various interferences with the satisfaction of physical and emotional needs. In other words, the excessive utilization of fantasy indicates areas of stress or conflict in need satisfaction in actual life. Although a direct transfer from individual to group phenomena cannot be made without safeguards, the essential function of fantasy in myth is assumed to be similar. In myth, as in individual fantasy, those human impulses and needs whose satisfaction in actuality is difficult or impossible of achievement find expression, either in relatively simple and straightforward wish fulfilment or in disguised and symbolic form. It is assumed that a fantasy theme must have public appeal in order to be perpetuated in folklore and that this fact will result in elimination of idiosyncratic elements of fantasy springing from deviant individuals and will insure the representativeness of the final product for the given society.

In all cultures there are limitations and difficulties in the way of successful expression of human impulses and in the satisfaction of human needs. We may think of these as due to: 1) the "natural" conditions of human life (of the biological organism and of his physical environment); 2) the necessary"social" conditions of human life (the fact of adjustment to other individuals in group living); and 3) the cultural rules and standards particular to a given group. Many of these limitations are, in a sense, universal in incidence, for example, the necessity to work for food, the necessity for sexual and emotional adjustments in the family unit, for control of hostility and aggression within the in-group. But the form in which they are cast and the relative severity of their impact will differ in accordance with environmental, social, and cultural variables. Many fantasy motifs in folklore are of such common occurrence that we can assume that they are related to general conditions of human life. Such, for example, would be the magical means of overcoming space by seven-league-boots or by travelling on a cloud or rainbow, the appearance of inexhaustible food supplies, supernatural marriages, magical weapons for conquest of rivals, magical curing, and many more.

However, the difference in treatment of fantasy elements as between different bodies of folklore are assumed to have some relation to actual differences in environmental conditions or in the social and cultural pressures characteristic of the groups in question. The particular fantasy themes emphasized in a given mythology should point to areas of strain and stress in actual life conditions. For example, the typical Zuni male fantasy of violent conquest over threatening female figures, as revealed in Benedict's analysis,[13] is presumably related to the stresses experienced by men in a female-dominated matrilineal society. Again, the preoccupation with in-group antagonisms and aggression in Zuni myths may be thus related to the apparent strictness with which explicit standards of mildness and cooperation are enforced in actual life. In the Navaho chantway myths the hero's continuous search both for dangerous experiences and for nurturant figures may prove to be likewise related to environmental and cultural pressures toward the particular brand of individualism characteristic of Navaho culture. It is for the clarification of problems of this order that we hope to utilize the psychological principles outlined above in dealing with the mythological data.

The analysis of value materials in the chantway myths will be approached in two complementary ways, one of which may be termed macroscopic and the other microscopic. First, the typical plot construction of the stories will be described with its variations. It is from the patterns thus delineated that the value themes will be drawn (see III). Secondly, the story content will be examined in greater detail to identify particular value elements and ethical principles as they appear in the mythological "explanation" of origins and in the sanctions and standards presented in mythological incidents (IV and V).

The analysis of plot construction and of the value themes revealed therein will necessarily be approached impressionistically.[14] This analysis will be documented by reference to the accompanying abstracts of the myths (VII), and the reader can compare the interpretations made with his own understanding of the mythological data. Themes which recur throughout the range of stories will be identified. The principal check on the validity of these value interpretations will lie in their congruence with ethnological findings and in the internal consistency of the resulting picture. Because of the fantasy nature of the mythological material, apparent contradictions between it and the ethnological picture are anticipated, but it is expected that such contradictions can be reconciled or explained in the light of psychological principles. Further, it is expected that such contradictions will point to areas of strain or uneasy adjustment between the demands of the socio-cultural system and the human needs of individuals living in it.

In the detailed examination of story content it will be possible to utilize more systematic methods for identifying value elements. Three principal types of evidence will be considered — the selfconscious "explanatory" statements made by the narrator to clarify or emphasize the significance of a mythological incident; the operation of sanctions in the dramatic action of the stories; and the regularities of interpersonal behavior portrayed in the stories as they point to standards of conduct. The nature of these types of evidence will be briefly indicated at this point, but more extended discussion of problems that arise in their use will be reserved for IV and V where their occurrence in the myths is analyzed.

In the study of mythology considerable attention has been devoted to
the occurrence of "explanatory elements" interpolated in the narrative
which explain how a mythological incident is related to present-day
beliefs or behavior.[15] Perhaps the most familiar of these are explanations of the origin of natural phenomena or of animal characteristics,
but social customs and ritual practices may also be accounted for in
this manner. In the chantway stories the narrator sometimes gives an
explicit statement of a moral rule and points out its origin in the action of the story. These explanatory elements represent self-conscious
value formulations of a different order from those found in the action
of the story itself, and they will collected and analyzed separately.

A second type of clearly identifiable value datum is found when the
dramatic action of the story calls forth positive or negative sanctions.
Sanction is here taken in its broadest sense, as the demonstration by
word or deed of approval or disapproval for an action or personality
trait. Such evidence of approval or disapproval constitutes one of the
principal operational indices suggested by Kluckhohn for the identification of values.[16] The stories provide an abundance of such material
in the penalties and punishments visited upon the hero as well as on
minor characters. The operation of both positive and negative sanctions
will therefore be analyzed. In connection with this analysis it will be
necessary to consider some special problems of interpretation that
arise from the fantasy character of the mythological material.

A third type of evidence bearing on values lies in certain patterned
regularities of behavior that seem to indicate role expectancies in
interpersonal relations. Such, for example, are the relationship patterns pictured between persons in certain kinship categories and the
reciprocal trickery and deceit practiced in relations with aliens. The
behavior portrayed seems to be implicitly accepted as appropriate or
proper even though it does not meet with explicit positive sanctions.
This type of evidence is judged significant in the delineation of standards of conduct, but it is more difficult to handle than is the material
on sanctions and, as will be indicated, it can be used only with certain
safeguards.

In the detailed examination of story content for the foregoing types
of evidence, various procedures for analysis were experimented with
and discarded as unworkable. One such procedure was analysis of the
content according to folklore motifs of the Aarne-Thompson classification;[17] another was content analysis by procedures similar to those
used in clinical psychology for projective materials, such as the
stories of the Murray Thematic Apperception Test.[18] Neither of these
approaches is oriented specifically to values; the motif classification
was not found to be sufficiently flexible while, on the other hand, the
projective test methods were too unstructured for the present purposes. The procedure finally utilized for ordering the mythological
data was similar in design to the topical classification of cultural
content used by the Human Relations Area Files (Yale cross-cultural
index).[19] A modified series of categories was set up, conditioned by

the mythological content and adapted to the purpose at hand. For example, topics dealing with material culture were eliminated and those dealing with interpersonal relations, personality traits, emotional reactions, different types of sanctions, etc., were expanded. The stories were systematically surveyed and the material in them was categorized according to such a scheme. In the detailed content analysis of V, the discussion of such topics as subsistence, sex, family relationships, and aggression will be based on the materials assembled in this way.

A concluding section (VI) will bring together the results of the impressionistic thematic analysis and those of the detailed examination of content to see to what extent they are in agreement and in what ways they may supplement each other. At this point it should be possible to draw some conclusions about the usefulness of these different approaches to mythological data. At the same time, the relationship of the mythological picture of values to the social and cultural forms of Navaho life will be reconsidered to see how the data of the present study bear on general problems in the functional relations between myth and other aspects of culture.

II. NAVAHO CHANTWAY MYTHS

The complex of ritual activities which constitute Navaho ceremonialism is directed toward control over supernatural forces for the welfare of the people. The chants or chantways represent only one ceremonial type but a type which holds an important position both in the formal ceremonial system and in the time and energy devoted to their performance. The chantways are performed to cure illness; they are held over a patient. Another smaller group of rites, known as blessingway rites, are performed to bring "positive blessings," protection and well-being. Although these blessingway rites are briefer and less complex than the curing ceremonials, in theory and in practice they form an essential part of the ceremonial system. Other principal classes of rites include divination to determine the cause of illness and to prescribe the proper ceremonial treatment, war and hunting rites (now obsolescent), and rites of passage (birth, initiation, puberty, marriage, death).[20]

Associated with most of these ritual forms are myths which tell how the ceremony in question originated. It is the origin myths of the curing ceremonials, or chantways, that are the subject of this study. These myths constitute a large portion of recorded Navaho mythology. Of an estimated 1500 published pages, less than one-third is devoted to various versions of the general origin myth, which recounts events of the emergence from the underworld and the exploits of the war gods in ridding the world of monsters.[21] The largest part of the remaining published material consists of chantway origin myths, which tell how the ceremony was obtained from supernaturals through the hero's exploits and trials. In theory these chantway myths branch off from the general origin myth at various points; some continue with a portion of their stories in common and later diverge to conclude their accounts of origin separately; in other cases the stories "meet" for a time at some common episode and again continue their separate courses. The total impression is of the weaving of single stories into an interconnected whole, although the pattern and connections are not formally systematized. Many episodes or types of episodes recur in different myths, and the significance of their recurrent use in plot construction will be discussed in the thematic analysis.

Abstracts of all available chantway origin myths have been prepared (see VII), with certain exceptions to be noted below. The attempt has been made to cover all published versions of a given myth. In addition, the unpublished manuscript collection of texts and translations by Father Berard Haile has been utilized.[22] Manuscripts in the Wetherill collection were also consulted but, because of their fragmentary form and often aberrant content, they have for the most part been referred to in footnotes rather than included in the abstracts.[23] The

11

published and manuscript sources have provided materials for abstracts of sixteen chantway myths plus the Enemy Way story.[24] A total
of somewhat over fifty versions were used in the preparation of these
abstracts. The number of versions available for the abstract of any
one story or portion thereof varies from one to eight.

Stories from Navaho mythology have been published since the 1880's
in widely scattered publications often difficult of access. This means
that in some cases there are several versions of the same myth recorded over a time span of fifty to sixty years. Some of the early versions are not completely identified but may be assigned to their proper
place in the body of chantway lore on the basis of their content. An
introductory statement to each of the abstracts in VII, gives notes on
the versions used as well as a summary of the story content and its
relation to other chantway stories. In view of the widely scattered
and uneven literature, it is hoped that the concordance of myths furnished by the abstracts and accompanying notes will prove useful in
its own right, independently of the value interpretations for which
they are here used.

The accompanying chart shows the place of these myths within the
total body of Navaho chantway lore. Navaho chantways may be divided
into three groups on the basis of similarities in ritual pattern, mythological associations and type of etiological factor against which the cure
is directed.[25] The largest group is that of the *holyway* chants, which
are employed when illness is traced to offenses against various supernaturals and holy people (such as lightning, thunder, winds, snakes, and
other animals). *Evilway* chants are used for curing sickness caused
by ghosts, either native or foreign. Upward-reaching-way, the myth of
which is not included in this study for reasons noted below, is the fun-
damental ceremony of this group. The Enemy Way rite used against
alien ghosts, although not a chant in itself, is associated with this
group. *Lifeway* chants, which are employed in cases of bodily injury,
constitute the third group, of which Flint Way is the representative
example. The complexities of Navaho ceremonialism do not, however,
allow the assignment of chantways to clearcut, separate compartments.
Although it is possible to specify certain chantways as belonging basi-
cally to one or the other of these groups, some may have variant forms
which allow their performance according to the ritual of another group
depending upon the purpose at hand.[26] Thus, Shooting Way is found in
both the holyway and the evilway groups in the accompanying chart.

The myths used in this study cover most of the important Navaho
chantways. A considerable number of those listed in the Wyman-
Kluckhohn classification are obsolete or obsolescent, and little is
known about their performance or about the accompanying myth (e.g.,
Dog Way, Raven Way, Awl Way). Several myths on which there is some
published material have purposely been omitted from this study. The
mythological backgrounds of Hand Trembling Way[27] and of Coyote Way[28]
are available in too fragmentary a form to be useful. The myth of Upward-reaching-way, or Moving-up-way, is largely concerned with

Navaho Chantway Myths

Wyman-Kluckhohn Chantway Classification	Versions of Corresponding Myth Utilized	
	In Abstracts	In Comparative Notes
Holyway Chants		
A. Shooting Chant Sub-Group		
Hail Way	Reichard, 1944a; Wheelwright, 1946a	
Water Way	Haile, 1932a (MS.); Wheelwright, 1946a (2 versions)	Coolidges, 1930; Wetherill, 1952
Male Shooting Way[29]	Newcomb and Reichard, 1937; Reichard, 1939; Reichard, 1934	Haile, 1947
Female Shooting Way		
Red Ant Way[30]		
Big Star Way[31]	Wheelwright, 1940	Wetherill, 1952
B. Mountain Chant Sub-Group		
Mountaintop Way[32]	Coolidges, 1930; Matthews, 1887; Wheelwright, 1951	Haile, 1946; Wetherill, 1952
Prostitution Way	Haile, 1931a (MS.); Kluckhohn, 1944; Pepper, 1908	
Way to Remove Somebody's Paralysis		
Moth Way	Haile, 1931b (MS.)	
Beauty Way	Haile, 1932b (MS.); Wheelwright, 1951	Coolidges, 1930; Curtis, 1907; Wetherill, 1952
C. God-Impersonators Sub-Group		
Night Way	Curtis, 1907; Matthews, 1902 (2 versions); Sapir and Hoijer, 1942; Stevenson, 1891; Wheelwright, 1938	Coolidges, 1930; Matthews, 1907; Wetherill, 1952
Big God Way		
Plume Way	Goddard, 1933; Matthews, 1897 and 1902; Sapir and Hoijer, 1942; Stevenson, 1891; Wetherill, 1952; Wheelwright, 1946a and 1946b (three versions)	Hill, 1938
Dog Way		
Coyote Way[33]		
Raven Way		

Wyman-Kluckhohn Chantway Classification	Versions of Corresponding Myth Utilized	
	In Abstracts	In Comparative Notes

D. Wind Chant Sub-Group

    Navaho Wind Way — Haile, 1932c (MS.); Hill and Hill, 1943a; Wheelwright, 1940 and 1946b; Wyman and Bailey, 1946 — Wyman and Kluckhohn, 1938

    Chiricahua Wind Way — Haile, 1932d and 1933 (Both MSS.)

E. Hand Trembling Way

F. Eagle Trapping Sub-Group

    Eagle Way — Newcomb, 1940a; Wheelwright, 1945 — Kluckhohn, 1941

    Bead Way — Hill and Hill, 1943b; Kluckhohn, 1941; Matthews, 1897; Reichard, 1939; Wheelwright, 1945 — Coolidges, 1930; Pepper, 1905; Wetherill, 1952

G. Group of obsolete Chants: Awl Way, Earth Way, Reared in Earth Way

Lifeway Chants

    Flint Way — Haile, 1943 (2 versions)

    Life Way

Evilway Chants (Ghostway)

A. Purification from Natives Sub-Group

    Upward-reaching-way

    Various evilway forms of chants appearing in holyway group, including *Ghostway Ritual of Male Shooting Way* — Haile, 1950

B. Purification from Aliens Sub-Group

    Enemy Way — Curtis, 1907; Haile, 1932b (MS.) and 1938a; Wheelwright, 1951 (2 versions)

    Two Went Back for Scalp Way

    Ghosts of Every Description Way

events of the general origin myth (events in the underworlds, the emergence, the first death, slaying of monsters), although it contains such additional incidents as changing-bear-maiden and the grinding skulls. Wyman and Bailey term this the basic myth of Navaho religion, from which the origin myths of most other ceremonials branch off at various points.[34] Because it thus duplicates the general origin myth, it falls outside the pattern of the other chantway myths and has not been included in this analysis.

The chart enumerates the mythological versions that have been collated in the abstracts as well as those to which comparative references are made in the introductory notes to the individual abstracts. The chart is adapted from the Wyman-Kluckhohn Navaho ceremonial classification.[35] To facilitate reference a separate list of the mythological sources used in the abstracts is also given at this point. (References which occur only in the comparative notes will be found in the general bibliography.) The chart, together with the references given above to myths of Hand Trembling Way, Coyote Way, and Upward-reaching-way, furnishes an index to the mythological materials connected with Navaho chantways.[36]

List of Mythological Sources

(Page numbers given here indicate length of mythological text. For complete references, see bibliography.)

Coolidges, Dane and Mary R.
    1930. Myth of the Mountain Chant. In *The Navaho Indians*, pp. 202-209.

Curtis, Edward S.
    1907. Legend of the Night Chant. In *The North American Indian*, pp. 111-116.

Goddard, Pliny E.
    1933. Game Story. In *Navajo Texts*, pp. 161-163.

Haile, Berard.
    1931a. Prostituting Way. Manuscript. 94 pp.
    1931b. Moth Way. Manuscript. 10 pp.
    1932a. Ceremony in the Water Way. Manuscript. 110 pp.
    1932b. Beauty Way. Manuscript. 91 pp.
    1932c. Navaho Wind Way Ceremony. Manuscript. 176 pp.
    1932d. Chiricahua Wind Ceremony of the Navaho. Manuscript. 147 pp.
    1933. Chiricahua Windway Chant. Manuscript. 259 pp.
    1938a. "Enemy Way Legend" and "The Group Dance." In *Origin Legend of the Navaho Enemy Way*, pp. 141-217.
    1943. Origin Legend of the Navaho Flintway. 319 pp.
    1950. Legend of the Ghostway Ritual in the Male Branch of Shootingway. 288 pp.

Hill, W. W., and Hill, Dorothy W.
    1943a. Frog Chases a Lewd Woman. In *Two Navajo Myths,* pp. 113-114.
    1943b. The Legend of Navajo Eagle-Catching-Way. Pp. 31-36.

Kluckhohn, Clyde
    1941. Episode from Eagle Way Chant Legend. In *Notes on Navajo Eagle Way,* pp. 7-9.
    1944. Prostitution Way Chant Legend. In *Navaho Witchcraft,* pp. 96-108.

Matthews, Washington
    1887. Myth of the Origin of Dsilyidje Qacal. In *The Mountain Chant,* pp. 387-417.
    1897. Natinesthani (Story of the Feather Chant). In *Navaho Legends,* pp. 160-194. The Great Shell of Kintyel (Beat Chant). In *Navaho Legends,* pp. 195-208.
    1902. "The Visionary" and "So, a Variant of the Visionary." In *The Night Chant,* pp. 159-171, 197-212.
    The Stricken Twins. In *The Night Chant,* pp. 216-265.
    The Whirling Logs. In *The Night Chant,* pp. 171-197.

Newcomb, Franc J.
    1940a. Origin Legend of the Navajo Eagle Chant. Pp. 50-77.

Newcomb, Franc J., and Reichard, Gladys A.
    1937. Myth of Male Shooting Chant. In *Sandpaintings of the Navajo Shooting Chant,* pp. 32-41.

Pepper, George H.
    1908. Ah-Jih-Lee-Hah-Neh, a Navajo Legend. Pp. 178-183.

Reichard, Gladys A.
    1934. Portion of Shooting Way Legend. In *Spider Woman,* pp. 194-195.
    1939. Legend of the Male Shooting Chant. In *Navajo Medicine Man,* pp. 38-73.
    Legend of the Bead Chant. In *Navajo Medicine Man,* pp. 26-36.
    1944a. The Story of the Navajo Hail Chant. 155 pp.

Sapir, Edward, and Hoijer, Harry
    1942. The Visionary. In *Navaho Texts,* pp. 137-259.
    A Legend of the Hollow Floating Log. In *Navaho Texts,* pp. 25-37.

Stevenson, James
    1891. The Brothers. In *Ceremonial of Hasjelti Dailjis,* pp. 280-284.
    The Floating Logs. In *Ceremonial of Hasjelti Dailjis,* pp. 278-279.

Wetherill, Louisa W.
    1952. Plumeway. In Wyman, *The Sandpaintings of the Kayenta Navaho,* pp. 88-89.

Wheelwright, Mary C.
    1938. Tleji or Yehbechai Myth. Pp. 1-13.
    1940. Myth of Sontso (Big Star). 13 pp.
    1945. Atsah or Eagle Catching Myth and Yohe or Bead Myth. 16 pp.
    1946a. Hail Chant Myth. In *Hail Chant and Water Chant*, pp. 3-45.
      Tohe or Water Chant (Versions I and II). In *Hail Chant and Water Chant*, pp. 55-100.
    1946b. Nilth Chiji Bakaji (Wind Chant) and Feather Chant. 15 pp.
    1951. Myth of Mountain Chant and Myth of Beauty Chant. 22 pp.

Wyman, Leland C., and Bailey, Flora L.
    1946. Navaho Striped Windway, an Injury-Way Chant. Pp. 213-238.

III. PLOT CONSTRUCTION AND VALUE THEMES

A Navaho chantway myth describes the origin of the associated curing ceremony, how it was obtained from supernaturals and made available for the use of earth people. The repetitive narrative pattern of these stories has long been recognized. They present the hero in some predicament from which he is extricated by supernatural aid. In this contact with the gods he obtains ritual knowledge and returns to teach the ceremony thus learned to his own people. The story is firmly linked with the ceremony and, depending on the purpose and thoroughness of recitation, may contain a detailed description of its proper performance.

In their interest in the complexities of Navaho ceremonialism, Navaho specialists have tended to concentrate their attention on the relation of myth to ceremony, to consider the myth in its function as warrant for and guide to chant performance. The present analysis proposes to use the material of these chantway stories for a different purpose, to see what light they throw on certain interests and preoccupations of the people whose literature they in part represent. Despite and within a relatively standardized formula, these stories present a surprising and gratifying fund of human material over and above their specific ritual associations. The patterns of plot construction reveal recurrent similarities of motivation and methods for resolving situations. The following analysis will attempt to identify these patterns and the value themes associated with them and to relate these themes to the actual circumstances of Navaho life.

In spite of a predominant preoccupation with the ritual correlates of Navaho mythology, some workers have directed attention to the life view and values reflected in these stories and to the psychological significance of their content. Reichard uses the content of both myth and ritual as an avenue to understanding the Navaho conception of the world and of man's nature; in them, for example, is embodied the Navaho conception of improving control over nature through knowledge.[37] Kluckhohn finds that the Navaho view the universe as orderly and lawful, and their attempt to obtain or maintain harmony in it is reflected in the myths as in other aspects of life.[38] On the psychological side, he sees the plots of chantway myths as furnishing a symbolic resolution of the intra-familial difficulties characteristic of Navaho society, and he points out how the mythological images of male and female characters mirror current conceptions of male and female roles in actual life.[39] Róheim specifically identifies oedipal elements in Navaho mythology and concludes, from this and other evidence, that the "spiritual life of the tribe is based on oedipal guilt feelings."[40] The work of these authors furnishes examples of how mythological materials can be related to native life experience. For the most part they have dealt with mythology

18

only peripherally or in conjunction with other data, although Róheim's
analysis relies heavily on myth and Reichard's interpretation of Navaho
religion is based on abundant data from both myth and ritual. The
present analysis will examine the mythological content for similar
purposes. Our approach to the mythological materials will be based on
recognition of the intimate connections between the mythological expressions of a people, their psychological manifestations and their
values.

The Pattern of Plot Construction

The chantway myths are hero stories; they recount the adventures
of a hero, more rarely of a heroine or of two brothers or sisters.
Typically, the hero experiences a series of misfortunes in which he
needs supernatural assistance if he is to survive. Sometimes he precipitates the misadventure himself by actively courting danger or intentionally disregarding prohibitions; sometimes catastrophe seems to be
visited upon him by external forces, apparently without his complicity
in provoking it; often responsibility for the mishap is left unclear and
indeterminate. As will be indicated later in the analysis, behind the
hero's seeming passivity in suffering catastrophe the stories show a
deep preoccupation with his active responsibility for provoking the
mishaps that plague him. Rejection by his family or ridicule and
scorn on the part of associates may set the stage for the hero's reckless behavior. His misadventures usually occur during sexual or
hunting exploits or while he is exploring merely out of curiosity.
Marriage may precipitate trials by a hostile father-in-law.

The hero's misadventures are usually bodily attack or capture by
animals, natural phenomena, supernaturals, or aliens. They may
leave him ill, destroyed bodily, transformed, or stranded in an inaccessible place. In this predicament the supernaturals come to his·
rescue or protect him from further harm. They restore him by ritual
treatment, and from contact with them he acquires ceremonial knowledge and power. Usually it is the restoration ceremony performed
over him as the patient that he learns in all its details. Then he travels freely among the gods collecting ritual information as he goes, and
from this series of supernatural contacts his own fund of power is increased. With each misadventure and restoration he gains in power
until, toward the end of the series, he has accumulated sufficient ritual
knowledge and power of his own to be able to protect himself with little
or no help from supernaturals.

In the final events of the story the hero returns to his own people,
without resentment for whatever part they may have played in his
misadventures. He teaches the ceremony he has learned, usually to a
younger brother, for the benefit of earth people and then departs to
live with supernaturals.

The relation of these stories to Navaho ceremonialism with its emphasis on curing is straightforward and explicit. Supernatural help for

the hero's illness or injury takes the form of ceremonial cure. Through the agency of the hero, knowledge of various means of ceremonial restoration is transferred to earth people, and this becomes embodied in the curing ceremonials practiced today.

From the standpoint of human content these hero stories have much in common with the hero myths of other cultures, times, and places, but they portray a selected set of attributes and actions. For the most part the heroes conform to the unpromising or "male Cinderella" type. They are presented at the outset of the story as rejected by their kin or somehow separated from the normal family group. They prove themselves and acquire power by undergoing trials and attacks, by a defensive rather than an overtly aggressive strategy. The superficial picture is of a passive, suffering hero, who is drawn into punishments, ordeals, trials, and contests, rather than of an active conqueror who undertakes feats of strength, a prolonged quest for a high goal, or subjection of rivals by cleverness and wits.[41] However, this image of the suffering hero has several variations which on closer analysis reveal what seems to be a covert preoccupation with the hero's own active share in provoking the mishaps which befall him. Whatever the provocation, the hero's deliverance is achieved through the miraculous intervention of supernaturals, who not only extricate him from danger but confer upon him the ritual power which will justify him in his people's eyes.

Navaho mythology has certain similarities with that of surrounding tribes, such as the Pueblo and Apache, as would be expected in view of the known historical connections between these tribes. Hero tales are widespread in North American Indian mythology, and those under consideration here have many features, both general and specific, that are similar to those in neighboring groups and in other areas of North America.[42] This study does not propose to enter into the many important and provocative historical questions raised by the existence of such similarities. Here we are interested in the manner in which the hero stories are elaborated within the body of Navaho mythology regardless of what may be the historical source of the materials out of which they are built. Although it is assumed that hero tales have a basis in certain universal psychological characteristics of mankind, it is of interest that important connections of these Navaho hero tales seem to extend to Plains Indian folklore and to the northwestern part of North America rather than to the Pueblos.[43] It is with these areas that the Southern Athabascans show general cultural relationship both in their manner of life and in presumed historical contacts.

In the foregoing pages we have outlined briefly the plot pattern of the chantway myths. Now we wish to consider in greater detail the constituent elements in this pattern. In their occurrence throughout the stories these elements show a range of variation, and the analysis of these variations should contribute to our understanding of the plot pattern as a whole. We shall attempt to identify the motivation that is operating in the problem situations of the stories and their means of resolution. For convenience the plot elements will be discussed under the following headings: *the hero's predicament*, his misadventures and the events leading to them; the outcome of this predicament in *the hero's rescue and acquisition of power;* and finally, the part played by *the hero's family situation and affinal relations* in these events.

A. The Hero's Predicament

The problem situation on which the dramatic interest of these stories centers is the unfortunate or dangerous predicament in which the hero finds himself. Usually this is not a single event but a mounting series of misadventures in which he becomes involved. The course of these adventures follows an identifiable pattern, and the mishaps themselves fall into a few well defined types.

The most dramatic crises occur when the hero is threatened with or actually destroyed by outright bodily attack from some external source, usually an animal, plant, or other natural phenomenon representing an unfriendly supernatural. Thus, he is "completely shattered" and his body parts scattered by a blow of thunder or lightning (Hail, Flint, Navaho Wind). He is "twisted into the ground" by an angry whirlwind (Navaho Wind, Chiricahua Wind), felled by shooting of cactus (Chiricahua Wind) or frog (Hail, Bead, Beauty), buried under a rock pile (Big Star, Beauty, Bead). He is attacked by bears, snakes, and birds during his witch father-in-law's attempts to kill him. These violent bodily attacks occur as the crisis of a major episode, or they are worked into the story as a series of minor incidents. They may accomplish the hero's destruction or leave him with lingering illness, and it is for restoration from these attacks that he needs supernatural aid. When the hero has accumulated sufficient power of his own, he is able to ward off the threatened attack, as in the witch father-in-law episodes.

In another form of attack, usually involving trickery and stealth, the hero is rendered helpless by transformation into animal form— coyote (Water, Shooting, Prostitution, Bead), snake (Big Star, Navaho Wind, Chiricahua Wind), or frog (Hail). His body is changed into that of the animal who has transformed him, and for restoration to his own form he needs the help of supernaturals and sometimes of his relatives.

The hero's mishaps sometimes take the form of capture and enforced separation from his own people. He is captured by aliens (Mountaintop), tricked onto a height from which there is no descent, as in the cliff nest of eagles (Bead), or stranded on a rock which grows into the sky (Big Star, Navaho Wind). In minor episodes he is captured and hidden away by water monster or spider.

By contrast with the bodily attacks and violence of the foregoing incidents is a second type of misfortune in which the hero is found in poor or lonely circumstances. He is a beggar, diseased or crippled, the butt of scorn and ridicule, and separated from or abandoned by his own people. As a poor beggar, he is dependent on and mistreated by Pueblo neighbors (Water, Prostitution, Twins[44]). He may be rejected by his family, lonely and scorned by them (Hail, Visionary,[44] Plume), forced to fend for himself (Twins) or brought up by animals (Mountaintop). Often this situation sets the stage for violent bodily accidents, but in some stories it constitutes the misfortune for which supernatural assistance is needed (Prostitution, Visionary, Plume).

The hero of the Chiricahua Wind Way voices a complaint: "Why is it that I suffer these hardships! It appears as though I were seeking the frightful things that are putting me to a test!" This exclamation embodies a crucial question that could be asked in all of these chantway stories. To what extent does the hero himself provoke the misadventures that befall him? Is it his own "fault," witting or unwitting, someone else's misdeed, or simply an impersonal circumstance that draws him into difficulty? The stories seem to be preoccupied with this question, to hint at its importance, but to leave its answer obscure.

An examination of the events leading to the hero's misfortunes may throw light on this question. These events follow several standard patterns. At one extreme is the wilful violation of known taboos. The hero ventures into forbidden territory in order to hunt or simply to find out why it has been forbidden. Thus, he encounters a series of mishaps when he repeatedly enters tabooed ground even while voicing his curiosity as to why it is tabooed (Navaho Wind), or he is threatened with destruction when he hunts in territory warned against in a dream (Chiricahua Wind). The hero of one version of Mountaintop Way is captured by Utes when he explores to the south in the direction forbidden by his father. The father-in-law trials typically occur when the new son-in-law ventures to the four directions in disobedience of his father-in-law's warnings. In some cases the hero risks violation of a taboo that is well know to him, as when he swallows deer intestines immediately after learning that they are forbidden and is himself transformed into a snake (Big Star).

A partial rationalization for such disobedience is expressed in one Shooting Way story (N&R)[45]: the hero takes pride in venturing into forbidden spots, "for he reasoned that he always came back restored and richer in lore for Earth People." The heroine of Beauty Way argues with herself when contemplating the last in a series of such transgressions; she protests "that she always returned safely and why should this be an exception." It may be noted that these consciously undertaken violations tend to occur toward the end of a series of adventures when the hero has already received power from supernaturals and thus has built up some confidence in his own ability to combat danger.

More frequent than this conscious and wilful disobedience of prohibitions are situations in which the hero seems to be drawn into danger only half aware of wrong-doing. Such, for example, is the impulsive shooting of whirlwind boy (Navaho Wind), the crippled twins' cry of joy that spoils their curing ceremony (Twins), acceptance of frog's challenge to race (Hail), adultery with thunder's wife (Hail), or the seduction of sisters by the smoke of bear and snake men (Beauty, Mountaintop). Similar also is the hero's obstinate insistence on launching his hollow log craft despite the protest of supernaturals; he does not defy a sepcific prohibition but he keeps his preparations secret for fear of intervention (Plume). This note of obstinacy recurs in other incidents — in the wayward gambler's disregard of his family's remonstrances (a favorite story opening), in the Visionary's refusal to be silenced by his brothers' scorn, in the crippled twins' persistent search for cure.

In the foregoing instances, transgression of prohibitions, whether intentional or not, typically meets with some form of violent attack or threat thereof. At the other extreme lie instances in which the hero finds himself in unfortunate circumstances for which he is apparently not responsible. In these situations, principally of poverty, desertion, trickery or ridicule, the gods take pity and rescue him. The hero is a poor beggar dependent on Pueblo neighbors (Prostitution, Water, Bead); the crippled twins are abandoned by their family as too great a burden (Twins); a boy is left behind in his family's flight from a hungry bear or abandoned as the offspring of an illicit sexual union (Mountaintop); the Visionary is scorned by his brothers (Visionary). At first glance these unhappy situations seem to be visited upon the hero without provocation on his part. Even here, however, there is sometimes a hint that the hero has erred in some detail, that he has perhaps overstepped his prerogatives in a questionable self-assertion. Thus, in one version of the Prostitution Way legend the hero and his grandmother are driven to a wandering existence in poverty by his offense of destroying Pueblo prayersticks. The twins are crippled by a rockfall when as children they assert their independence and explore in curiosity (Twins). Profession of visionary ability is discounted as undue claim to supernatural power (Visionary). This note of surreptitious self-assertion is echoed in the taunt of dove maidens to the hero of Navaho Wind Way when he is stranded on sky-reaching-rock: "Isn't it true that you used to value yourself very much? It's quite clear now that you are only an ordinary person."

Thus, the events which lead to the hero's misfortunes seem to contain an element of overt or covert self-assertion. It should be remembered that these misfortunes in their turn ultimately result in the hero's acquisition of ritual power, and later, in the discussion of value themes, we shall have opportunity to consider the beneficent aspects of these apparently presumptuous acts.

B. The Hero's Rescue and Acquisition of Power

Once the hero has met with accident, trial or test, his rescue is dependent on the goodwill and help of supernaturals. The manner of obtaining help varies with the nature of his predicament, but it results invariably in a transfer of power to the hero himself, both for his personal benefit and, ultimately, for the use of his people.

When the hero is rendered helpless by a bodily attack, his representative, often a member of his family, may apply to supernaturals for his restoration (Flint, Navaho Wind, Chiricahua Wind). The supernatural must be approached with the proper offering before he will consent to perform the necessary ritual, and he may be reluctant to lend his services. Often, after a series of unsuccessful petitions, the secret of the proper offering is revealed by some lesser supernatural such as the messenger fly or bat. In other cases intervention is undertaken voluntarily by the gods without request from earth people. They observe the hero's plight and take pity on him, as when they construct and guide his hollow floating log (Plume), or when they provide the scorned beggar hero of Prostitution Way with sex and hunting magic. Aid volunteered in this manner is not confined to major rescues; when the hero is in a tight spot or embarking on a dangerous exploit, minor animal characters, such as spider, bushrat, toad, bat, or fly, offer magical means of escape or protection. The two most prominent helpers of this kind are messenger fly, who acts as doorguard to the gods and defies their anger in order to help earth people, and the wind monitor who accompanies the hero on exploits to warn him of danger and advise how to circumvent it. The wind monitor usually becomes active after the hero has experienced major catastrophes. His presence may be thought of as a manifestation of the hero's own accumulating knowledge and power; he has learned to listen to the advice of a "wind informant along his earfold."

Another manner of receiving supernatural aid occurs less frequently. In some cases the hero stumbles by accident into supernatural surroundings. He is stranded on sky-reaching-rock and emerges into the sky (Big Star). The heroine in flight from her bear or snake husband arrives unknowingly in the subterranean home of his people (Beauty, Mountaintop). Once having entered these surroundings, the hero or heroine becomes involved in the supernatural contacts through which ritual power is acquired.

Except in those instances when the gods freely volunteer help, they show apparent reluctance and annoyance at the petitions and claims of earth people. "Earth surface people are not allowed here," is the stock inhospitable greeting with which the petitioner is met. In these circumstances it is only by virtue of having found the way through obstacles into the gods' sanctuary, by some special claim on their favor, or by the compulsion of correct offerings that supernatural aid is obtained. This mythological picture of supernatural aid obtained by coercion accords with the principles of Navaho ceremonialism; in actual ceremonial performance ritual actions have as their objective the compulsory invocation of supernatural aid.

In their relations with the hero, the supernaturals thus manifest a double aspect. At some times they are pictured as irascible, inhospitable beings unconcerned about or even hostile to the welfare of earth people, while at others they seek out and succor the hero in his misfortune. It should be remembered that the attack on the hero comes most often from offended supernaturals. Frequently one group of gods is ranged against another group in strife over the hero, as in the division between hostile and friendly winds (Chiricahua) or thunders

(Hail). This pattern assumes clearest form in the war between the thunders, in which one group of thunders rescues the hero after he has been attacked by the opposing group; the peacemaking ceremony for the war thus provoked becomes the curing ritual in which the hero is restored (Hail). This double aspect of the supernaturals is seen again when lesser supernaturals — intermediaries, animal helpers, wind informants — voluntarily aid the hero in opposition to the wishes of more important gods. Big fly, in his position as messenger or door-guard of the gods, thus acts in league with the petitioner, advising him even at the risk of rousing his patron's ire.

Usually it is when the hero has, wittingly or unwittingly, trans-gressed prohibitions that help must be sought with offerings and the reluctance of the gods overcome. On the other hand, their aid may be freely volunteered when the hero's predicament seems to be visited upon him by accident, when he is discovered in unfortunate circum-stances apparently through no fault of his own. However, there is not a one-to-one correspondence between the source of the hero's diffi-culties and the manner in which supernatural help is obtained. We have pointed out the possible covert participation of the hero in bring-ing himself to a sorry plight which superficially seems to be due simply to external circumstance. The obscurity with which both of these plot elements are handled — the responsibility for misadventure and the manner of rescue — may point to a concern about different aspects of the same psychological problem, i.e., the extent of the actor's own responsibility for his misfortune and in the face of this whether and how supernatural protection can be expected.

From his contacts with the gods not only does the hero receive relief for his immediate misfortune but he obtains power for his own future use. The gods perform a ceremony to restore the hero, and in the course of its performance over him as the patient he learns it in all its details. Usually a series of ceremonies is required before re-storation is complete. Later he travels freely among supernaturals collecting further ritual knowledge and power from these contacts. In those stories that recount a series of adventures, the hero may thus gradually accumulate a fund of power so that in the end he is able to ward off dangers substantially by his own efforts or with the coopera-tion of animal helpers. Toward the end of such a series of adventures he is often found established with his own wind monitor to warn him of danger and direct his actions, as in his successful struggles with a witch father-in-law.

The power thus invested in the hero is, however, not for his use alone. The standard conclusion to these stories brings the hero back to his family to teach his ceremonial knowledge for the benefit of earth people. He instructs some member of his family, usually a younger brother, in the conduct of his ceremony. The obligation to return to his family, and through them to make the fruits of his supernatural experience available to earth people, brings us to a consideration of the significance of the family situation as portrayed in these stories.

Before this is undertaken, brief note should be made of some exceptions to this pattern of concluding events. The powers for sexual attraction and hunting magic obtained by the hero of Prosit1tution Way are not thus transferred to his people for public use at the conclusion of the story. These powers are of a somewhat different order from those used in curing disease; they are for private use and personal gain. In the Prostitution Way story the hero has been living in poor circumstances with his (foster) grandmother. He returns to her and, although she also participates in the benefits of his new magic, the story does not specify how this knowledge is to be perpetuated for earth people. The story of the Eagle Way for trapping eagles is similarly atypical. At its conclusion the hero returns to live with his first wives, and he himself practices the eagle-trapping ritual that he has learned from supernaturals. Although these stories account for the origin of the ceremony, they do not tell how the ritual knowledge is to be communicated to earth people.

C. The Hero's Family and Affinal Relations

The chantway myths emphasize the fact of the hero's separation from his family; to undertake his adventures he departs from home. In the course of his wanderings he may engage in sexual liaisons and marriage, thus establishing for himself a new set of affinal relationships. There are certain well defined patterns for the manner of his separation from his family and return to them after his supernatural experiences, as well as for the kind of affinal ties set up by his sexual adventures. To complete our outline of the chantway stories, we shall consider how these family relationships are handled in plot development.

A statement of the hero's relations with his parental family is usually given at the outset of the story. Most typically he is then living with mother, father, and siblings. He may become estranged from his family by some action of his own, or he may simply leave them for hunting adventures and travels. In the former case, intra-familial tensions are clearly indicated. By some wilful or stubborn action, the hero provokes his family's rejection. In the face of remonstrances he gambles away his family's property (Hail, Visionary, Plume) until their patience is exhausted and he has to leave. His characterization as a "wayward, roving gambler" (Visionary) epitomizes the qualities of obstinacy, rebellion and irresponsibility that drive him from home or make him unacceptable to his people. Similarly sister heroines provoke their people's wrath and rejection by making unacceptable marriage choices (Mountaintop, Beauty).

Rejection for an offense committed represents one type of the hero's separation from his family. In other cases his departure is motivated by an impulse toward exploration or self-assertion, but it does not cause harm to his kin except as they regret his absence. He leaves his family on hunting expeditions (Mountaintop, Chiricahua Wind), to explore surrounding territory and satisfy his curiosity (Prostitution, Flint, Navaho Wind), or in search of ritual knowledge (Plume, Shooting). The desire to explore may be combined with disobedience of his father's instructions (Mountaintop). Impelled by curiosity the stricken twins are caught by a rock fall, and as a result of their crippling they are abandoned by their family. The action of these heroes is similar to that of the war gods in the general Navaho origin myth; as children or young men they are "difficult to control" and wander away from home in search of adventure. In many of the stories it is implied that the hero meets accident because he is thus inwardly impelled to leave his family to satisfy his curiosity or to seek adventure.

By contrast with the above types of family separation, in some cases the hero is already established away from his family when the story action begins. He is living with a foster mother, referred to as his grandmother, at the opening of the story (Water, Prostitution); he may have been abandoned as a child (Prostitution, Mountaintop) or chosen by supernaturals for his role (Water).

The pattern of separation from family appears, thus, in three variations, ranging from active rejection because of the hero's offense, through his departure on his own impulse, to a mere statement of his living apart without further explanation of the events leading thereto.

In those stories in which the hero has not been actively rejected, he sometimes maintains contact with his family through his adventures. They may be instrumental in obtaining his restoration, and he returns to them before starting on further adventures. In stories that recount the exploits of brothers (Shooting, Big Star), each actor undertakes his adventures alone, but when the hero falls into danger his brother stands ready to assist. Even the rejected hero may retain some tie of affection with a family member, such as a special relationship with a sister or niece (Plume, Visionary).

Whether or not the circumstances of separation from the family have been explained at the opening of the story, the fact of the hero's return to them is usually specified. This fact is so standard that mention of it may become a mere formality. In many stories, however, the details of his return and both his own and his family's attitudes toward it are clearly set forth. Toward the end of the hero's visit with supernaturals he may be subjected to tests or temptations which if not successfully surmounted would prevent him from seeing his home again. He is required to identify correctly his god protector (Visionary) or places on earth (Visionary, Flint), or he must demonstrate his perfect knowledge of the ceremony before he is allowed to return to his family (Visionary). In the sky he is invited to marry an eagle wife but is advised that if he does so he will never see his family again (Bead). In minor incidents he is warned not to accept food or tobacco from various animal protectors "or he will become one of them," the implication being that he will not then be able to return to his people (Hail, Mountaintop, Beauty). Loneliness and sadness over separation from home are expressed, and particularly joy at reunion. The hero or heroine is at first not recognized by his family but when identified is embraced and welcomed joyfully. They make no reference to his former misdeeds if this was what drove him from home. The two sisters of Beauty Way and Mountaintop Way approach their home fearfully, but in their wish to return they are willing to risk again their family's anger; they find that ill will is no longer harbored against them. Whether the original offense is felt to be the hero's (e.g., excessive gambling) or the family's (e.g., abandonment of crippled twins, rejection of vision claims), no resentment is expressed on either side.

The homecoming of the hero is effected in a spirit of reconciliation. His return with a gift of supernatural powers may be considered as a means of making amends for his offense against them or for his wilful parting from them. At the same time it provides demonstration of his own powers, a justification of his original ambitions and self-assertion. He now returns not as a child but as a responsible adult with superior powers.

The conclusion of the chantway stories takes the hero back to live with supernaturals after he has imparted his ceremonial knowledge to earth people. In his contact with the gods he has become like them and finds himself no longer at ease in his own home. In one story he lives apart until a ceremony is performed over him because the "odors of his people's lodge" have become unpleasant to him (Mountaintop). He becomes restless on earth and longs to return to the gods. This final alienation underlines what seems to be the double aspect of the hero's return with power — on the one hand he offers his knowledge as a gift of reconciliation to his people, and on the other he has vindicated himself by becoming too holy to remain with them.

Before this sequence of events is completed to bring the hero back to his family, he has in most of the stories contracted marriage arrangements or engaged in sexual exploits which institute for him a new set of affinal or pseudo-affinal relationships. The sexual adventures which he undertakes provoke trials and difficulties of a particular kind. As we have seen, in many of the hero's misadventures his antagonists appear in the form of distant or impersonal forces (animals, plants, natural pehnomena, gods, or more rarely, aliens). What the particular trial episodes now to be considered hold in common is their concern with personal relationships within the domestic family. Here his antagonists become more personalized; they represent family members. The following episodes will show how the myths give expression to the intra-familial tensions that are generated by these sexual adventures.

Witch Father-in-law.[46] In the course of his adventures, usually toward the end when he has gained some ritual power of his own, the hero may be subjected to trials by a malevolent father-in-law. The relatively complicated series of events comprising these witch father-in-law episodes recurs with great stability and frequency (Plume, Navaho Wind, Chiricahua Wind, Eagle, Enemy, Shooting-Ghostway). The episode opens when the hero discovers a family living apart,

consisting of father, mother, and daughter. The visitor is immediately
greeted as a son-in-law, but in offering this apparent welcome the
father acts deceitfully and secretly plots the hero's destruction. The
reason for the father's malevolence is sometimes explicitly stated:
since he is a witch and since witches commit incest, he is married not
only to his proper wife but also to his daughter; he is thus jealous of
the new son-in-law. The father-in-law, while protesting good will,
attempts the hero's destruction by a series of treacherous attacks.
The hero is usually warned not to explore to the four directions from
his new home or not to venture into some particular place. In typical
fashion the warnings are disregarded, and the hero finds himself confronted by fierce bears, a snake, cannibal birds, lightning or some
other threat of attack. Either these antagonists have been sent by the
father-in-law, or, if in animal guise, they represent the father-in-law
himself in animal transformation. In these encounters the hero is advised by wind or some personal monitor how to combat the attack by
his own audacity or trickery. In some cases he has the help of his
new wife who tells him the secret of her father's power (e.g., that it
lies in his medicine bundle or name). "Poisoned" food and tobacco are
also used as weapons in these encounters between father-in-law and
son-in-law. The father-in-law serves the hero poinsoned food which
he refuses. As though in premonition of the forthcoming struggle the
hero may first offer his own "poisonous" tobacco to the old man and
demonstrate his ritual power by reviving him when he falls unconscious
(Shooting-Ghostway, Plume, Eagle). The hero is able to circumvent
all attempts on his life and the father-in-law is finally forced to admit
his superior power.

Retaliation for Unacceptable Marriage. A second type of episode,
in which the central characters are women, presents another facet of
the family conflicts provoked by marriage. In a sense these episodes
represent the obverse of the hero's situation; they express tensions
that may be generated within the woman's parental family by her marriage. Here the woman suffers the wrath of her own family for a marriage choice unacceptable to them. In the two stories whose central
characters are women (Beauty, Mountaintop), the family separation is
caused by the flight of the sister heroines from the anger of their kin
at their marriage to snake and bear old men. Again when the hero
tricks non-sunlight-struck Pueblo maidens into marriage (Prostitution,
Water), they dare not return home without his magical protection for
fear of retaliation. The women's angry people threaten "whipping or
beating to death" as punishment for their action.

Offended Husband. Still another set of trial episodes deal with
retaliation for adultery. The angry husband attacks the hero who has,
wittingly or unwittingly, committed adultery with his wife. In three
chantway stories (Hail, Water, Flint) the hero thus offends against and
is attacked by thunder. In a similar episode an angry buffalo husband
attempts retaliation (Shooting, Flint). Whether or not the hero triumphs
over the offended husband, in none of these incidents does he remain

with the women he has thus usurped. The hero sometimes finds himself in the position of the offended husband. In order to steal his wife, Coyote maliciously transforms the hero and takes his form (Prostitution, Shooting-Ghostway) or strands him on sky-reaching-rock (Big Star). The plot interest hangs on how with supernatural aid the hero is able to regain his own form or return to earth and take revenge on Coyote.

In the types of conflict just cited the antagonists are brought into relationship by marriage or sexual affiliation; the actors are in an affinal or pseudo-affinal relationship. A survey of all the myths used in this study reveals that fourteen out of a total of eighteen stories contain one or another of these episodes involving conflict over marriage or with affinal relatives. Moreover, this type of episode provides major plot interest in eleven of these stories (Hail, Water, Shooting, Big Star, Mountaintop, Beauty, Plume, Eagle, Flint, Enemy, Shooting-Ghostway). In only four stories (Visionary, Twins, Bead, Moth) are such episodes unrepresented (at least in the versions available for study), but one of these, Moth Way, deals with the same problem of family disruption by marriage in a quite different and striking manner. The story of Moth Way is not one of the typical hero chantway stories. It tells how the expedient of brother-sister marriage was devised for just this purpose, to prevent family disruption by marriage. Because of great love for the children they have raised, parents are reluctant to let them be taken from them by marriage with aliens, so they propose that the brothers and sisters marry to keep them within the family. These incestuous marriages bring tragic consequences; those who have participated are, like moths, impelled to self-destruction in the fire.

It should be remembered that, as events in the hero's series of trials and adventures, these sexual episodes take place within the larger framework of the hero's separation from and reconciliation with his own parental family. The mythological treatment of parental and affinal relations highlights the perennially recurrent human problem of family disruption and reconstitution as it concerns the relations both of parents and children and of husband and wife.

Value Themes

With the foregoing outline of plot construction in mind, we shall now turn to the task of identifying the major value themes expressed in this body of chantway myths. For reasons indicated in the Introduction, "value theme" has been chosen as a convenient designation for the value elements that we here seek to delineate. The term "theme" is taken as particularly appropriate to the literary form of our data. In these stories we find that certain basic ideas are subjected to variation and development. These ideas contain both existential and normative elements; they involve notions about the natural laws operating in human existence as well as notions about desirable states of being or

modes of action. In order to clarify the significance of the value themes
that appear in the stories, supporting reference will be made to ethnological data. The chantway myths are themselves a living and functioning part of Navaho culture, and it is in this context that the themes
embodied in them assume their fullest meaning. Our discussion of the
mythological value themes will indicate how these symbolic expressions are functionally related to the cultural forms and psychological
manifestations of actual Navaho life experience.

The chantway stories recount vicissitudes in the life experience of
the hero and the means whereby he acquires a measure of control over
the forces in his environment. Their pattern of plot development
makes dramatic use of circumstances and problems that are inherent
in the process of growth from childhood into adult status. The stories
show concern with the dangers of life and the means of warding off or
counteracting them. These dangers take the form of illness and bodily
destruction and, in the Navaho conception, ritual power is the means of
prevention or cure. The stories also deal with problems of family
relations in both parental and affinal settings. The hero's attempts at
self-assertion and his increasing assumption of responsibility form an
undercurrent linking these plot elements. Separation from his family
to undertake his own hunting and sexual adventures, acceptance of the
discipline and responsible participation required to learn ritual, and
finally reconciliation with his family and the gift to them of his ritual
knowledge — these can all be viewed as steps in assuming the responsibilities of an adult role in Navaho society. The mythological themes
will be discussed under four headings corresponding to the major elements in this pattern: concern with health and illness; acquisition of
ritual knowledge and power; the ties of family relationships; and finally the hero's self-assertion and assumption of responsibility as they
are related to the other elements of this pattern.

A. Health and Illness

Health, illness, and death are matters of universal human concern,
but the form which this concern takes may vary in different cultures.
The Navaho have centered their religious practices and rituals on the
act of curing and the effort to maintain health. It is no surprise to
find that the value attached to health and the means of maintaining it
furnishes a central theme in the stories that recount the origins of
curing rites.

Although the prominence given to the problem of health and illness
in the chantway stories is expectable, the manner in which it is handled
merits further consideration. Illness or injury is caused by an attack
which emanates from an external agent rather than from within. Loss
of consciousness, with or without bodily destruction, and crippling from
objects shot into the victim's body are the most common effects. The
violence of the onslaught and the resulting total incapacitation mark the
severity of the experience. The suddenness and unexpectedness of

attack seem also to obscure the hero's awareness of its cause. However, we have seen that the hero plays covertly a considerable role in bringing these afflictions upon himself. The range of variation in recognizing his personal responsibility for the illness suffered has been pointed out. At one extreme is his reckless defiance of known prohibitions, but even when the transgression seems unintentional there is indication that hidden impulses of self-assertion are operating.

The mythological picture accords with actual Navaho practice in tracing the cause of illness to transgression of rules or taboos.[47] The myths, however, seem to go further in depicting a predominantly defiant spirit in these violations; they are presented as transgressions on the rights of supernaturals. Sudden and traumatic illness is pictured as a punishment for wilful wrongdoing. Thus we find existential and normative elements mingled in the Navaho conception of the cause of illness. The transgression of supernatural rules and taboos operates as a natural law to cause illness or injury, but the violation of these rules involves the ethics of interpersonal relations with supernaturals.

The form of illness suffered in the myths is similar to a type which seems to be common in Navaho medicine, i.e., certain hysterical manifestations which involve fainting, loss of consciousness, paralysis, etc.[48] However, the myths picture this type of ailment, which presumably has important psychosomatic components, almost to the exclusion of other forms of illness. The incapacitation resulting from attack by witchcraft in the myths is of this order; the hero feels unaccountably weak and loses powers of speech and mind. It should be noted that the psychological background and latent functions of witchcraft beliefs in actual life[49] are congruent with a strong psychosomatic component. If it is correct to identify the physical symptoms portrayed in the myths as centering on psychosomatic ills, this fact should lend some weight to interpretation of the psychological significance of the mythological content.

Restoration, or cure of illness, is effected by ritual action in the myths as in actual life. In the stories, correct ritual treatment, once obtained, is automatically effective. There seems to be no conception of an ailment beyond the bounds of treatment but only the problem of obtaining the correct treatment. Thus, the hero can be restored even though he has been completely shattered and his body parts scattered. It is striking that on no occasion is illness or injury considered hopeless. These conceptions of universal treatability and automatic effectiveness do not preclude the necessity of continued or repeated treatment when symptoms of illness persist. The hero may require a series of ceremonies until he or the supernaturals conducting them are satisfied that a complete recovery is assured. In these mythological representations of automatic and infallible means of cure, fantasy mechanisms of wish fulfilment seem to be at work.

In the real life situation it is more difficult to judge the extent of confidence in treatability. However, the theory of Navaho ceremonialism is in accord with the mythological picture. It provides a detailed

classification of etiological factors in illness, each with the appropriate choice of ritual treatment. In practice also the employment of
diagnostic techniques and of repeated efforts to find a successful
treatment support the confidence in treatability that is conveyed in the
myths.[50]

Health and illness are opposite facets of the same human problem,
and although the Navaho curing ceremonials deal with both, these two
facets receive somewhat different emphasis in the various phases of
the total ceremonial complex. In the myths we find more attention devoted to disease than to the positive state of health. The stories contain detailed descriptions of the events leading to injury and illness
and of the desperate situation of the hero when he is thus overcome.
On the other hand, it is in the ritual poetry and in the instructions for
ritual procedure that accompany these stories, rather than in the story
action itself, that conceptions of health and measures for regaining
health are spelled out. Here, as in actual life, we find restoration of
harmony as the keynote to the procedures that restore health.[51] The
conception of health as a state of harmony is mirrored in the plot
construction of one story already cited; in Hail Way restoration of the
hero is finally accomplished in the ceremony of peace-making between
the opposing groups of supernaturals that have come into conflict over
his original misadventure. The return of the hero to his family may
also be thought of as a symbolic and temporary restoration of harmony
in the familial bonds disrupted by his departure.

From the foregoing discussion it can be seen that the mythological
value theme pertaining to maintenance of health contains both existential and normative elements. The state of health is presented as desirable and much effort is expended for its attainment. Sudden and
traumatic illness is conceived as the consequence of and supernatural
punishment for ritual transgression. Cure is effected automatically
by application of the correct ritual. These conceptions combine beliefs about the operation of natural laws and about proper standards of
interpersonal relations with supernaturals.

B. Power and Knowledge

Our discussion of illness and curing has inevitably touched on conceptions of supernatural power and its place both in causing illness and
in curing it. We wish now to consider the mythological representation
of the nature of ritual power and the process of its acquisition.

In these stories the hero is faced with the problem of obtaining
supernatural aid to effect his rescue or restoration. The key to its
solution is knowledge of the proper approach to supernaturals in order
to enlist their assistance. For the most part the gods are pictured as
reluctant to contribute their services until compelled to do so when
approached in the correct ritual manner and with proper offerings.
Access to supernatural aid requires knowledge of and ability to provide
the necessary offerings. The power that the hero gains in his

supernatural contacts, whereby he is enabled to avoid further catastrophe to himself, is knowledge of the appropriate ceremonial equipment and ritual actions. When he learns the ceremony conducted over
him, it thereby becomes his own property, his own source of power to
compel supernatural aid in the future. Ritual knowledge gained from
the supernaturals becomes a personal possession, a kind of property,
which can be communicated to others at the will of the possessor.
Thus, power in general consists of both tangible and intangible property, i.e., possession of the proper ritual objects and knowledge of
ritual techniques. Both are valued for the services they can command.

The conception of knowledge as power conveyed in the myths is
borne out in practice. Knowledge of the appropriate appeal to the
supernaturals is the means of obtaining their help, and with it goes the
power of control over adverse circumstances. The compulsion of the
proper word and act to bring divine aid is a cornerstone of Navaho
religion.[52]

On the other hand, we have seen that in some cases supernaturals,
or more usually their intermediaries, offer help freely; or the gods
may be ranged in conflict with each other, some acting as voluntary
protectors of the hero and others hostile to him. Big fly or bat may
offer the secret of access to the god who can cure the hero. Talking
God may come voluntarily to advise the hero's family of what has
happened to him, or he may act as the hero's protector in his search
for supernatural aid and during his visits among hostile supernaturals.
The background of remote and disinterested supernaturals who can be
moved only by the compulsion of proper ritual is supplemented by the
presence of a few key figures who are active in bringing help to the
hero or in opening the avenue for his gaining it himself. Thus, the
supernaturals in the myths present a double aspect, both helpful and
forbidding, nurturant and indifferent. Their disinterest accords with
the belief held in actual life that supernatural aid is obtained by compulsion. Their offers of voluntary help, on the other hand, seem to
represent the wish fulfilment functions of myth.

The contrast between nurturant and indifferent supernaturals reflects two aspects of the same psychological problem; the hero's
relations with the gods play out, in these repeated and stereotyped
forms, ideas of dependency on more powerful figures.[53] In the myths,
as in the ritual activities of actual life, the hero learns to use an
active rather than a passive solution to the problem of power. He
gains his own power to control the forces on which he is dependent. As
he successfully undergoes trials, he emerges with the supernatural
power that has been communicated to him. The power thus accumulated
serves as protection in subsequent encounters; he becomes invulnerable to attacks that would previously have destroyed him. Ultimately
he makes his ritual power available for the benefit of others by teaching his ceremony to earth people.

The extent of the hero's personal holiness is discovered on his return home. After these supernatural contacts he no longer feels at

ease with his own people and ultimately he departs to dwell with the gods. This mythological detail raises a question with respect to the status of ceremonial practitioners in actual life. They hold a position of respect and responsibility above the average citizen,[54] but they do not seem to be considered personally holy and akin to the supernaturals in a sense that would divorce them from everyday life. Nor does there seem to be evidence that the practitioner is personally immune from illness and accident. By his close association with ritual equipment and activities, the practitioner runs a greater risk of offending by ritual transgression. The extent to which he is able to withstand the dangers of this position may be likened to the growing invulnerability of the chantway hero as he builds up his power.

The mythological theme relating to power represents an instrumental value. Ritual power is desirable as the means whereby the end state of health may be attained and maintained. Here again, as in the health theme, we see a mixed value conception which contains an important existential component. Power results from possession of tangible and intangible property, i.e., ritual objects and knowledge of ritual techniques. It is conceived as an automatically effective means of protection and restoration. The supernaturals are compelled to restore health by the proper words and acts. The value of ritual power extends beyond the personal benefits which accrue to its owner; when the ceremony is taught to earth people, its benefits become potentially available to the whole Navaho community.

C. Family Relationships

The plot pattern of the chantway stories gives an important place to difficulties arising in intra-familial relations. These difficulties are presented in two recurrent situations: in the hero's separation from his own parental family and in the family readjustments consequent upon marriage, both of which have already been discussed as they function in plot development. Tensions arising in the family appear as an undercurrent running through the mythological material, and the way in which these tensions are handled points to the value placed on achieving harmony and solidarity in family relations.

We have indicated how the hero's separation from his own family, which forms the framework of the typical story, occurs often in situations where defiance or rejection play a prominent part. The family unit is disrupted by tensions generated within it. These are pictured as originating either with the hero himself (defiance, waywardness, seeking for independence) or directed at him by other family members (scorn and rejection). Often the attribution of "fault" is not clearcut and both parties are seen as contributing to the separation. The later reconciliation of the separated member, brief though it may be, serves as a symbolic restoration of balance and harmony within the family.

The management of intra-familial tensions poses problems in all human groups, and concern with these problems is not peculiar to the

Navaho. But the conditions of the Navaho physical environment and the particular forms of social structure with which problems of group and environmental adjustment are mediated seem to put a premium on maintaining an harmonious family group.[55] Both in the hunting and collecting economy pictured in the myths and in the present day seasonal-nomadic herding and agricultural economy, the isolated, extended matrilineal family group must serve as an integrated and largely self-sufficient unit. The demands for harmonious cooperation and responsible action by its members are great if the group is to function successfully as an economic unit. However, the social form of matrilocal residence determines the point at which disruption of the family unit inevitably occurs, i.e., when the growing sons become of an age to "seek their own fortunes." It is this tension point that is represented in the hero's separation from and reconciliation with his parental family.

A second point of tension occurs in the adjustments required between the new son-in-law and the family group into which he marries. The problems arising in this situation are presented in plot construction in two complementary forms — in the witch father-in-law episodes and in the punishment of daughters for an unacceptable marriage choice. In a matrilineal and matrilocal family organization the incorporation of a son-in-law into the family group creates problems of adjustment for both the new husband and the members of the existing family. In Navaho culture the rule of mother-in-law avoidance provides means of dealing with some of the strains arising in this situation. The mother-in-law taboo is referred to in these myths but does not provide material for plot development. The witch father-in-law episodes reflect another aspect of the same problem, one that has been mentioned but not emphasized in ethnological analysis, that is the jealousies and tensions evoked between the men of the new family unit.[56] These tensions must be harmonized if successful operation as an economic and social unit is to be achieved. That the new son-in-law is felt to upset the affectional balance of the existing family unit is underlined by the fact that he interrupts his witch father-in-law's supposed incestuous relation with his own daughter.

These various mythological representations of intra-familial tension are expressions of an underlying value theme which emphasizes the desirability of maintaining harmonious family relations. This theme is portrayed in two familial areas. Within the parental family the tensions operating when children break away from consanguine bonds are represented in the difficulties of the hero's departure from home and in the possessiveness of parents which leads to the attempt at brother-sister marriage. Points of tension in the new family established by marriage are represented in the witch father-in-law episodes and in the punishment of daughters for choosing mates unacceptable to their families. As in the case of health, the myths make principal use of the negative side of this theme in plot construction; they emphasize the points at which family disruption occurs. Its positive side is reflected in the hero's reconciliation with his family. Existential elements are less prominent in the expression of this theme than in those of health and power, although they enter into the injunction against brother-sister incest which is believed to lead to "insanity."

D. Self-assertion and Responsibility

The chantway myths attribute to the hero certain character traits which assume importance in the process of establishing his adult status. Emancipation from the protection and control of his parental family requires some assertion of his own needs and desires. Acquisition of ritual power provides him with practical means of self-reliance and at the same time demonstrates his growing ability to assume responsibility. It is by this discipline that he is transformed from an irresponsible adventurer to one who has learned to heed the warnings of the gods and who can use his knowledge for the welfare of the community.

We have noted how the thread of self-assertion in the hero's activities is manifested in a range of expressions from simple desire to investigate to a defiance of family and group rules. Sometimes independence is forced on the hero by his family's disapproval or rejection. In other instances it is more positively sought in a spirit of curiosity and adventure. In both of these circumstances restlessness and seeking after excitement may be present. Characteristic is the persistence, obstinacy and even defiance with which he pursues his course. Not only his family but also the supernaturals become objects of this defiance. He offends against his family by gambling away their property or he ventures in disobedience of their instructions. More often it is the authority of supernaturals that is flouted by reckless violation of ritual taboos. These actions are directed against forces that seem to be felt as constricting. Punishment for defiance and aggression is experienced in the attacks and trials suffered by the hero. At the same time these trials provide the avenue whereby he acquires power of his own. His self-assertive actions have desirable consequences; they lead ultimately to achievement of ritual power and independence.

Self-assertion, as pictured in these stories, has both destructive and beneficent potentialities. Its harmful aspects appear, for example, in the hero's irresponsible gambling away of his family's property, his infringement on sexual rights of others, and his excesses in hunting. These destructive manifestations are subjected to punishment and control, and ultimately they are replaced by the beneficent effects of his return with ritual knowledge. The destructive elements in self-assertion are exemplified in the extreme by an incident in the Mountaintop Way story. The boy raised by owl is sent back to his own parents by the owl man, who has begun to fear his developing power as a hunter with the bow and arrow that was given him in childhood. With his own kinfolk the boy "becomes dangerous to people"; he shoots an old man, an old woman, a boy and girl, and has to flee from his people's anger.

They pursue him with intent to punish and are dissuaded from this only
by evidence that he has acquired the protection of companions. This
incident is not properly a part of the chantway hero's adventures. Owl
boy is a brother of the young man who later becomes the hero, but who
likewise "becomes troublesome" as he grows up. The boy who becomes
dangerous to his own people appears elsewhere as a popular incident in
Navaho myth; in all versions he escapes as an outcast and goes to live
with aliens (Ute, Sioux).[57] This owl boy incident epitomizes the destructive side of the growing boy's self-assertion, and its uncontrolled aggression meets with community sanctions.

The complex of attitudes and actions subsumed by the theme of
self-assertion, interlocking as it does with other value emphases on
health, power, and family relations, presents a tempting springboard
for considering some of the psychological implications of the mythological material.[58] The hero is introduced as a young man at the age
when he is confronted with the need to establish his own independence
and manhood. As such he is driven by an impulse toward independent
action. He explores in curiosity and against authority, with greater or
less realization that he is risking disaster by so doing. The disaster
met in these attempts is phrased as punishment for violation of rules,
whether intentional or not. At first the punishing agent takes a relatively impersonal form, a supernatural who has been offended. This
agent is almost invariably male. Punishment is visited in the form of
catastrophic illness or injury. At some point in the series of such
adventures, and usually after he has accumulated some supernatural
power of his own as a result of them, the hero becomes involved in
struggle with a more personalized opponent — the witch father-in-law
or the offended husband — in a setting that is frankly sexual. In this
encounter he successfully overcomes his antagonist. This pattern
viewed psychologically seems to reflect concern with problems of authority and independence, of how the hero is to extricate himself from
both the domination and the safety of his consanguine kin group and how
he is to prove his manhood and his ability to establish himself in marriage. The punishments that he suffers in this process are those of
illness and injury, threats most feared in Navaho culture.[59] In psychoanalytic terms, both the form and the agency of these punishments
would identify them as castration threats. The hero is successful in
combatting these threats, but the story does not end here; rather it
brings him back to his own family with the proof and fruits of his success in the form of ceremonial power. This return with the gift of
ritual knowledge may be interpreted, again in psychoanalytic terms, as
restitution for his unconscious hostility toward the forces of domination
that he has successfully combatted.[60]

So far we have dealt principally with the young man's extrication
from the security and domination of family ties, and we have seen how
in this context self-assertion may function as a valued personality
trait, even though in the short run its aggressive-destructive manifestations are punished. Equally important is the process whereby he

develops self-reliance and responsibility. The hero is often presented
at the outset as irresponsible or reckless. The trials suffered leave
their mark; by them he is taught to recognize proper authority and to
respect ritual rules. He learns to listen to the voice and advice of
supernaturals. The learning of a ceremony is an arduous undertaking
and requires close and serious application. This is discipline in the
full sense of punishment for the sake of training. The result is ability
to protect himself, and specifically to ward off attack by the threatening father-in-law or the offended former husband of his wives. Thus
proving his ability to establish himself in marriage, he returns to his
own people not merely as an adult in his own right but with the gift of
supernatural power which implies assumption of responsibility for the
welfare of his people.[61]

The function of discipline in the young man's training is reflected
in other mythological incidents as well as in practices of actual life.
In one story the reluctant hero is urged by his grandmothers to race
ceremonially for various kinds of "property." A frequent episode in
the mythological accounts of the fire dance is that of the reputedly lazy
boy whose grandmother offers him as a runner and whose unexpected
prowess is due to secret practice in racing. In actual life, training in
hardihood and responsibility is an important part of the young boy's
education, and the traditional device of early morning racing and rolling in the snow is symbolic of this general attitude.[62]

The mythological transformation of the young man's irresponsibility
to responsibility has significant parallels in similar stories from
Navaho life. After describing such ideal qualities as fortitude, industry, responsibility in making decisions, and dependability, Reichard
continues:

> "These qualities are the ideal; but, oddly enough, the prototype in several
> biographical descriptions of successful medicine men is a youth who has, of
> all the good qualities, primarily intelligence but who, until he starts his pro-
> fessional training, is the Navaho idea of a wastrel. He assumes no respon-
> sibility. He resists the admonition to marry and settle down. He may work,
> but he is sometimes lazy, at best unsteady. He is a rover, traveling widely,
> becoming a professional visitor, usually at a home where there is a de-
> sirable girl or a bevy of attractive women.... He does not invest such prop-
> erty as he may gain, but spends it in dissipation, particularly gambling, al-
> though he may gain by the same means. An old man, reformed, boasts of
> youthful philanderings and tolerates those of his grandson or nephew, but
> does not condone their irresponsibility for the results of their dalliance.[63]

It is not suggested that discipline and responsibility are problems
only for the young man who becomes a ceremonial practitioner nor that
the chantway myths reflect principally the attitudes and values of those
who know and use them in this practice. Rather it would seem that the
psychological problem of establishing independence and responsibility
is a concern of young men in general and of other members of the
society for them. It is perhaps most strikingly demonstrated in the
requirements for and demands upon ceremonial practitioners. But the

complex of attitudes associated with self-assertion and responsibility
is based in the conditions and structure of Navaho society. The environmental conditions and economic basis of Navaho life require
initiative, industry, and mobility in gaining a livelihood. The relatively
isolated position of the family group imposes the necessity for cooperation between members but also, in large measure, for independence
and self-reliance of the individual.[64] The particular phrasing of Navaho
individualism, as contrasted for example with the close-knit, communal
interdependence of Pueblo life, is congruent with the importance given
to self-assertion and personal responsibility in the myths.

The foregoing analysis has indicated character traits that contribute to the youthful hero's success. The value themes thus represented
center on the two qualities of self-assertion and responsibility, both of
which are pictured as desirable. A measure of self-assertion is necessary to break away from familial bonds and establish an independent
adult status. However, this can also be dangerous, and when carried
to an extreme in destructive acts it meets with sanctions. Young men
who indulge in reckless and irresponsible behavior must be taught to
recognize proper authority; by submitting to discipline they acquire
power with its attendant responsibilities. It is through self-assertive
acts tempered by the lesson of discipline that responsible adult status
is achieved.

IV. EXPLANATORY ELEMENTS

The discussion of value themes as presented in the typical and re-current forms of plot construction has necessarily been wide-ranging and impressionistic. We shall now turn to a somewhat more systematic and detailed examination of story content. Ultimately we shall want to see to what extent this examination substantiates the picture of the im-pressionistic analysis and in what directions, if any, it may extend and amplify the formulations already arrived at. The procedures for analyz-ing the details of story content and the reasons for using them in con-junction with an impressionistic analysis have been outlined in the In-troduction. In this chapter we shall deal with the "explanatory" state-ments interpolated by the narrator in his account of mythological events.

As is not unusual in mythology, the chantway narrator sometimes in-terrupts the flow of his story to explain the intended significance of what he has been saying or to comment on the correspondence or discrepancy between what happens in the story and what happens or should happen in everyday life. These explanations and cautionary statements do not oc-cur frequently nor with any apparent regularity. The point at which one narrator pauses to interpret may be passed over without comment by another. The way in which the same story, episode, or incident may thus in some cases be used as explanation of the origin of some natural phenomenon and in others be told simply for its narrative value is well known.[65] Although such digressions do not appear frequently in the Nav-aho material, as compared to some other bodies of mythology, they seem to have a special importance when they do occur. They are chosen as points meriting further emphasis or clarification, either for traditional reasons or because of the interests of the story teller.

The data that concern us here are, then, any generalizing statements that break into the continuity of action and depart momentarily from the story to set forth some current belief about the nature of things in the world, some precept for action or rule of conduct, as well as any expla-nation of the origin of such beliefs and precepts. "Explanatory element" is the generic term usually applied to statements of this kind that appear in the mythological narration. A particular type of explanatory element, i.e., cautionary statements that warn against certain actions and point out the penalty for committing them, will be of special interest for the present purposes. We shall bring together the scattered data of this kind and attempt to assess its significance for a value analysis.

In a sense the chantway myths as a class may be considered prima-rily as explanatory tales, since they describe the origin of present-day ceremonies. The conduct of curing ritual over the hero sets the pattern and acts as a guide for current ritual practice. Those portions of the myths that describe ritual acts are thus regarded as explaining their origin even if this is not explicitly stated. This general explanatory function is often indirectly reflected by special designation of those ritual actions that today differ from this initial performance. Although quantitatively this explanation of ritual forms a large part of the mythological material, we do not propose to deal with it here in detail. For reasons already indicated, the myth abstracts have centered on the human content of the stories and no attempt has been made to summarize the lengthy descriptions of ritual performance. This general explanatory function of the chantway myths and their explicit relation to illness, health, and curing should not be lost sight of in examing their content for other occasional and specific "explanations."

Health

The importance of health, well being, and harmony implicit in the total form and purpose of the chantway myths finds expression in a number of explicit statements about the source or "cause" of illness or death. Thus, it is specifically stated that infraction or disregard of ceremonial rules or the misuse of ritual will result in illness. Wheelwright's version of "The Visionary" presents this warning during the hero's instruction in ceremonial lore: he is told that the gods will punish negligence by sending disease and plagues (locusts, grasshoppers), and it is emphasized that humans must obey the ceremonial rules and keep ritual objects holy in order to keep well and happy. When the hero of Eagle Way is presented with the choice of learning alternative rituals, he is warned that earth people will get disease and develop bad habits if they use the witchcraft way of eagle trapping (Eagle N). The Visionary warns his younger brother that he must learn the ceremony exactly or he will become blind, warped, and twisted (Visionary Mb). Transgression of certain taboos, apparently not related to specific rituals, also results in illness. In the Beauty Way story the heroine is captured by squash plants when she strays into a garden, and the narrator takes this occasion to give a general warning that sickness will result if one lies down in a (corn) field (Beauty H). The hero of Chiricahua Wind Way is instructed that eating certain parts of deer will cause illness — eating the head will cause nosebleed and head swelling; the heart, bleeding; and eating portions of the digestive tract will cause one to be turned into a snake (Chiricahua Ha). Frog warns the hero against disease contracted by immersion in water (Plume Ma).

Implicit in the foregoing mythological statements is the idea that illness is an undesirable state of affairs. At the same time that infraction of ritual rules is identified as the cause of illness, a warning is given against such violations. These statements indicate that both the end state of illness and actions which lead to this state are negatively valued. In the discussion of fertility and ritual below, we shall see that transgression of ritual rules may also lead to other unfortunate consequences.

A few statements point to the source of illness or death in the "meanness" of supernaturals. First Man and First Woman are considered mean and from them will come epidemics, coughs, and colds (Shooting

N&R). The worm man who emits stinging insects claims that he is to blame if earth people get sores around the mouth, ears, face, or on the body (Hail R).

Finally, two explanatory elements merely identify the forms of illness pictured in the myths with contemporary manifestations. The origin of "fits and spells" is identified with the "fit" experienced by Holy Girl during the hero's recital of ritual information he has obtained from Sun (Shooting N&R). In another story the patient is "seized with hypnotic convulsions" during the singing and this is given as the explanation why patients fall into a trance today (Twins).

Fertility

Fertility with its opposite, threat of famine, also becomes a focus for explanatory statements. The hollow log trip of Plume Way in which the hero learns to raise crops serves to introduce corn raising to his people or to explain the origin of corn and pumpkins. The hero of Hail Way departs with his sister to live with supernaturals, he to have charge of rain and she of plants for the benefit of earth people (Hail W). The heroine of Beauty Way is put in charge of cloud, rain, mist, and vegetation for earth people (Beauty H). Changing Woman's gifts to earth people from her home in the west are cloud, rain, pollen, and dew (Shooting N&R).

Ceremonial transgressions may cause crop failure as well as illness. We have noted how the Visionary is warned that ritual negligence will be punished by plagues (locusts, grasshoppers) (Visionary W). The permanent ceremonial pictures cannot be given to humans who are not as "good" as the gods; if they quarreled over a picture and tore it, this would cause drought and crop failure (Visionary Ma). It is for this reason that the pictures are given in the form of sandpaintings. Ritual and taboos connected with the preparation and use of corn and other foods are detailed in the story of Plume Way, and the infringement of these taboos is said to bring damage to the crop by frost and flood or to cause the corn to "consume itself" (Plume Mb). The latter threatened action is compared to the results of the ritual error of feeding meat to the ceremonial masks, which would cause men to eat each other (Plume Mb). Following the hero's successful race with frog in Hail Way, an apparently irrelevant instruction is given not to make dumplings when planting, or hail will ruin the corn (Hail R). In Wheelwright's version of the same incident it is explained that tying a toad in a garden is thought to bring rain (Hail W).

Drought is also explained as the result of anger on the part of supernaturals. Four sisters mutilated for adultery depart to the north with a curse for their husband who had thus punished them and with the warning that when they turn their faces south there will be drought (Water Wa). Likewise, supernaturals offended by refusal of their gifts of food predict scarcity of food or severe weather; when there are many pinyons there will be snow and cold and people will freeze to death (Hail R).

The foregoing explanatory references reflect a positive valuation of fertility, a factor which did not assume importance in the plot construction of the stories.[66] Although this material does not lend itself to quantitative treatment, it is interesting to note that agricultural fertility receives roughly as much emphasis as health in these explanatory references. The contrast of Navaho ceremonial interest in curing with Pueblo emphasis on fertility[67] tends to obscure the real importance in both groups of the respective secondary element of this pair. Pueblo ceremonialism also functions for curing, and the natural harmony which Navaho ritual seeks to establish or restore includes in important measure the fertility of nature.

Ritual Observance

In the cautionary statements referring to health and fertility, the actions which result in undesirable consequences are ritual violations — neglect or misuse of ceremonial knowledge and infraction of ritual taboos. Similarly in the story content it has been seen that ritual transgressions bring down punishment on the offender. The importance of ritual in general and of certain specific ritual acts is underlined by additional cautionary references.[68] In some of these the penalty for transgression is not specified. Thus, at the conclusion of Enemy Way, Black God explains that ghosts will try to persuade people not to observe the proper taboos and warns against giving in to this; the ceremony will be a means of self defense in the future (Enemy H). The hero is warned that the ceremony must not be forgotten (Mountaintop W), that punishment will result if he tampers with the ceremony (makes it up or plays with it) or if he neglects to keep this ceremonial knowledge alive (Hail W). If he forgets any of the ceremony, that part will revert to the gods (Hail W; Navaho Wind Wa). The bear's awkward gait is attributed to his disregard of instructions not to lie down during a ceremony; he suffers a paralytic stroke and is restored but his gait remains awkward (Chiricahua Hb). In another version of this same story both bear and snake neglect to make pollen offerings and stagger off "without getting their full sense" (Chiricahua Ha).

Explanation of the origin of sandpaintings reveals some Navaho ideas about the importance of and means of preserving sacred knowledge. The pictures are shown to the hero drawn or painted on some kind of material, but in this form they are taken back by the gods and are to be reproduced by earth people in sand. This is to prevent quarreling over them as material possessions (Visionary Ma; Shooting Ra) and to guarantee knowledge and use of them to anyone who has sufficient interest to learn the sacred lore (Shooting Ra). Elsewhere the source of sandpainting materials is specified. After his defeat of insect, weed, and rock enemies, the hero sends trophies from these encounters to earth people; pounded rocks from the rock enemies are to be used for sandpaintings (Bead R).

Additional ritual prescriptions specify that sacrifices are necessary for ceremonial treatment (Shooting N&R), that the presence of a menstruating woman destroys the efficacy of the prayersticks (Visionary S&H), that dumplings are not to be brought into a Hail Way ceremony (Hail R). In one version of the Visionary, Talking God lays down the rule that a ceremony must be stopped at once if a death occurs while it is in progress (Visionary W); in other versions when death occurs in such circumstances the holy ones debate whether to stop their ceremony but apparently do not follow this rule (Visionary S, S&H). Navaho respect for and avoidance of death also figure in an injunction received from supernaturals during the hero's sky visit; pregnant women "must not see people that are hurt, or dead people, or animals, and this was the first time that men knew this" (Water Wa).

Sex and Family Relations

Another group of explanatory elements refers to sex, marriage, and family relations. The origin of sexual attraction and of differences between male and female genitalia are described in Prostitution Way together with the woman's injunction that compensation must be made for sexual intercourse (the marriage payment) to avoid a "bad outcome" (Prostitution Ha). The action of the story carries out this injunction; the hero kills antelope for the people of his non-sunlight-struck brides, and this is said to be the origin of the saying, "If a person marries he goes into debt" (Prostitution Ha). Another version of this plural marriage is taken as occasion to explain the origin of sororal polygyny; it is said that the sun also had two wives, "That's why policemen can't stop it — it is something written down back there" (Prostitution K). At the conclusion of this story the hero makes the prediction, "Everywhere on the earth there shall be prostitution" (sexual excess) (Prostitution Ha).

Sexual activities are referred to, but in a manner less clearly identifiable as explanatory, in other contexts. It is said that Begochidi, the *berdache*, "bothers" people when they are about to shoot game, when they urinate, or when they are about to have intercourse, by putting his hand to their sexual parts (Moth). The old snake man who seduced the heroine of Beauty Way and "strapped" her to him with a snake is said to bother people in similar fashion (Beauty Hb).

The Beauty Way story contains an ambiguous reference to husband-wife relations. When the heroine is about to leave her snake husband's home to return to her family she is detained by the singing of a corn kernel; the narrator explains that on this account "leaving is not hurriedly done"[69] (Beauty H). In this same version the necessity for leaving is explained: because her snake husband has performed a ceremony over her it would be improper for them to live as husband and wife (Beauty H).[70] The traditional penalty for adultery (mutilation by cutting off nose or ear) figures in one version of Water Way; when the women thus mutilated turn their faces south there will be drought (Water Wa).

In several cases (principally in the witch father-in-law episodes) the mother-in-law taboo is observed in the action of the story, but in only one does the arrival of the new son-in-law become the occasion for explaining this custom. The father of the hero's buffalo wives is reluctant to accept their new husband, but their mother believes the daughters' story and offers to depart, thus instituting the mother-in-law taboo as a means of showing respect (Flint Hb).

In one version of Prostitution Way, joking occurs between the hero and his grandmother; he teases her about her resplendent visitor, Talking God, and intimates that he must be her husband (Prostitution H). This incident is cited as the origin of the joking relationship between grandmother and grandchild.

Brother-sister relations, which have been identified as a point of psychological tension in Navaho family relations,[71] receive some explanatory treatment. In the hero twins' ceremonial treatment by supernaturals, daughters of their protector shape and mold them to look as beautiful as their brothers; their exclamation, "Behold our ugly brothers!" is said to explain the fact that a girl will speak of her younger brother as ugly no matter how beautiful he is (Twins).[72] The story of Moth Way in its totality serves to demonstrate the tragic consequences of sexual contact between brother and sister. The narrator concludes, "Therefore there is absolutely a mutual fear of their lower parts between brothers and sisters, the mere thought of such a thing is to be feared" (Moth).

Aggression

The problem of aggression in interpersonal relations receives attention in several references whose phrasing seems to reflect a certain acceptance, or even fatalism, in acknowledging its existence. In the hero's contests of skill with White Butterfly, his opponent admits defeat only after an argument. The narrator explains, "That is the way it always is when people play together, one gets beat and then they get mad at each other" (Prostitution K). The hero's quarrel with Coyote for having stolen his wife is settled by Big Star with the admonition that there will always be different kinds of people in the world and "they must make the best of it" (Big Star). When the supernaturals argue over the order of songs in a ceremony, the narrator explains, "Accordingly too people at present engage in arguments" (Shooting-Ghostway). The fear that humans would quarrel over sandpaintings if given to them as material possessions has been cited above. Recognition of "meanness" has also been noted as a permanent attitude of First Man and First Woman who send disease; by contrast Changing Woman has "no meanness left" in her and sends rain and other necessities for fertility. The winds warn earth people that when they sound, "No person must bother us because there will be meanness in us" (Chiricahua Ha). On the other hand, the hero of Navaho Wind Way gives a warning apparently at variance with this when he departs to live with supernaturals as part of the wind; he says that it will make him angry if his people flee from the wind in fear (Navaho Wind Wa).

Aggression is occasionally explained as a justified retaliation for harm suffered. The danger of toad's ill will when his children have been injured is recognized; unless they are restored "he will feel badly toward us and we may die" (Hail W). The rock wren explains his eagerness for the fight: "It is because I am attacked that I am fierce" (Big Star).

Irresponsibility

The "aimless wandering" of the heroine of Beauty Way provokes the disapproval of her snake protectors, presumably as evidence of irresponsibility or indolence. This attitude is crystallized into an explanatory statement, however, only in the equivocal statement that if anyone stays out over four nights it is concluded that he "must not have done anything good" (Beauty H).

Property

Among the explanatory elements already cited, two concern property or material possessions — the prescription of the marriage payment and the belief that earth people would quarrel over sandpaintings. The possession of property is used as a standard of comparison in a reference to Apache aliens; the fact that Navaho runners win valuables from them is given as the reason why the Navaho have ever since been richer than their neighbors (Mountaintop M). These references indicate the importance attributed to the possession of property, particularly as it is useful for sexual and ritual purposes.

Animal Origins

By comparison with some other bodies of mythology, explanations of animal origins or characteristics occur only rarely in these ceremonial myths. Insofar as they simply identify the source of contemporary animal characteristics, they contribute little to an understanding of values. For example, the presence of bees on earth is attributed to the action of the hero in his war with stinging insects. From this encounter he saves some of the defeated bees to be sent through the sky hole for earth people (Bead W, R) with the admonition that they are to multiply for earth people but not become harmful again (Bead M) or that they are to be useful to men in ceremonies (Big Star). On the promise of an old bee woman to be friendly, he leaves some for honey and for their wax, which will take away pain and heal wounds made by eagles' claws (Eagle N). (Likewise the origin of tumbleweed is accounted for by the weed and grass seeds sent to earth after this encounter [Bead R]; and from the hero's defeat of rock people came rock fragments to be used for sandpaintings [Bead R].) At a ceremony conducted by the gods, snake is naked and has no place to put the medicine administered to him; he puts it in his mouth for safekeeping and that is why snakes are poisonous (Visionary Mb).

Miscellaneous

A few miscellaneous references to omens and the power of names complete the enumeration of explanatory elements in the chantway myths. The Navaho belief in omens [73] is reflected in a supernatural's instructions to the hero that ringing ears or twitching nerves are warnings to be still and wait for a message, "for usually our minds prevent the message coming through" (Big Star). Talking God warns the hero that when his voice is heard in the future it will be a warning or ominous sign that something will happen to him or his people on that day (Visionary Mb).

In the witch father-in-law episodes the hero may gain knowledge of his father-in-law's name for magical use, [74] but it is only in the Mountaintop Way story that the significance of such knowledge is explicitly stated: the heroine is protected from her bear husband's attempts to seize her because he does not know her name, "which would give him power over her" (Mountaintop W).

This survey has shown a scattering of explanatory statements in the chantway myths which tend to cluster around certain life activities and interests. Health, fertility and ritual are subjects which most frequently receive this type of treatment, but "explanations" also deal with sex, marriage, family relations, aggression, irresponsibility, property, and omens. The suitability of this material for value study merits some further discussion.

By the very fact of being singled out for special attention, the subject matter that becomes crystallized in explanatory statements may be assumed to have some special importance to the native narrator. For one reason or another this material is chosen for emphasis. From the recordings alone, it is not always possible to determine whether this emphasis reflects a general focus of interest in Navaho culture or springs from personal preoccupations of the narrator. However, when a similar explanation is offered in several different contexts, as the warning that disease or famine will result from ritual negligence, it may be assumed that this represents a cultural rather than individual interest. The circumstances of narration, of native informant vis-a-vis the anthropologist, may also affect the narrator's need to explain a given item in the story. The reference to sororal polygyny as "something written down back there" to explain "why policemen can't stop it" seems to be such an attempt to interpret the force of custom to an outsider. It is within limitations of this kind that items thus chosen for "explanation" are assumed to have value significance.

The term "explanatory element" implies an attempt to clarify by reason the existence of the phenomenon in question. The fact that such explanations may not fulfill logical requirements does not controvert this essential intent. An explanation of origins may rest on an appeal to tradition rather than on a rational tracing of causal connections. The origin of corn is referred to the occasion when a mythological hero is

taught to raise crops, or the occurrence of trance during ritual treatment is referred to similar seizures experienced by mythological characters. The origin of natural phenomena may simply be attributed to a
mythological incident in which the animal or natural phenomenon in
question figures, as in the sending of bees and tumbleweed to earth after
the hero's war with stinging insects. The foregoing explanations of origins are existential in nature. Others, although stated in causal terms,
introduce a normative component, as when various punishments are attributed to disregard of ritual rules. Often the explanatory element has
an artificial or forced quality; it seems inadequate or inappropriate to
the phenomenon it purports to explain. It is rationalizing rather than
rational, an attempt to give the facade of reason to phenomena whose
deeper significance is not recognized.

This rationalizing quality is perhaps most apparent in explanations
which fuse normative and existential elements in a single statement,
which give a rule of conduct and the reason why it should be observed.
Precepts, warnings or cautions are linked, either explicitly or by implication, with the unfortunate consequences that are expected automatically to result if the warning is not heeded. They can be recast in an
"if....then" causal statement. Thus, if ceremonial rules or taboos are
disregarded, illness or crop failure will result; compensation must be
made for sexual intercourse by the marriage payment to "avoid a bad
outcome"; the prohibition on brother-sister incest is explained by the
disastrous consequences which once resulted from such a practice.
Few, if any, prescriptions for action are presented without some such
attempt to identify a reason for their observance.

This type of cautionary statement which specifies not only the action
to be avoided but also the penalty for infringement would seem to have
particular usefulness for value analysis. These warnings present, as
it were, a double focus of value judgment; both the action and the punishment which it would precipitate are indicated as undesirable. In the
data cited the most common actions warned against are misuse of ritual
or disregard of ritual taboos. The penalties threatened are illness and
crop failure, both of which are realistic points of concern in Navaho
life. As the focus of Navaho ceremonialism, it is not surprising that the
positive value of health should be thus explicitly indicated in the ceremonial myths. Similarly the importance of fertility, which forms a secondary focus of interest in Navaho ceremonialism, receives recognition
by explanatory treatment. It may be noted, however, that the famine
threatened as penalty in these explanatory statements applies to crop
failure rather than to lack of game. In the action of the stories this situation is reversed; there it is by withholding of the game supply that
earth people are punished for transgressions.[75]

Turning attention from the penalty to the enjoined action, we find that
the bulk of cautionary statements warn against misuse of ceremonial
knowledge or disregard of taboos. That maintenance of ceremonial rules
and taboos should thus be valued is implicit in the psychological nature
of ritual itself, which acts to reduce emotional insecurity and anxiety.[76]

When it thus serves a psychological need, ritual activity comes to be valued in and of itself. The thematic analysis demonstrated the importance of the hero's responsible and disciplined action in his relations with supernaturals. In these cautionary statements of the specific punishments that will follow from violation of taboos and improper use of ritual we see again, and in a slightly different context, the importance attached to proper ritual observance.

V. SANCTIONS AND STANDARDS

Introduction

In this chapter we shall examine the myths in greater detail to see what can be learned from the dramatic content of the stories about the valuation of specific actions, character traits, and life situations. Although the material to be examined is the same as that employed in the impressionistic thematic analysis, a more systematic approach to this material will be attempted, with the purpose of identifying specific mythological elements that indicate the presence of value judgments. We shall assemble and discuss the mythological elements that show the operation of sanctions and that otherwise indicate standards of conduct. It is hoped that this analysis will provide some confirmation of the value themes already identified and will at the same time amplify and extend the thematic analysis with more specific content.

The "explanatory elements" discussed in the previous chapter were found to contain statements which set forth a rule of conduct together with the expected penalty for its violation. Such explanations presented an explicit and self-conscious statement of sanctions. The penalty was seen as resulting automatically from commission of the act. The relationship implied was causal and necessary, existing in the nature of things. But the "nature of things" included man's relations with the supernaturals, and many of the penalties were phrased as punishments imposed by the gods.

The occurrence of sanctions and beliefs about their operation can provide us with information about the value judgments of a society. Sanction is here used in its general meaning: a reaction showing approval or disapproval of an action or mode of behavior.[77] This reaction may be expressed in word or deed by members of the society; it may be attributed to the gods, as in the supernatural sanctions just referred to; or it may reside principally in the emotional reaction of the individual, as in the internal sanction of guilt. Whatever their locus, sanctions occur in response to actions that are considered desirable or undesirable. Explicit evidence of approval or disapproval, as in the imposition of sanctions, has been suggested by Kluckhohn as one of the convenient indices to value phenomena,[78] and we shall examine the mythological content for evidence of this kind.

Before embarking on our analysis, it may be well to consider some of the characteristics of social sanctions and anticipate some of the problems that will arise in attempting to identify their operation in literary materials. The cross-cutting classification of sanctions into positive and negative, organized and diffuse, will be useful in viewing the mythological material. Because negative sanctions tend to be more definitely formulated than positive ones, we may expect a clearer expression of negatively valued actions, what is to be avoided or guarded against, than of positively valued actions. In many cases, standards of the desirable are implicit in or may be deduced from standards of what is undesirable, but in this process they do not emerge with the same specificity and clarity as the negative standards. We shall be prepared, then, to find our attention directed predominantly to negative values.

The distinction between diffuse and organized sanctions is of particular interest in the analysis of literary materials. Organized sanctions are expressions of approval or disapproval, by word or deed, that are applied according to a definite and recognized procedure, as for instance the traditional Navaho penalty of mutilation inflicted on a woman guilty of adultery. By contrast, diffuse sanctions are spontaneous expressions of approval or disapproval by members of the society acting as individuals. Organized sanctions, clearly presented as such, play little part in the plot construction of the myths, although they appear, as does the penalty for adultery just noted, in incidents not essential to the plot development. On the other hand, diffuse sanctions do play a significant part in plot construction, but the attempt to identify them presents certain difficulties.

In literary material we have two problems in determining the value significance of diffuse sanctions. The first is whether an individual act of punishment or reward also represents group sentiment. In the absence of commentary by other actors in the story or by the narrator himself, it is difficult to judge whether a given action represents, for example, an individual impulsive act of revenge or a retaliation that is recognized as a justified penalty by group standards.[79] To some extent we shall have to rely on collateral evidence within the story itself (such as supporting actions or statement by other actors) and from ethnological sources in estimating the value significance of such material.

A second problem arises in judging the significance of the actor's success or failure in his enterprises. When may success be attributed to virtuous conduct; when is failure due to displeasure or punishment by gods or men? We are assuming that accidental good or bad fortune may be relegated to a minor role in myths, except insofar as they may embody native existential beliefs about chance. As human creative products, occurrences in the myths may be assumed to be in a sense controlled, so that they represent what their communal authorship wants them to represent and external chance factors do not intrude. Our problem here depends partly on the nature of fantasy as it operates in myths. If a bold and rebellious action meets with success, does this represent a fantasied wish fulfilment of desired but forbidden impulses? Or does it mean that the rebellious act is thereby condoned or approved? In general we have felt that collateral supporting evidence, internal or external to the myths, is necessary to warrant the latter interpretation, and this was the assumption used in the thematic analysis.

In our analysis of diffuse sanctions in the story content we shall have to make judgments in both of these areas: whether a given reaction represents a social sanction or is merely an individual reaction without significance for group values, and whether success or failure is to be taken as token of approval or disapproval. In this area our conclusions will have to be stated tentatively and as matters for further investigation.

The distinction between religious and secular sanctions also warrants some attention in the light of the material to be examined. Religious or supernatural sanctions may be distinguished from other diffuse sanctions by the fact that they rest on a system of religious beliefs and are implemented by gods or supernatural forces. In the primitive or folk society a separate area of religious belief is not so easy to demarcate as in complex societies. Even in the latter, where secular and rational controls seem to play a large part in interpersonal relations, these secular sanctions may be referred to a basic view of life which is in a sense religious in character. In the Navaho myths it is impossible to segregate the secular from the religious. Human and divine actors and activities are intimately interwoven. It is often difficult to distinguish whether a particular mode of behavior portrayed in the myths is considered appropriate for supernaturals, for fellow human beings, or for both. The gods are drawn into the human community where they play their part as figures of authority and power, whether this be in protective, malevolent, or neutral roles.

Although the following analysis will rely largely on the operation of sanctions, the action of the myths contains other material relevant to standards of conduct. Certain regularities of interpersonal behavior portrayed in the myths, for example behavior in relation to specific categories of kin, carry an implication of appropriateness even though they do not call forth explicit positive sanctions. We may think of these as role expectancies in interpersonal relations. In some cases deviation, within limits, from role expectancies is allowable, or role alternatives may be culturally patterned. If myth is accepted as a "communal product," the role behavior pictured therein is also in a sense communally sanctioned, except insofar as it represents fantasies of the "culturally disallowed." Where possible, ideal patterns of this kind will be identified in the mythological material and will be compared with similar ethnological material. In the thematic analysis this type of data has been utilized, but we shall call attention here to some specific patterns, particularly in the areas of kinship behavior and relations with aliens.

In choice of topics for our survey of sanctions and standards, we are governed by the mythological data. Certain subjects were found to recur from story to story and to be dealt with in similar fashion in different contexts. The sequence in which they will be discussed is to a certain extent arbitrary. We have chosen to begin with material on subsistence and property and to proceed to interpersonal relations as they are seen in sex and marriage, family and kinship relations, and, finally, in relations with non-kin and aliens. Material on character traits will be discussed as it occurs in relation to the foregoing topics.

Subsistence and Property

A. Subsistence

Success or failure in hunting game provides the central plot interest in two stories (Navaho Wind, Chiricahua Wind), and it is pictured as an important means of subsistence in twelve others (Water, Shooting, Big Star, Mountaintop, Prostitution, Moth, Visionary, Twins, Plume, Eagle, Bead, Flint). By contrast agriculture is of major interest only in the story that purports to explain the introduction of crops (Plume), although some agricultural activity is pictured in five others (Water, Prostitution, Beauty, Navaho Wind, Eagle). Families that are described as living in poverty obtain their meager livelihood by hunting woodrats or birds and gathering wild seeds; their means of subsistence does not include agriculture, nor do they hunt large game. Marriage to a stranger who has better knowledge of hunting and material culture techniques brings more comfortable circumstances (Big Star, Eagle). Ritual for hunting (Prostitution, Mountaintop) and eagle trapping (Eagle) is learned and prized. The hero of Mountaintop Way is spared by the Utes so that he may teach them how to use the stalking equipment and ritual that he has just acquired from his father. The hero learns hunting ritual from supernaturals (Prostitution) or from his malevolent father-in-law (Plume).

In the thematic analysis we have noted how the hero is punished by supernaturals for hunting in forbidden territory, or merely for venturing into it to satisfy his curiosity. The supernaturals also control and regulate the amount of game taken by a hunter. They withhold game as a punishment for ritual transgressions or lack of proper respect, or simply to enforce limits of moderation. The able and careful hunter who never kills game wantonly is viewed with approval (Flint), while the hunter who kills to excess incurs the anger of the gods (Chiricahua B), becomes ill (Plume Wc), or must be taught the error of his ways by supernatural instruction (Bead K). The gods withhold game when they consider that a hunting party has killed sufficient deer or in punishment for the slaughter of magpie and crow (Visionary). The supernatural keepers of game explain how they value game greatly and agree to release only enough to sustain the hero (Chiricahua Wind). Excess in hunting seems to be considered an expression of lack of respect for supernatural sources of provision, and in this respect it is similar to ritual transgressions. The hero of Chiricahua Wind Way is initially punished for excess in hunting (Version B) or for ridiculing supernaturals (Version A) by having his game withheld. He is preoccupied with this hunting failure and subsequently indulges in a series of impulsive or consciously disobedient acts in hunting, whereby he is drawn into contact with supernaturals, punished by them and finally emerges chastened and with power of his own. The hero of Navaho Wind Way is punished for committing a series of prohibited acts, among which are hunting in forbidden territory and eating the entrails of the deer he has killed. Violation of food taboos occurs in a minor hunting incident when the hero misuses his animal hosts' raw food; again game is withheld in punishment.

Although agriculture appears not infrequently in the story content, it does not assume the importance in plot development that hunting does. In several minor incidents the hero finds frog or toad at work in his garden (Water, Prostitution, Navaho Wind). Corn, "the gift of life," is given to the sisters of Eagle Way with instructions from supernaturals that it is to be carefully guarded. Corn grinding provides a setting for flirtation or for the marriage test whereby a maiden is selected by her success in tossing a cornmeal ball. The heroine of Beauty Way finds crops in the underground home of the snakes and in her ignorance she encounters difficulties in cooking them. In the latter references corn and crops are principally associated with feminine activities. There is only one story in which agriculture plays a major role. At the conclusion of his hollow log trip the hero of Plume Way obtains knowledge of gardening and the associated ritual and brings it back to his people. In one version the corn brought back relieves famine that had commenced at his departure and serves to wipe out the original offense of gambling for which he had been rejected (Plume G). The second portion of the Plume Way story deals in a parallel fashion with hunting; it is devoted to the hero's acquisition of hunting powers from his evil father-in-law, Deer Raiser.

The foregoing references indicate the important place that the stories give to hunting activities. Hunting is pictured as a valued means of subsistence. In addition certain rules of conduct for hunting are indicated. Ritual transgression and excess in taking game are pictured as punishable offenses subject to supernatural sanctions. In the previous chapter we noted how, except for taboos on eating certain parts of deer, hunting activities were not subjected to "explanatory" treatment. On the other hand, fertility and crop failure did become a focus for explanatory and cautionary statements; the evil consequences of ritual misuse of corn are specified and drought and crop failure are threatened as punishment for ritual transgressions. Thus, while both hunting and agriculture play important roles in the myths, they receive differential treatment. Hunting adventures provide material for plot development, and it is from the operation of sanctions in the action of the stories that we reconstruct rules of conduct for hunting. For the most part agricultural activities do not provide material for plot development; they are not so firmly woven into the dramatic fabric of the stories, and our notion of values associated with agriculture comes from a different source, from the cautionary statements that specify drought and crop failure as themselves a punishment for ritual transgression.[80]

B. Poverty

In the thematic analysis poverty was seen to be one of the factors contributing to the hero's misfortunes. His poverty provides opportunity

for exploitation by Pueblo neighbors (Prostitution, Bead). In the eagle's
nest story of Bead Way the hero is presented as a poor beggar or slave
whose condition is taken advantage of by the Pueblos to trick him into
the dangerous feat of obtaining eagle feathers from a cliff nest. He is
forced to comply, or he accedes to their demand on promise of food. In
his own words: "I lead but a poor life at best. Existence is not sweet
to a man who always hungers." In the only version in which the hero
chooses voluntarily to undertake the feat, he measures the promised reward of riches (jewelry and horses) against the possibility of being
tricked, and he decides to risk it (Bead H&H). The Pueblos plan to
leave the helpless Navaho stranded in the nest after he has thrown down
the eagle feathers to them. This situation constitutes the predicament
from which supernaturals rescue him, and with the power thus gained
he later retaliates by winning valuables from his Pueblo tormentors.

The disadvantages of poverty which place the individual in such a
vulnerable position, open to trickery and exploitation, are also demonstrated in the Prostitution Way story. Here the beggar hero is subjected
to scorn, teasing, and ridicule for his poverty and exploited sexually by
Pueblo women. From this situation likewise the supernaturals rescue
him; from his visit with them he acquires three kinds of power — love
magic, hunting magic, and the power to transform property (e.g., poor
furnishings into fine). With the love magic he seduces maidens and
acquires wives. The marriage payment is made with antelope killed by
his newly acquired hunting magic. He uses the power to transform
property to improve the furnishings of his home for his wives. As noted
in the previous chapter, this incident is cited as "explanation" for the
origin of the marriage payment.[81]

Two versions of Water Way (Wa, Wb) repeat the ridicule of the beggar hero by Pueblos and his retaliation by sexual conquests. In these
and a third version (Water H) the hero is also ridiculed among his own
people not only for his poverty but also for a self-inflicted, disfiguring
skin disease which earns him the name Rough Skin. In the preparations
to expose himself to ridicule, his "grandmothers" induce him to race
ceremonially by promising valuables (horses, sheep, soft goods, jewels).
In the story of the stricken twins, poverty leads their family to abandon
them when their accidental crippling makes them too great a burden.
Because they are poor and lack offerings their petition for cure is refused by the gods until their supernatural kinship is established or until
they have won the necessary valuables by trickery from the Pueblos.
Here also the twins are mocked and teased for their poverty and deformity by both the gods and the Pueblos.

In these incidents poverty, sometimes combined with physical deformity, is presented as an undesirable condition which provokes ridicule and exploitation, but from which the hero may be released by
supernatural aid. Paralleling this external sanction of ridicule for
poverty is a personal emotional reaction on the part of the actor himself which ranges from modesty to shame when in his lowly condition
or poor appearance he is confronted with persons of high estate. When

the hero discovers and approaches a well furnished home, he puts aside
his poor moccasins and possessions in shame before entering (Hail,
Plume). His shame in these instances is apparently mingled with sexual
shyness, since in these visits he is either seduced or welcomed as a
son-in-law. Similarly the mother of the crippled twins is shy in the
presence of her supernatural lover who is "too fine a man" for her lowly status (Twins), and wandering sisters are at first reluctant to accept
the favors and hospitality of their unknown resplendent benefactor (Eagle).
Evidence of modesty is not limited to sexual situations but appears also
in other relations with supernaturals. In the test of kinship the crippled twins choose the poor bow and arrow as suitable to their poor es-
tate (Twins), and in the hollow log story the hero's grandmother is
sceptical that supernaturals would visit "such poor people as we" (Plume).

Standards of property and youth are applied in judgments of an unknown suitor. In Enemy Way, sister heroines are refused to tattered
and decrepit old men suitors (bear and snake), but their magical transformation to handsome and well attired youths reassures the maidens,
"for surely....such finely dressed, handsome men could mean no harm."
The hero of Navaho Wind Way is enticed by a beautiful maiden to her
well furnished home, but he is saved from seduction when she is transformed into an ugly old woman and her fine furnishings turn to rags
(Navaho Wind).

These references to poverty and wealth give us a fuller picture of
the values attached to the possession of goods. We see again the association of property with supernatural power that was discussed in the
thematic analysis. Offerings are needed to approach the gods and, in
turn, power acquired from supernaturals can be used to obtain property.
Further than this, poverty is presented as an undesirable state, one
which lays the subject open to ridicule and exploitation. Possession of
material goods is shown as a means of sexual conquest. Property is
needed for the marriage payment. Old age, deformity and poverty are
associated with sexual rejection, while youth, fine clothes and a handsome appearance win acceptance.[82]

The use of trickery and deceit in the foregoing account of property
dealings is noteworthy. The Pueblos do not hesitate to trick a helpless
Navaho, and the Navahos retaliate in kind. The Navaho beggar who was
tricked into the eagle's nest (Bead) later uses his newly acquired ceremonial power to defraud the Pueblos of their valuables. Trickery is
also used without such initial provocation, as when the crippled twins
bring plagues to the Pueblo crops so that they can use their magic to
get rid of the pests and then collect the reward. Even within the in-
group valuables are stolen when needed for ceremonial offerings; the
hero of the hollow log trip lies when he assures supernaturals that he
has the proper offerings and then has his niece steal them from neighbors (Plume). The secret of proper offerings for a god is learned by
deceit; big fly and other intermediaries repeatedly reveal these secrets
to earth people under promise that their masters not be informed of the
source of their knowledge (Twins, Navaho Wind, Chiricahua Wind, Bead,

Flint, Enemy). The trickery and deceit used in property dealings does not meet with negative sanctions, nor are they made into moral issues. Rather, they seem to be expected on both sides, and they often accomplish positive results, such as obtaining cure. The significance of deceit and trickery in interpersonal relations will be considered at greater length later. For the present we wish merely to point out their presence in property dealings.

C. Responsibility

This discussion of subsistence and property presents a convenient springboard for considering standards of personal responsibility and industry as they appear in the myths. In the thematic analysis we have shown how the hero is transformed from a self-willed and irresponsible youth to one who undertakes and fulfills serious ceremonial obligations for his people. In the action of the stories we find sanctions imposed for excessive gambling and other evidence of unfavorable attitudes toward irresponsibility, indolence, and lack of direction in life activities.

One of the stereotyped incidents used to begin a story is the hero's rejection because of his excessive gambling (Hail, Visionary, Plume).[83] He gambles away his family's possessions (Hail, Visionary, Plume). His people remonstrate with him to no avail (Hail). They threaten physical punishment of whipping or death, which he escapes with supernatural help, and he is thus driven from home into solitary wanderings (Hail, Plume). Such gambling carried to excess and the irresponsible loss of the property belonging to others provokes punishment. In other contexts gambling does not of itself call forth sanctions. In betting contests of skill the hero often fares well. After losing his body parts to frog in one race, he is aided by supernaturals to win in a second (Hail). In his successful contests with White Butterfly (also known as the Great Gambler), the contenders bet their possessions, their wives, and even their own bodies, and the hero wins by trickery and supernatural aid (Water, Prostitution).[84] It is in the description of this contest that the narrator stops to explain how such games lead to quarreling (see Explanatory Elements, above). Runners for the Navaho win valuables from Apache aliens (Mountaintop). In these incidents gambling is presented as an accepted and often successful activity. It is only when it becomes excessive or irresponsible that it meets with disapproval, which is expressed in organized community sanctions threatening whipping or death.

There is some indication that excessive absorption in games, whether or not betting takes place, is viewed as dangerous. On two occasions a child is stolen while its protectors are absorbed in a game (Big Star, Navaho Wind). A heroine meets disaster when she insists on participating in the rolling stone game of rock wrens which has taken her fancy (Beauty). Jicarilla Apache invited to a corral dance are late because they have stopped to play or gamble on the way (Water, Mountaintop). These actions do not meet with organized sanctions, as in the case of the hero's excessive gambling, but they are pictured as leading, at least in the first two examples, to an unfortunate outcome. Similarly, a self-willed insistence on satisfying curiosity leads to disastrous results. The hero or heroine disregards warnings of supernatural protectors (eagles, snakes) to explore to the four directions and repeatedly meets disaster — by letting loose uncontrollable storms, being captured, shot, transformed or buried by animal attackers (Beauty, Bead). Disapproving attitudes toward such self-willed and irresponsible behavior are indicated by the Beauty Way story. The heroine's snake hosts complain about the trouble her stupidity and wilfulness cause them and voice disapproval of her aimless wandering (Beauty). She justifies her actions as satisfying her curiosity and reassures herself with the thought that she always returns safely. When accosted by owl she responds to his questions with evasion, explaining her presence simply as aimless wandering. Owl rejects this explanation with the admonition that she does not like "one that wanders about with no purpose in view."

Thus, the hero's adventures appear in two different, but not contradictory, guises. From his point of view his actions are motivated by persistence, courage, and audacity, sometimes masked by ignorance, and they ultimately bring rewards of ritual power. From the viewpoint of supernaturals these same actions provide opportunity for testing and developing his ability to accept supernatural discipline and to act responsibly. We have noted that toward the end of his series of trials he obtains a supernatural monitor who directs his actions, as in the successful evasion of witch father-in-law attacks. In Wetherill's version of Plume Way this condition for final conferring of ceremonial power is explicitly formulated; not until the malevolent father-in-law sees that the hero "has at last learned to heed a warning" does he teach him the ceremony. In other cases the hero must demonstrate his knowledge and responsibility before being allowed to return to his own people with it (Visionary). A parallel transformation from irresponsibility and indolence was found in the recurrent, stylized incident of choosing messengers for the fire dance (Hail, Water, Mountaintop), where the reputedly lazy boys perform successfully as runners (see above). In the course of ritual instruction, the learner is transformed from apparent laziness to responsibility. A younger brother of the hero who appears slovenly, ugly, and stupid is urged by his grandmother to learn the ritual when the elder brothers fail; since he has been memorizing the songs while pretending to sleep, he is successful and thenceforth takes more care of his personal appearance.

Among the supernaturals irresponsibility is not condoned. Little sorrow is expressed by their fellow supernaturals when crow and magpie are killed by hunters, since they would not heed warnings but let themselves be irresistibly drawn by freshly killed meat (Visionary). When the hero's supernatural protector forgets his duties and becomes absorbed in dancing, his charge is stolen by hostile gods (Visionary).

In summary, a negative valuation of irresponsible behavior is indicated by two types of evidence in the foregoing material. Negative sanctions of expressed disapproval or threatened punishment are imposed when the indolence and irresponsibility go beyond bounds. At the same time these qualities are pictured as leading to physical disaster while their opposites, industry and responsibility, bring success in feats of physical skill or in ability to learn ritual.[85]

Sex and Marriage

Some of the sexual content of the chantway stories has been discussed in the thematic analysis, particularly the significance of the hero's marriage as a step in attaining adult status in family relationships. We have also noted that acts of adultery and seduction figure prominently in the stories. Sexual incidents involving adultery, seduction, or marriage are of interest for plot development in all of the myths except one (Visionary). In thirteen stories they constitute major episodes (Hail, Water, Shooting, Big Star, Mountaintop, Beauty, Prostitution, Moth, Plume, Eagle, Flint, Enemy, Shooting-Ghost).

Adultery brings disaster, or threat of disaster, to the hero. (The term adultery is here used in its dictionary definition: sexual intercourse of two persons, either of whom is married to a third person.) In six stories the hero commits adultery and is attacked by the offended husband (Hail, Water, Shooting, Big Star, Prostitution, Flint). This happens whether it is the hero (Water) or the unfaithful wife (Hail, Shooting, Flint) who takes the initiative in making sexual advances. That the husband's attack is conceived as justified retaliation with group sanction rather than merely individual revenge is indicated in several cases by the context. The anger and retaliation of the offended husband is expected. Although eager to protect the hero, supernaturals claim they are powerless to ward off the impending attack (Water), or after restoration from a first attack, the supernaturals who side with the hero warn that the offended husband still holds a grudge (Hail). When the hero commits adultery with a singer's twelve wives in revenge for ridicule, he is warned that punishment is inevitable, that it must take place as ordained (Water). Demonstration of the hero's own power finally dissipates the grudge held by the offended husband (Flint). In the marriage to buffalo women (Shooting, Flint) the hero's new in-laws warn him of the power of his wives' former husband; his new father-in-law admonishes him for the great fault he has committed in taking the wives of such an important person (Flint). When the hero's companions commit adultery with the wives of their hosts, the party is sent away with curses (Shooting). The offending wife is sometimes punished — by thunder attack (Flint), or by subsequent desertion (Prostitution).

In other incidents the hero finds himself in the position of the offended husband. Coyote transforms him and steals his wife (Prostitution, Big Star). Although the trick is temporarily successful, the hero regains his own form with supernatural help and retaliates by blowing Coyote's hide back onto him (Prostitution) or by killing him (Big Star). When his wives are stolen by White Butterfly, the hero uses supernatural aid to defeat him in contests and finally kills him (Water, Prostitution). Sometimes his anger and jealousy cannot be assuaged, and he punishes his wives also by desertion (Prostitution, Water) or by killing them (Prostitution), later taking out his anger by indiscriminate seductions (Prostitution).

Sanctions against adultery are thus acted out in the stories. The traditional penalty of mutilation imposed on the woman is mentioned in an explanatory element but does not occur in the story action. There is some indication that, despite disapproval, the outcome of an adulterous relationship depends in some measure on the relative power of the two contending men. Thus, the hero is able to keep his buffalo wives when he demonstrates his superior power (Shooting, Flint), or to regain those stolen by White Butterfly (Water, Prostitution). It is through his accumulation of power that the hero is finally able to render ineffective the continued retaliatory grudge of the offended husband (Hail, Water, Flint).

Seductions, whether or not they involve adultery, may show either the man or the woman taking the initiative. Those in which the hero makes the advances serve as demonstration of his magic power and as retaliation for slight or ridicule suffered, as in the butterfly seduction of non-sunlight-struck Pueblo maidens (Water, Prostitution, Enemy). The woman is pictured as drawn by forces beyond her power to resist although aware of her wrongdoing (Water, Prostitution, Enemy). In the seduction of sisters, the younger voices premonition of evil: she is reluctant and questions whether it is safe to follow the sweet smell of smoke with which bear and snake are enticing them (Enemy); and again in the butterfly seduction she complains, "In vain I try not to want it (the butterfly), in vain it dissatisfies me" (Water Hb).

In these seductions the woman fears her family's wrath and punishment for her unacceptable marriage (Water, Prostitution, Enemy, Beauty, Mountaintop). Similarly the mother of the stricken twins fears to tell her family of her relations with the resplendent stranger, Talking God, who is "too fine a man" for her (Twins). When their family threatens violent retaliation (beating), the women have to flee to the protection of their new husbands (Water, Prostitution, Enemy). Even when the woman herself takes the initiative in the seduction, her family may voice their disapproval (Eagle, Flint). We have noted that the family's anger at these unacceptable marriage choices which separate the woman from them or bring an undesirable spouse into their group is congruent with the social requirements of matrilocal residence. In the extended matrilocal family it is of crucial importance that the new member be acceptable to and accepted into the woman's family group. The sanctions observed in the story action indicate that a woman's free marriage choice, without her family's assent, is considered undesirable, nor do such liaisons or marriage in the stories usually survive.

The myths also present a contrasting marriage type in which the hero, visiting as a stranger, is invited into the woman's family. The family group is pictured as isolated and anxious for a new son-in-law, and the hero is immediately welcomed as such. He neither takes the

initiative nor appears to be reluctant; the arrangement is engineered by
the woman's father. This type of marriage occurs most frequently in
the witch father-in-law episodes, where the father's welcome proves to
be deceitful and the new son-in-law is subjected to trials (Plume, Eagle,
Enemy, Shooting-Ghost). It is, however, not limited to these; sometimes the new husband is welcomed without trickery (Big Star, Bead,
Plume Wa), or the father-in-law does not become hostile until the hero
tries to leave (Prostitution, Navaho Wind, Chiricahua Wind). The comparatively passive hero drawn into marriage by circumstances or the
machinations of the new wife's people finds a counterpart in autobio-
graphical material,[86] and it is congruent with Navaho matrilineal and
matrilocal family structure. The mythological emphasis on the father-
in-law's hostile actions may be functionally related to strains and tensions which are generated in such a structure. In the fantasy of myth
the forbidden aspects of these tensions, e.g., the incestuous attraction
between father and daughter and the consequent rivalry with the new
son-in-law, are apparently allowed an overt expression that would be
unacceptable in actual life.

The passive role of the hero in sexual relationships noted above finds
other expressions in the myths. He is seduced by women whom he does
not know are married (Hail, Shooting, Flint). The dangerous, tempting
woman is personified by the parallel characters "The Woman Who Dries
People Up," Changing Bear Woman, and Hunger (or Thin Woman), who
are said to harm their lovers. These women participate as beautiful
maidens in corn grinding and win a marriage test by successfully tossing an unbroken ball of cornmeal to the man of their choice (Navaho
Wind, Mountaintop). The hero is impressed with the fine home to which
the beautiful maiden (Woman Who Dries People Up) brings him, but he
wakes in the morning to find her turned into an old hag and himself
stranded on a sky-reaching-rock; he flees in desperation and escapes
only with the aid of helpful animals, one of whom stops the old hag's
pursuit by defeating her in a race (Navaho Wind). Changing Bear Woman
and Hunger are said to give their lovers sores or starve them to death.

This nightmare fantasy of the beautiful, seductive woman who turns
to a destructive old hag in the morning occurs frequently in Zuni myths.[87]
It does not have such a prominent place in the Navaho chantway myths,
occurring only in the two stories noted above, nor does it seem to occur as frequently in the total body of Navaho mythology as it does in the
Zuni myths. An allied incident is found in the Navaho coyote cycle, in
which Changing Bear Maiden becomes destructive as a result of her
sexual relations with Coyote. The association of both of these dangerous
women, Changing Bear Maiden and The Woman Who Dries People Up,
with witchcraft seems to enhance their power to evoke dread. Rather
than this image of the woman who is dangerous and destructive in herself, the chantway myths emphasize the image of the seductive woman
who leads the man into conflict with the men to whom she rightfully
belongs.

Certain aberrant sexual episodes occur in the stories which will be more fully dealt with in the discussion of family relations. These are, for instance, the abortive attempt at brother-sister marriage, the incestuous bond between father and daughter in the witch father-in-law episodes, and marriage to a wife's sister. Here, however, the attitude toward offspring born to such aberrant unions should be noted. There are three instances in which the infant is abandoned in shame — the offspring of the witch father-in-law and his daughter, who is later raised by owl (Plume S& H), that of a hero's deceitful marriage to his wife's sister, also raised by owl (Mountaintop), and the monster infant born as a result of Coyote's adulterous relations with the hero's wives (Prostitution).

Legitimate marriages as pictured in these stories are shifting and short lived. The hero contracts a series of unrelated marriages or sexual liaisons. In his wanderings, although already married, he is welcomed into a new household as son-in-law, where he lives until he grows restless again. He may leave one wife, or wives, for an interlude with another and later return to the first attachment. Marriage is usually terminated by the hero's restlessness; he simply leaves. On a few occasions jealousy over a wife's adultery brings the relationship to an end, as in two of the hero's marriages to non-sunlight-struck Pueblo maidens in Prostitution Way. The stories do not reveal group attitudes toward these actions. Personal responses are sometimes evoked by the hero's departure, e.g., the rejected wives are disappointed or the father-in-law angered. The fact that negative sanctions are not apparent may signify acceptance of these shifting sexual relationships. Census data compiled for a small Navaho community show in actuality a pattern of shifting marriages with frequent separation or divorce.[88]

Termination of marriage also occurs when the husband has performed ritual over his wife (Beauty, Big Star). In the Beauty Way story the impropriety of continuing as husband and wife after this has occurred is pointed out in an explanatory detail. In another story, after singing over his wife to cleanse her from the effects of Coyote's adultery, the hero is told by the gods that he should not return to her (Big Star). These actions are consonant with the Navaho conception of the relation between singer and patient as a kinship tie which precludes sexual contact.[89]

Polygyny, although merely touched on in the myths, bears some mention here. In four stories there is one or more polygynous marriage or liaison (Water, Prostitution, Eagle, Flint). In all cases these unions involve sisters, who usually maintain a solidary relationship with each other in the marriage. The frequency of polygyny would in itself seem to reflect an accepted cultural pattern. At one point the narrator explains, as it were for the benefit of his white listener, that the custom of having two wives is "written down back there" (Prostitution). One puzzling exception to this acceptance of sororal polygyny is the incident in Wheelwright's version of the Mountaintop Way story in which a hero schemes to replace his own wife with her sister by pretending death in order to return in disguise. This is a variation on the Navaho tale of Coyote's marriage to his own daughter and carries the implication of such an illicit relationship. In the absence of evidence that such disapproval attaches to the marriage to a wife's sister and the abundant evidence to the contrary, a possible explanation of this incident may be that the narrator intentionally substituted this character to avoid an objectionable theme of father-daughter incest. In this incident the first wife's sister is not seductive; rather the husband takes the initiative. The solidary relationship between sisters usually evident in these polygynous marriages is reflected here in the action of the younger sister, who immediately communicates to the older her suspicions about the identity of her new husband. In one version of the seduction by buffalo women this solidarity is underlined by the elder sister's explanation for bringing her younger sister along, that she "did not trust to do it alone" (Flint Ha). In only one instance is hostility between sisters of a polygynous marriage indicated, and solution of the difficulty takes an unexpected form. The wives quarrel and, distressed at "this new phase of their married life," they commit suicide by disappearing into a spring (Prostitution P).

Although sororal polygyny and harmonious relations between the co-wives are clearly reflected in the action of these stories, the appearance of such discrepant details as the illicit marriage to a wife's sister and the suicide of sister co-wives raises some questions of interpretation. From the data of the myths the significance of these aberrant incidents is not apparent. A possible explanation for treating marriage to the wife's sister as illicit has been advanced. The reason for the drastic means of avoiding friction in the second incident is obscure; another version also terminates this marriage violently by the hero's forcing his wives into the water (Prostitution Ha). There is some reason to think that sororal polygyny is a fairly recent development,[90] and the appearance of these discordant incidents may be the result of some ambivalence surrounding this custom.

In summary, the myths present two types of sexual situations which provoke negative sanctions. These are a man's adultery with a married woman and a woman's unacceptable marriage choice. In the former case the sanction takes the form of retaliation by the woman's offended husband, in the latter punishment by the woman's own people. In addition there is evidence that the internal sanction of shame is active in certain cases of aberrant sexual unions. We have noted the injunction against continuing a marriage when the husband has performed a ceremony for his wife and how this is carried out in the action of one story. The occurrence of polygyny and of short lived, shifting marriages is accepted without comment in the myths and seems to reflect customary standards operating in actual life. The nightmarish fantasy of sexually dangerous women is more difficult to interpret in value terms. Along with evidence of the hero's passive role in some other sexual incidents, this may point to an important component in the young man's image of women, but the material here analyzed is provocative rather than conclusive on this point.

Family and Kin

The foregoing discussion of sex and marriage has touched at several points on relations within the actor's parental family, as in references to incest and to the relation of sisters in sororal polygyny. This section will review the mythological material on family and blood kin relations as it seems to reveal on the one hand accepted attitude and action patterns and on the other sanctions for unacceptable behavior between kin.

Most of the myths indicate directly or by implication the family situation of the hero or heroine. The stories are about equally divided between those which specify a complete family group of mother, father, and siblings (Hail, Big Star, Mountaintop, Beauty, Twins, Navaho Wind, Chiricahua Wind, Flint) and those in which the hero's family is incomplete. The relation between siblings may be the chief family tie shown (Shooting, Visionary, Eagle, Bead, Shooting-Ghostway), or to relatives through a sister (sister's daughters) (Enemy). The hero and a maternal figure, mother or foster grandmother, constitute an isolated family group in two myths, both of which concern sexual powers and do not entail the hero's teaching of a ceremony to his own people (Water, Prostitution). Various versions of the Plume Way story include several of these relationships by introducing the hero as residing with his family but living apart with a grandmother and niece and ultimately returning to teach his brothers ceremonial knowledge.

The central importance of the family, the pattern of the hero's separation from it and his subsequent return with ceremonial power have been described in the thematic analysis. It was seen that the ostensible reason for separation varied from a punishing rejection by the family to active exploratory curiosity on the part of the hero, but that underlying this range of forms there seemed to be a covert preoccupation with the hero's own attempts to break away from family bonds, whether he did this straightforwardly or by provoking punishment and rejection. Recognition of family ties figured thus at the beginning of the story and again at its conclusion when the hero was reunited with his people.

The positive aspect of family ties is demonstrated by the joy with which the hero is welcomed home regardless of the original reason for separation. He is careful to avoid any actions in his contacts with supernaturals that would prevent return, such as marriage (Bead) or eating the food of his animal hosts (Hail, Mountaintop, Navaho Wind). He is sometimes subjected to tests which he must pass successfully if he is to see his people again (Hail, Visionary). Sorrow is evinced at the original separation (Mountaintop, Prostitution, Beauty, Visionary) and again on his final departure to live with the gods (Hail, Mountaintop). His family is worried and troubled when they fear he has met mishap, and the father makes every effort to rescue him (Navaho Wind, Chiricahua Wind, Flint). Remorse is shown for causing harm to one's own people (Visionary, Water, Prostitution, Flint). The hero is troubled by the slaughter of his relatives, in which he has been unwittingly instrumental, and organizes a retaliatory raid (Enemy).

A. Parents and Children

Within this general atmosphere of positive family ties, there is sometimes more specific representation of the parents' desire for or fondness of children. The parent eagles show their gratitude for the hero's protection of their children (Bead). Parents become angered by or try to avenge the death of their children (Hail, Chiricahua Wind, Enemy). The hero of Navaho Wind Way comes upon crazy people who are doing "an ugly thing"; they throw their children into the fire and then revive them. The possessive love of parents for the children they have raised is illustrated in the disastrous extreme by their unsuccessful attempt to keep them within the family by brother-sister marriage (Moth). Even though a new mother denies knowledge of the father of her children, the family feels that it is good to have their number increased (Twins).

Desertion of children occurs in three types of situation — in illicit marriages, under economic stress, and as a negative sanction directed against irresponsibility. The abandonment of offspring of an incestuous or irregular marriage has been taken as evidence of shame at such a union. Thus, the child of a girl by her witch father is abandoned to be raised by owl (Plume S&H), as is the child of the stealthy union between a man and his wife's sister (Mountaintop). The monster born when Coyote steals the hero's wives is thrown away at birth (Prostitution). Children are abandoned when parents are unable to care for them — when the family flees from a bear in famine (Mountaintop) and when they are unable to support the economic burden of the crippled twins (Twins).[91] In both cases the children return later to their parents with supernatural power, but they make no overt attempt to shame the parents for their action.[92] Finally, desertion or rejection of children is used as a negative sanction applied against the hero's irresponsibility, as when he gambles away his family's property (Hail, Visionary, Plume). The owl boy who becomes dangerous with bow and arrow is threatened with punishment and driven off by his own people (Mountaintop).

Certain aspects of the relation of the male hero to his parents, and more particularly to his father, have been considered in the thematic analysis. To the extent that later attitudes toward authority are patterned on childhood experience within the family, the images of authority should reveal something about the young boy's attitudes toward his father and other adult males in the family group. As we have seen, the hero's discipline is usually effected by supernaturals rather than by his own father. Disobedience of the actual father occurs only rarely, as when the hero of Mountaintop Way disregards his father's instructions not to hunt to the north. Often the authority for the prohibition remains anonymous; it resides in ritual taboos, impersonal prohibitions against trespass, the force of natural and social hazards, and ultimately in the power of supernaturals. The hero's self-assertive defiance of authority provokes immediate punishment by the offended supernatural. But in the long view, these very punishments provide the means and discipline for the hero's growth in ritual knowledge and ability to take care of himself.

In the few cases in which the father is at the same time a supernatural, he assumes a magically protective and nurturant role. Talking God thus advises the crippled twins in their search for cure and magically provides them with food and covering (Twins). The sun father is constrained to help his sons and give them magical powers once their identity is established (Shooting, Plume Wc). In these stories the actual father is not shown as the authority who disciplines or punishes a son;[93] this is left to supernatural figures or the wicked father-in-law. On the other hand the father does seek aid for a son who has met mishap (Navaho Wind, Chiricahua Wind, Flint). In these stories the actual father is presented as solicitous for and protective of the son's welfare, or he is absent from the action entirely.

Thus, the mythological material indicates a double conception of the adult males, as punishing and retributive authorities and as protective figures. These two facets of the father image have been discussed in the thematic analysis, where their congruence with the results of projective tests given to modern Navaho young men was pointed out. A counterpart of this double image seems to be represented in the hero's own ambivalent attitudes toward authority resulting on the one hand in his audacious actions which necessitate appeals for help and on the other in his submission to discipline.

Conflicting attitudes in the father-daughter relationship become manifest in connection with the daughter's sexual activities and marriage. When daughters bring home an unacceptable "earth person" as husband, their father complains that this is the result of their wandering at night, that they should have stayed home (Eagle). We have already noted other occasions on which daughters are punished for an unacceptable marriage choice. A father questions his daughters closely about their delay at the spring when getting water, suspecting that they have met a man (Prostitution). In this case the father is eager to find their suitor and institutes an exhaustive search to identify his footprint; he is pleased when he finds the hero and invites him to his home "to make the marriage sure" (Prostitution). In the witch father-in-law episodes the hero is cordially welcomed as a new husband for the unmarried daughter, and the father is shown as concerned about her marriage.

Some of the witch father-in-law episodes clearly reveal contradictory elements underlying the father's concern and eagerness for his daughter's marriage. The occurrence of father-daughter incest is specified in three of these episodes (Plume, Enemy, Shooting-Ghostway) and the father's jealousy is offered as explanation for his attack on the daughter's new husband, despite his original cordiality. Moral condemnation of such an incestuous relationship is evident in the literary treatment of these situations. The father-in-law is identified as a witch by virtue of this incestuous relation as well as by his other illegitimate activities (cannibalism, traffic with the dead). Incest is a "symptom" of witchcraft, and attitudes toward it are intimately connected with the general fear and condemnation of witchcraft.[94] In Plume Way the hero finds neighboring people who confirm his suspicions of the father-in-law's evil intentions, and the father-in-law himself is finally brought to "admit his evil ways." In the two other versions of this episode the wife warns her new husband of her father's intentions and helps him to evade attack (Enemy, Shooting-Ghostway). She knows her father's witch ways and claims that "he really is no good" (Enemy). The fact that the hero ultimately triumphs over the wicked father-in-law is taken as cause for satisfaction (Plume, Shooting-Ghostway), and when not thus successful, the hero is left with anger and resentment at being outwitted and proceeds to take revenge for the wrong done to him and his kinsmen (Enemy). Further consideration of witchcraft as a condemned and forbidden means of conducting interpersonal relations will be postponed to a later section; here it is sufficient to note the condemnation of incest and its intimate connection with witchcraft in Navaho thought.

The mother-daughter relationship appears in the stories only in connection with reception of the daughter's new husband. The mother withdraws from the group in observance of the mother-in-law taboo (Flint, Shooting-Ghostway), but the daughter goes to consult her when the father is rendered unconscious by the new son-in-law's tobacco (Plume, Shooting-Ghostway). A grandmother[95] intercedes to calm the grandfather's anger when the daughter brings home a new husband; she points out that the new son-in-law may bring valuable things which they desire (Eagle).

The relation between the hero and a maternal figure receives considerable attention although this woman is more often a grandmother than the hero's own mother. The hero lives alone with his grandmother or mother in poor circumstances. They are dependent on each other; she gathers plants and cooks for him, and he hunts woodrats or birds. After the hero has acquired power over property, he takes care to provide for his mother or grandmother (Water Wb, Prostitution). He does not tell her about his plans but he returns to her after his adventures (Water, Prostitution, Plume) and confides in her (Water Wa). In the hollow log story, the grandmother complains that he makes his plans in secrecy, and he protests fear that she would have interfered with his trip had he told her (Plume Mb). The relation of the hero to a mother figure is thus pictured as close, with each in some measure attending to the needs of the other, but with the boy shielding his plan of action from interference.

The grandmother figures sometimes assume a more authoritative, directing role, particularly in connection with the youth's training for physical skill and hardihood. Two old women designated as grandmothers direct the hero to race "for property." It is the grandmother, too, who urges her reputedly lazy grandson to race at the fire dance or to learn the ceremony when others have failed (Hail, Water, Mountaintop, Visionary). In these incidents she appears as a behind-the-scenes tutor prodding the young man on to accomplishment.

In the analysis of explanatory elements the joking relationship between grandmother and grandson was noted. The hero of Prostitution Way teases his grandmother about her resplendent visitor, Talking God (Prostitution H). In Navaho culture this relationship permits joking of a sexual nature,[96] and it may be significant that the two stories in which the hero undertakes sexual exploits on his own initiative are those in which he lives only with a grandmother (Water, Prostitution). In one of these it is not only the hero who profits by his newly acquired love magic; the grandmother also indulges in sexual excesses with the Pueblo young men (Prostitution K). Sexual freedom and absence of negative sanctions against sexual exploits are noteworthy in these particular stories.

B. Siblings

Sibling relationships in their various forms and combinations are perhaps more prominent in the chantway stories than any of the family relationships hitherto discussed. If the thematic analysis is correct in identifying the psychological focus and preoccupation of these stories in the problems of breaking away from parental ties to establish independence, this emphasis on sibling relationships is appropriate and expectable. Siblings of the same sex are faced with similar problems, and one would expect to find a certain solidarity and community of interest vis-à-vis adults and current life problems, as well as tensions due to sibling rivalry. For siblings of different sex the similarities due to age status are complicated by factors of sexual attraction and taboo. As we shall see, the mythological material is consistent with these expectancies and reflects both solidarities and tensions in sibling relationships.

The bond between brothers is most clearly demonstrated in the stories where they participate alternately or together in adventures or stand ready to aid each other in time of danger (Shooting, Big Star, Mountaintop, Twins, Plume, Navaho Wind, Bead, Shooting-Ghostway). When both brothers participate in adventures, those of the older may be emphasized (Shooting); or the adventures of the older brother may constitute one chantway myth (Navaho Wind) and those of the younger another (Big Star). The crippled twins participate equally as joint heroes (Twins). Sometimes the brother appears at the opening of the story to support the hero and start him on his adventures. Thus, the hero's brothers help to rescue him from his first false start in the hollow log (Plume Mb), or the hero consults with a brother about undertaking the eagle's nest feat (Bead H&H). Two brothers learn the ritual of hunting from their father and hunt together (Mountaintop). The hero's younger brother helps to rescue him from a coyote transformation (Shooting-Ghostway). In these activities the brothers support each other, but it is usually the younger brother who comes to the hero's aid, warns the family of mishap, or tries to secure supernatural assistance (Shooting, Big Star, Plume, Navaho Wind, Shooting-Ghostway).

One of the most constant elements in the chantway story pattern is the return of the hero to teach to a brother, or brothers, the ceremony he has learned in his travels. Of the ten stories which specify the hero's teaching of the ceremony for benefit of earth people, seven have him teach it to a brother (Hail, Mountaintop, Visionary, Plume, Navaho Wind,

Bead, Flint). In six cases (all of the foregoing except Hail Way) one or more versions specify that it is a younger brother who learns the ceremony. The sister heroines of Beauty and Mountaintop Ways also teach their ritual knowledge to a younger brother.

The few examples of strife between brothers stand out strikingly against this predominant mood of harmony and mutual support. In two versions of the hollow log story the hero's brothers participate in the threat of violence to punish him for gambling away his own and his relatives' property (Plume G, Ma). It is, however, only in the story of the Visionary that estrangement and reconciliation between brothers becomes material for plot development. The hero's brothers reject him because of his vision claims; they ridicule him and try to exclude him from their hunting party. (By contrast, the hero's sister supports him, and her husband is ready to place credence in his vision claims.) Not until his visions are validated by the supernaturals do the brothers come to believe the hero's claims and then they are overcome with remorse; they weep in sorrow at his departure to the gods and pray for his return. Although the hero chides them for their poor treatment of him, he nevertheless returns later without resentment to teach them the ceremony he has learned. Sanctions against fraternal strife seem to be operating in this story; the brothers are humbled by demonstration of the hero's favor with the gods and are brought to a complete reversal of their scornful attitude. Although this incident raises the problem of rivalries underlying the surface solidarity of brothers, the myths do not offer conclusive evidence on this question.

The discussion of sororal polygyny has indicated that sisters also maintain a harmonious relationship. The resort to suicide, used in one story to terminate the difficulties that have developed between sisters of a polygynous marriage, may be evidence of the strength of this standard. Sisters appear as central characters at the opening of the Eagle Way story and again in the latter portion of Enemy Way, at the conclusion of which they separate to become the heroines respectively of the Mountaintop and Beauty Way stories. These sister pairs, like those of the polygynous marriages previously noted, have strong ties of affection and mutual dependence.

Most of the sister pairs are engaged together in sexual incidents of seduction or marriage. In two such incidents, the butterfly seduction (Water, Prostitution) and that by bear and snake old men (Enemy, Beauty, Mountaintop), the sisters' mutual dependence is heightened by the knowledge that their wrongdoing will make them outcasts from their families. In these episodes it is the younger sister who voices doubt of the wisdom of their action, but she follows the lead of the older (Prostitution, Enemy). When Coyote assumes the hero's form in order to steal his wives, it is again the younger wife who suspects something amiss (Prostitution). In other decisions the younger defers to the older — when sister heroines wonder whether with the passage of time it is safe to return home in view of their family's former threats (Beauty); and when the hero asks Turquoise and White Shell Woman for some of the corn

entrusted to them by Talking God (Eagle). In the relations of younger
and older sisters a puzzling detail is introduced when one sister makes
a mistake in a kinship term of address. The older sister is so distracted by the butterfly that entices them from their underground chamber that she addresses her younger sister as "older sister," and the
younger protests that this is an "ugly way of calling me relative"
(Prostitution Hb).

The relationship between brothers and sisters in Navaho culture has
been identified as one of particular ambivalence and strain involving
both deep affection and tensions which become apparent only in indirect
forms, as in witchcraft stories or accusations.[97] Bonds of affection and
trust between brother and sister are clearly represented in the mythological material, as is also the rule for sexual avoidance. Although
these myths do not connect witchcraft with the brother-sister relationship, they do contain reference to a patterned joking which may similarly
be evidence of strain in the relationship.

Bonds of solidarity and trust are demonstrated in a range of brother-
sister relations in the chantway stories. A brother or a sister may
support a sibling of opposite sex who is under attack by other family
members. When an unmarried mother refuses to reveal the father of
her twins, her brother takes her side to stop the family's questioning;
he maintains that she knows no more than she tells (Twins). Con-
versely, the sister of the Visionary supports him against the other
brothers, and her husband is the only member of the hunting party who
shows sympathy with his vision claims (Visionary). Among the family
members it is only the sister who is sorry when the hero is sent away
for gambling to excess (Hail). A sister wakes the hero to tell him of
the presence of strange creatures whom he tracks and finds to be buffalo; this act starts him on a sexual adventure with buffalo wives (Flint).
The hero's sister accompanies him on a second visit to the gods despite
parental protests, and she ultimately departs with him to dwell permanently with the supernaturals and to share his responsibility as intermediary for earth people (Hail). Two pairs of brothers and sisters,
Holy Man and Holy Boy, and Holy Woman and Holy Girl, participate
together in the Shooting Way story; and the brothers watch out for the
welfare of the women.

The brief story that recounts the disastrous effects of brother-sister
incest presents vividly the temptations to sexual contact and the reasons
for strict avoidance (Moth). This story is unlike the other chantway
myths in its brevity and in the absence of a single central character; it
has the flavor of a simple moral tale. Here brother-sister marriage is
not explicitly phrased as resulting from the force of sexual attraction
between brothers and sisters but rather from the desire of parents to
keep close to themselves the children whom they have raised and whom
they love, "because you love your children and they themselves love one
another." The experiment is disastrous; those who participate later
rush madly into the fire like moths, and the two groups of men and
women have to be separated by a rock ledge so that they cannot see one

another. The resulting taboo is explicitly stated: "Therefore there is absolutely a mutual fear of their lower parts between brother and sister, the mere thought of such a thing is to be feared." In both the action and the subsequent statement of the rule, this is the most forceful formulation of a moral rule that appears in the chantway stories. In his comments on this story Father Berard indicates the extension of this rule to the larger group of clan relatives.[98]

The tension and ambivalence between brothers and sisters may also be reflected in an obscure recurrent detail that seems to combine elements of prideful affection and joking disparagement. In three stories the ritual performed over the hero in his visit to supernaturals includes shaping of his body to make him beautiful (Prostitution, Twins, Plume Wc). This is done by young women who in one case are referred to as his sisters (Prostitution H) and in the others as daughters of a supernatural (Twins, Plume Wc). They press his limbs and shape him to look like themselves (Prostitution H, Plume Wc), or to make him as beautiful as their own brothers (Twins). They address him as younger brother and joke about how ugly he was before (Prostitution), or after the transformation they exclaim, "Behold our ugly brothers!" (Twins). This incident is given as explanation of the fact that a girl will speak of her younger brother as ugly no matter how beautiful he is. Similar incidents of shaping and beautifying appear in the general Navaho origin myth when the war gods have passed tests in the home of their sun father. The women, in this case their half-sisters, joke about their appearance, and this incident is cited as the origin of joking "when brothers and sisters and first cousins meet."[99] Although these actions apparently violate the taboo on physical contact between brothers and sisters,[100] in this very fact they may represent a fantasy expression of the forbidden physical attraction in this relationship. Their association with joking accords with the psychological function attributed to joking relationships, which operate as a safety valve for ambivalent tension points within the kinship circle.

One further kinship bond is given some prominence in the chantway stories. This is the relation of the hero to his sister's daughter. In terms of the kinship structure this may be considered an extension of the bond between brother and sister. In a matrilineal society this relation may assume considerable importance, and traditionally in Navaho culture the mother's brother has some responsibility for the sister's child in education and discipline, in marriage choice, and in property inheritance.[101] In two stories the hero has a close relationship with a niece (Plume, Enemy).[102] The hero of Enemy Way, who is said to have raised his two nieces, shows great affection for them. He offers them in marriage to the young man who can pass the suitor test of capturing the turquoise and white bead scalps of two non-sunlight-struck Taos maidens. This marriage test serves two functions — to secure suitable husbands for the nieces and to provide revenge for the slaying of his relatives who were tricked into a previous raid on Taos.[103] The close relationship to a niece appears in two versions of the hollow log story;

in both she stands by the hero when he has been rejected by his family (Plume Ma, G). In one the hero lives apart with his grandmother and niece; he is torn between his responsibility to hunt woodrats for her food and his desire to embark on the hollow log trip (Plume Ma). In this version she connives with him to steal the sacred objects for offerings, and it is her pet turkey who accompanies him on his trip. In the other version the niece gives the hero her necklace to wager in gambling, and it is she whom he sends to the storage pits on his return to discover them magically replenished with corn to relieve famine (Plume G).

In summary, the mythological material pictures certain regularities in family relationships. The recurrent appearance of these patterns in the action of the stories forms the basis for their tentative identification as accepted standards of kinship behavior. Thus, we see portrayed in the stories the strength of family ties, solidarity between siblings of the same sex, and the protective attitude of a man toward his niece. In some cases these standards of kinship behavior receive further confirmation from the evidence of negative sanctions operating when they are not adhered to. Discord between brothers or between sisters was seen to provoke the internal emotional sanction of remorse. These kinship patterns also receive confirmation from ethnological reports of the conduct of kinship relations in actual life.

In some kinship relationships the myths picture conflicting or ambivalent attitudes. In the father-daughter relationship, incestuous desires are imputed to the father alongside of his desire to see his daughter established in marriage. Likewise the force of sexual attraction between brother and sister is vividly pictured. In both cases such incestuous activities meet with negative sanctions. The myths reveal two components, one protective and the other punishing, in the young man's father image. Similarly, conflicting elements are evident in the young man's relationship to his grandmother; this is pictured as a mutually supportive one, but it also contains elements of reciprocal sexual joking and of direction and control by the grandmother. Although clear-cut negative sanctions appear only in connection with incest, nevertheless the fantasy representation of conflicting attitudes in all of these relationships draws our attention to them as possible tension points in the kinship system. The tensions in brother-sister relations, and to a lesser extent in grandparent-grandchild relations, have been discussed in the ethnological literature but those in the father-daughter and father-son relationships have not received the attention that this mythological evidence would indicate they deserve.

Some Aspects of Interpersonal Relations

In the preceding section we were concerned with patterns of relationship within the family group. We now propose to enlarge the focus of attention to consider mythological material that deals with interpersonal relationships in a wider sphere, with certain action and attitude patterns toward non-relatives and aliens. The myths present a considerable number of situations in which either friendliness or hostility are expressed in interpersonal relations, and it is this material that we shall examine in the following pages.

A. Companionship and Hospitality

The typical isolated circumstances of Navaho life, whether this be the hunting and gathering subsistence pictured in the myths or the semi-nomadic sheepherding economy of the present day, requires a high degree of self-reliance in practical affairs. And there may be considerable periods of time which call for emotional self-sufficiency; the threat of loneliness is ever present.[104] Under the conditions of relative isolation between family groups, the problem of loneliness, the manner of relating to strangers, of offering or receiving hospitality, and of treating petitions for help assume special importance.

The concept of motion has been identified as a significant motif running through many aspects of Navaho life.[105] In the form of restless and ceaseless traveling it appears throughout the chantway stories.[106] To cite only the most striking examples — the hero and his grandmother travel to some fifty-seven places in their flight from Pueblos (Prostitution); the stricken twins travel persistently from one holy place to another through sixteen refusals of help by the gods (Twins); sister heroines flee through unknown surroundings to escape their bear and snake husbands (Beauty, Mountaintop). Usually the hero travels alone on his adventures. He leaves a younger brother behind in order to hunt alone (Shooting, Mountaintop); he is rejected by his family and forced to fend for himself (Hail, Visionary, Plume); or he voluntarily undertakes exploration alone out of curiosity (Prostitution, Chiricahua Wind, Flint, Shooting-Ghostway).

In undertaking these travels, whether enforced or voluntary, there seems to be some pleasure or satisfaction in the act of setting out and accomplishing alone the adventures of the cycle. This fact is consonant with the emphasis on self-assertion identified in the thematic analysis. The travels and adventures are solitary from the point of view of human companionship, but they are ultimately accomplished only with the help of protective supernaturals who furnish aid. Thus, the hero is not represented as completely self-sufficient.

Despite the apparent satisfaction in solitary travels, the hero is often lonely for new companionship or homesick for his family and home. He tires of walking around in one place and decides to take a circle trip and visit on the way, thinking that he "might see some people and if he does, stay one night with them" (Prostitution K). The heroine of Beauty Way disobeys the instructions of her hosts not to wander, with the protest, "Why should I be lonesome! Why should I stay in one place for no reason whatsoever!" (Beauty H). When living alone, the hero sights a fire in the distance; he immediately explores in curiosity and finds a family group where he is welcomed as son-in-law (Plume). Prior to this he has been lonely on his hollow log trip; he sings a song of grief and is comforted by the presence of his pet turkey (Plume). The hero returns to his mother restless, sad, and lonely after the loss of his wives and soon starts out in further search for a woman of his dreams (Water Wa). Loneliness and the theme of curiosity and venturesomeness are intertwined; loneliness and boredom furnish motivation for a continuous search for new adventure and companionship.

The practical difficulties of solitary existence are sometimes apparent. The rejected hero of Hail Way has to live off the countryside and make his own poor clothing, and the crippled twins would perish without the magical provision of food and covering by their supernatural protector. The plight of solitary women is even more difficult. Turquoise Woman and White Shell Woman have trouble obtaining food until Monster Slayer appears to advise them and take them to his home; when he leaves them to marry corn maidens, they wonder how they will be able to get food and live (Eagle). Heroines fleeing from their snake and bear husbands make no attempt to subsist by themselves but accept the hospitality of the first strangers whose homes they enter (Beauty, Mountaintop).

The hero may express loneliness specifically for his home and family or for the supernaturals with whom he has visited. When starting out in disobedience of his father's instructions the hero of Mountaintop Way looks out over the country of his people and, overcome with sadness at its beauty, sings a song. In his sky visit the hero is homesick and disobeys instructions not to look down through the sky hole at his earth home (Big Star). He submits to tests to be allowed to return to his family (Visionary), or he refuses to marry an eagle wife until he has seen his family again (Bead). The joy with which the hero is welcomed on his return has already been cited. Likewise he expresses sadness at parting from the supernaturals who have befriended him. In his loneliness he returns to their home but is disappointed to find no one there (Hail, Eagle). The hero and the gods express mutual sorrow at parting; at home he is sad and lonely for them (Visionary). In the usual conclusion to the chantway stories his newly established bonds with the supernaturals prove to be stronger than his ties to home and family, and he departs to dwell with them permanently.

A lonely wanderer may be received with hospitality by strangers. Monster Slayer voices a welcome to visiting corn maidens, "We are alone and it is pleasant to have visitors. You are welcome whenever you want to come" (Eagle). Helpful animals offer their homes as refuge to the fleeing hero or heroine. The welcome of the hero when he happens upon an isolated family in his wanderings is likewise cordial; they express desire for a new son-in-law. However, such hospitality is not always straightforward. The hearty welcome may cover hostility, as in the evil father-in-law episodes. Often the father-in-law's deceitful flattery is immediately recognized (Plume, Enemy, Shooting-Ghostway), but on other occasions his hostility does not become apparent until the hero tries to leave (Shooting, Chiricahua Wind). Reluctant acceptance is accorded the new husband brought home by the corn maidens or buffalo women (Eagle, Shooting, Flint). The grandfather of the corn maidens objects to their new husband because earth people "always break our rules," but he welcomes him with deceitful flattery, saying that he is glad to see him, that earth people "are polite and keep all rules and tenets strictly" (Eagle).

When a stranger arrives he is immediately offered food or tobacco. This puts him in a difficult position if he distrusts the proffered hospitality. The hero is warned by his monitor that the evil father-in-law is offering poisoned food or tobacco (Plume, Eagle, Shooting-Ghostway). He refuses food or tobacco offered by animal protectors (Water, Eagle); if he ate their food he would become like them (Hail, Mountaintop). If he eats the food of the dangerous Woman Who Dries People Up he would never be able to leave her (Navaho Wind). The heroine is warned not to eat in the snake home she visits (Beauty). Sometimes the hero obviates this difficulty by offering his own tobacco first (Shooting, Water, Mountaintop, Plume, Eagle).

So far we have seen suspicion of strangers juxtaposed with apparent hospitality. In other situations the reception of strangers is frankly hostile. Aliens are not freely accepted. Old men of an alien tribe are not welcome to join a war party (Enemy). Marriage to aliens is refused because this would take children away from their parents (Moth). The Pueblos are unfriendly toward and exploit a poor Navaho beggar (Water, Prostitution, Twins, Bead). Supernaturals are inhospitable and reluctant to admit earth people amongst themselves. They are pictured as jealous of their powers which are only grudgingly and under pressure made available to unworthy mortals. The typical greeting by supernaturals is, "Earth people are not allowed (or not welcome) here" (Water, Beauty, Visionary, Plume, Navaho Wind, Shooting-Ghostway). The hero is granted admittance only when his errand is satisfactorily explained, usually by an intermediary from amongst the supernaturals themselves who is acting as his protector (Water, Shooting, Prostitution, Chiricahua). The supernaturals are surprised at the presence of mortals because earth people have never before gained entrance (Twins). The reasons given for refusal center on the unworthiness of earth people: the Indians are a "bad people" and the gods do not want them amongst them (Visionary); earth people are "no good" (Chiricahua Wind) or do not observe the rules properly (Eagle). Reluctance to admit mortals is allied to refusal of help except under the compulsion of proper offerings. Entrance to the home of a god is gained by knowledge of the proper formula to appease the doorguards, just as his intercession for cure is secured by the proper ritual offering. In the face of this inhospitality, access to the gods is often gained by trickery and deceit. Big fly or bat tells earth people the secret of his master's offering, at the same time pledging them not to divulge the source of their information (Navaho Wind, Chiricahua, Bead, Flint, Enemy). The hero's protector deceives the dangerous whirling-tail-feather, persuading it to stop whirling so that the hero can enter (Shooting).

These contacts with supernaturals involve a special element that is not usually present in relations between earth people. The supernaturals are different from earth people in their holiness and power, and the visitor approaches the powerful gods as a petitioner for help. Perhaps the closest analogue in actual life is application to a ceremonial practitioner for his services. Such applications, too, must observe the proper ritual forms. Under the compulsion of public opinion the singer must be "more generous and hospitable than the ordinary Navaho,"[107] an obligation that may cover some fear that he like the gods will begrudge the use of his powers.

In the foregoing situations the supernaturals are pictured as responding with emotions that are understandable in human terms. In other situations they similarly display human weaknesses. When left out of festivities they respond with anger and even sulking. Uninvited guests complain or retaliate for this slight. In various stories frog, winds, owls, snake, big dipper, spider, Coyote, and water sprinkler thus object to being excluded (Hail, Visionary, Twins, Chiricahua Wind). Big snake complains that they always leave him out when they have a merry time (Visionary). The offended gods have to be pacified with offerings (Visionary, Chiricahua Wind) or their share of the gifts (Twins). In retaliation the uninvited gods steal the hero (Visionary), steal the voices of participants (Visionary), or strike the gathering with lightning (Chiricahua Wind). These incidents seem to reflect desire for sociability as well as for the offerings that accrue from such gatherings. Similar incidents are not duplicated in the ceremonies held by earth people, although they take care to send out runners with invitations when a big public dance is held (Water Wa, Shooting, Mountaintop, Bead).

The foregoing data deal with attitudes toward companionship and loneliness as they are represented in the myths, as well as with the manner of receiving strangers. Of the hostility and distrust underlying an apparent readiness to extend hospitality to strangers more will be said in the following section, although it may be noted here that both the hospitality and the basic distrust of strangers fit with observational evidence of Navaho society.[108] The material on companionship and loneliness does not present clear value standards. Both sides of the problem are evident — on the one hand pleasure in independence and self-sufficiency, and on the other loneliness and the desire for companions. These attitudes are congruent with the circumstances of Navaho life which place a premium on self-sufficiency but by this very fact often present situations when the help of others is urgently needed. It may be remembered that self-reliance and independence were identified as central emphases in the thematic analysis, and the above material reinforces the impression that this constitutes a problem area in Navaho culture.

B. Aggression

Running through the material on relations with strangers we have seen a pronounced thread of hostility and suspicion. We shall now consider the form that these hostile interpersonal attitudes take when expressed in overt acts of aggression. Our attention will focus principally on acts or tendencies toward action which have a harmful or destructive intent. In popular usage the conception of aggression includes elements of initiative and vigor in meeting and overcoming obstacles. Such elements have already been considered as they operate in the hero's self-assertion and will not be further discussed here. First, we shall consider aggression in extra-familial relations, but this will ultimately lead back to tensions within the family and kinship circle. Because the stories center on the hero and his activities, our examples will in largest part come from those aggressive acts which are directed at or emanate from the hero. In lesser measure conflicts between the supernaturals or amongst earth people also furnish data on aggression.

The amount of material on aggression in the stories is large, and for convenience of description it will be necessary to impose a somewhat arbitrary organization. Different types of aggressive activity will be distinguished as they appear and are labeled in the myths. Hostility comes to overt expression principally in the form of attacks, contests, quarreling, war, trickery and witchcraft, and the appearance of aggression in these various forms will be described.

The central aggressive acts of the myths are the series of attacks suffered by the hero in his adventures. These attacks are, however, provoked by the hero's own self-assertion which, as we have seen in the thematic analysis, contains a more or less clearly defined aggressive-destructive component, e.g., in the disregard of family responsibilities, in infringement of sexual rights, and in violation of taboos. The counter-aggression takes the form of bodily attacks in which the victim's body parts are scattered, objects are shot into him, he is captured and rendered powerless, or he is changed into animal form. The offended husband retaliates for adultery with an attack which shatters, or attempts to shatter, the hero totally (Hail, Water, Flint). He is likewise attacked bodily for venturing on forbidden territory (Shooting, Big Star, Beauty, Navaho Wind, Bead, Flint), or for other ritual violations (Shooting, Mountaintop). For similar violations he is captured (Shooting, Beauty, Mountaintop, Plume, Bead) or transformed into an animal (snake or antelope) (Big Star, Plume Wc, Navaho Wind, Chiricahua Wind). Other offenses for which the hero is attacked are excess in hunting (Chiricahua Wind, Bead), his impulsive shooting of a wind child (attack by the father wind) (Navaho Wind, Chiricahua Wind), and his disrespectful ridicule of wind's fawn meat (Chiricahua Wind). We have indicated that these attacks seem to be recognized as expectable and justified. When the offended husband seeks to avenge an act of adultery the hero is warned that his punishment is inevitable and must take place as ordained (Water). The new buffalo father-in-law admonishes the hero for his "great fault" in taking the wives of such an important person as their chief (Flint Hb) and in another version indicates that he can expect the chief's retaliation (Flint R). Punishment for the violation of forbidden territory or of ritual taboos is likewise apparently expected.

The hero's brother pleads with him not to violate a food taboo by eating a snake (Big Star). After he has been transformed into a snake, the hero's family explains that this is why he had been warned not to trespass (Navaho Wind). The killer of whirlwind boy is told that nothing can help him against the power of the angry father (Big Star), or in other instances he himself anticipates punishment (Navaho Wind, Chiricahua Wind). The winds accuse him of having killed the child without cause (Chiricahua Wind). The whipping threatened by a woman's family for her unacceptable marriage choice is similar to these experiences of the hero in that the punishment is provoked by her own act and takes a physical form (Water, Prostitution, Enemy, Beauty, Mountaintop).

In these attacks we see that the aggressive aspects of the hero's actions meet with counter-aggression on the part of the offended persons or supernaturals. This counter-aggression is phrased as punishment and is felt to be justified. It constitutes retaliation rather than revenge.[109] In some cases, such as the retaliation of an offended husband for adultery, the sanctions on which the retaliation rests are diffuse. Others in which the whole group participates tend to be more organized, such as the threat of public whipping for an offense which affects the whole family or community.

The sense of the supernatural punishments is that the hero must be taught proper conduct, and it is from the restoration after such attacks that he gains his own power by learning the ritual performed over him. In some cases, in place of bodily attack, the hero is immediately captured for violation of taboos and taken to the sky to be taught proper behavior and use of his powers (Shooting, Bead K). The attacks suffered are thus, in a sense, purifying or, perhaps more properly, disciplinary and educational. They do not, however, have the same phrasing as the Christian idea of conscious atonement or self punishment. The trials are not entered into with full awareness and intent. The hero complains at having to undergo such hardships; he has only dim awareness that he brings them on himself. Suffering the attack is not automatically purifying but provides means for gaining power in the act of rescue or restoration. The hero profits by the knowledge that he gains rather than by the suffering he undergoes.

Certain attacks on the hero are apparently unprovoked, or insufficiently provoked by him, and seem to spring from the inherent "meanness" of his adversary. In the discussion of explanatory elements we have noted recognition of this "meanness" as a character trait of certain supernaturals[110] — winds, First Man and First Woman. These pseudo-explanatory references were congruent with a certain fatalistic acknowledgment of the existence of aggression. Other supernaturals characterized as "mean" are Coyote (Big Star) and Big God (Prostitution).[111] Because of this the hero is warned not to go near Big God's home. This designation of "meanness" implies recognition of a hostile disposition, a constant tendency toward aggression in some persons. Similarly the father-in-law is specified as "evil" (Plume) or "no good" (Enemy), a characterization which carries in addition a negative moral judgment of his witchcraft activities.

Coyote is a character who commits aggressive acts out of his own ill temper or perversity. He transforms the hero and takes his form in order to steal his wife (Prostitution, Shooting, Shooting-Ghostway) or strands him on sky-reaching-rock for the same purpose (Big Star). Coyote's trickery is sometimes successful (Prostitution, Big Star); in other cases it rouses the wife's suspicions so that she refuses to live with him (Shooting, Shooting-Ghostway). Even after his restoration and return the hero bears a lingering grudge against Coyote (Prostitution, Big Star, Shooting-Ghostway). This becomes occasion for the protecting supernatural's admonition that there will always be different kinds of people in the world and "they must make the best of it" (Big Star). Coyote is oversensitive to slight or disapproval and in minor incidents acts aggressively with little or no provocation. He sneaks into a ceremony when not wanted (Hail, Visionary), and he steals the voices of participants when not admitted to a gathering (Visionary), the hero's mind and speech (Navaho Wind), songs intended for the hero (Flint), or even the hero himself (Visionary). His perversity is noted: "It will avail nothing to be angry with Coyote, wrathy words and loud commands will not influence him" (Visionary).[112]

It should be noted that in the total body of Navaho mythology Coyote appears not only as a trickster but also as a beneficent figure, particularly at the time of emergence when he takes initiative in establishing the natural phenomena of the world. This aspect of his character is expressed in the first portion of the Shooting Way story when he takes a helpful and directing hand in events. In his character the hostile elements in aggression become blended with the positive, as we have similarly seen in the analysis of the chantway hero's character.

Another expression of aggression appears in the formalized contests of racing and trials of skill employed as the means of settling contending claims (Water, Prostitution, Navaho Wind, Eagle, Enemy), or merely as a demonstration of power (Hail). It is by these means that the hero wins back his wives stolen by White Butterfly (Water, Prostitution) and that frog saves him from the claims of the Woman Who Dries People Up (Navaho Wind). Similar trials of skill constitute part of the suitor test imposed by the hero to win his nieces, although the victors, snake and bear old men, prove unacceptable for other reasons and are not awarded the maidens (Enemy). The woman's marriage contest of tossing an unbroken cornmeal ball to the chosen man also has this element of skill (Navaho Wind, Eagle). These contests provide a formalized and controlled situation for acting out individual aggression and settling the point at issue, which is usually a sexual claim (recovery of wives or suitor test). The aggressive components are given explicit recognition in an explanatory element attached to the argument which arises in the hero's games with White Butterfly; the narrator explains that "when people play together, one gets beat and then they get mad at each other" (Prostitution K). Trickery and deceit are employed in these contests. With supernatural help the hero evades his opponents' doorguards by a storm or by putting them to sleep; he wins the games of strength and skill with the help of animals who manipulate the game pieces (Water, Prostitution). White Butterfly on his part vainly employs "wizardry" shooting and in defeat tries to trick the hero into killing him with a magic ax which will rebound on the wielder. Trickery and witchcraft shooting are employed in races (Water, Prostitution, Hail, Navaho Wind). Frog shoots hail into the hero's joints to delay his running and urges him to touch the magic ax which will kill the wielder (Hail). Cloud, rain and wind are used to throw an opponent off the race course (Hail, Navaho Wind), or one of the contenders urinates to cause his opponent to slip (Water, Navaho Wind). The woman wins the marriage test by surreptitiously adding egg to her cornmeal ball or binding it with cord to keep it intact (Navaho Wind, Eagle). Akin to the trickery in these formal contests is the ingenuity of toad and turtle when subjected to retaliatory attack by Pueblos for taking jeweled scalps (Enemy): when put into a heated pot, toad urinates to form a pool to protect them; turtle's shell breaks the heated pot in which they are enclosed or protects them from blows.

So far we have considered principally acts of aggression by individuals. Aggression is also pictured in the myths as a group phenomenon, in raid and warfare and in other hostile relations with aliens. Raid or warfare plays a part in six stories (Hail, Mountaintop, Big Star, Eagle, Bead, Enemy). All of these involve aliens (Pueblo or Ute) or a different kind of people (stinging insects, etc.) except for one case when the war is between opposing groups of supernaturals (Hail). In addition, four stories have substantial incidents showing hostile relations with Pueblo aliens which do not develop into violence but are played out with trickery (Water, Prostitution, Twins, Bead).

The only internal strife which breaks out into group violence is the war between two groups of thunders who are ranged against each other over the question of protecting the hero (Hail). One group is led by the thunder husband whom the hero has unwittingly offended by adultery, the other by the thunder who was summoned to restore the hero. Although disagreement and even conflict between supernaturals appear in other stories over helping the hero, the division between protective and hostile supernaturals is most clearly shown in this case. The reason for the opening of hostilities is not entirely clear; the protecting thunder organizes a war party because the opposing thunder "has uttered that which is evil." Although other supernaturals allow the hostilities to proceed, there is some expression of disapproval and the slaughter is not allowed to get out of bounds. Changing Woman refuses to participate with the admonition, "Surely I bore my children (to subdue) monsters, not to be in the midst of it," i.e., not to participate in war. Talking God, Calling God, and Begochidi intervene to stop the slaughter and again Changing Woman protests that peace should be made. They are tired of war and "many are sick and wounded and all are poor." But peace negotiations are difficult because each side fears that it is too dangerous to make overtures. Once the token of peace is accepted, however, their anger is ended and a peace ceremony ensues. However, the offended thunder still harbors a grudge, but his second attack on the hero is dissipated by substituting words of peace in the ritual.

In the war with stinging insects, weed and rock people, which occurs in three stories (Big Star, Eagle, Bead), the hero acts as peacemaker as well as conqueror. These people are the traditional enemies of the eagles and hawks who have protected the hero, and he subdues them with magic obtained from supernaturals. One version of the episode indicates that the hero is himself eager for the fight, "He wants to go pretty bad. Thinks there is a lot of fun in it" (Bead K). In the end he brings these traditional hostilities to a conclusion and sends the remaining enemies to earth with instructions that they are not to become harmful (Big Star, Bead). He cures the wounded eagles and hawks (Big Star, Bead). At the same time he admonishes the eagle and hawk people not to provoke attack; the rock wren has claimed that it is because he is attacked that he is "fierce" (Big Star).

The story of the Enemy Way rite has as its principal action raiding and war against the Pueblos. Here, too, raiding is undertaken apparently in a spirit of adventure. The initial provocation does not lie with the Pueblos, but hostilities are prolonged out of revenge. Raids are proposed by the hero's evil father-in-law to demonstrate his powers and shame the hero, or they are undertaken by toad and turtle to get the jeweled scalps of non-sunlight-struck maidens. Ultimately the hero organizes a raid himself to avenge the death of his kinsmen or the bird children killed in preliminary encounters. Whereas the participants take enjoyment in the adventure, there is here also some effort on the part of directing supernaturals to limit the slaughter. Talking God tries to dissuade the attackers, saying that he stands for everything peaceful and that the Pueblos are a source of offerings for him. The Enemy Way rite itself is a means of purification and defense against the evils resulting from warfare, viz., the enemy ghosts which have "swarmed from the slaughter."

Hostilities with Utes are pictured in the Mountaintop Way story. Here the Utes are the aggressors and, although successful in capturing the Navaho hero, or heroines, they are ultimately outsmarted by the prisoner's escape with valuables. The hero escapes with the aid of supernaturals at the moment when his Ute captors are about to kill him.

These incidents of warfare convey an impression of exhilaration and enjoyment on the part of the participants. The existence of traditional enemies and the spirit of revenge are prominent. At the same time there is a note of warning from supernaturals or the participants themselves to avoid excess and to set some limits to the slaughter.

Trickery and deceit figure in warfare. ". . . Anything is allowable in warfare on an enemy, especially a foreign enemy."[113] But they seem also to be a constant ingredient in Navaho-Pueblo relations, even in peaceful circumstances, and to be expected by both parties. Navaho-Pueblo relations are most often pictured in the myths in the situation of the poor Navaho beggar who is dependent upon Pueblos for his very livelihood (Water, Prostitution, Twins, Bead). He endures their taunts and ridicule and is exploited by them, but through ritual power or magic bestowed by the gods he is able to turn the tables and retaliate for his bad treatment. In these dealings trickery is used on both sides. The hero who has suffered taunts and mistreatment tricks non-sunlight-struck Pueblo maidens from their underground chamber (Water, Prostitution). The beggar-slave is tricked into the feat of obtaining eaglets from a cliff nest where his Pueblo tormentors plan to leave him stranded; on his return with ceremonial power he tricks the Pueblos out of their valuables and ascends with them to the sky (Bead). The crippled twins approach the Pueblos armed with secret power to cause and relieve famine in order to obtain their valuables (Twins). They are met with taunts and rejection until their restorative powers are needed. The Pueblos offer to pay for magical relief of the famine, but at the same time they plot to kill the twins and regain their valuables. In these situations trickery and deceit are employed by both parties without apparent compunction.

This discussion of aggression in inter-group situations has stressed attitudes of suspicion and deceit. Similar attitudes were also found operating in relations with strangers not specifically identified as belonging to an alien tribe. We have noted the suspicion toward hospitality offered by strangers, the grudging hospitality of supernaturals, the deceit employed to gain entrance to them, and the trickery used in formal contests. We have alluded to Coyote's trickster role and the treachery in the evil father-in-law's attacks on the hero. These trends reach a climax in the witchcraft activities of these two figures. Before pulling together the threads of suspicion, trickery, and deceit that run through much of the mythological material and trying to assess their general role in interpersonal relations, we shall consider in somewhat more detail this crucial form of aggressive action.

Witchcraft is specified in comparatively few instances in the myths, although it seems justifiable to equate with it certain activities similar in form and situation.[114] The agents whose activity is specifically identified as witchcraft are frog or toad (Hail, Beauty), White Butterfly (Water, Prostitution), Coyote (Shooting-Ghostway), and the evil father-in-law (Plume, Eagle, Enemy). When the heroine strays against instructions, toad angrily denounces the presence of an earth person and shoots mudballs at various parts of her body (soles, hip joint, small of back, shoulder blades, hollow of head); she is lamed and felled by this witchery (Beauty). Big fly warns against having toad cure her, insisting that he cannot be trusted and may merely make her condition worse. The shots turned back on him are given as explanation of his awkward gait. Similar shooting, although not specified as witchcraft, occurs when the hero of Bead Way strays in disobedience of warnings; buzzard and eagle people, or frogs and toads, shoot their arrows into his joints. We have noted how witchcraft shooting is similarly used by White Butterfly in his attempt to defeat his opponent in racing, but the shots are avoided or thrown back on him (Water, Prostitution). Although not specified as witchcraft, similar shooting by frog in a race defeats his opponent (Hail).

Although Coyote is represented as "mean" and a trickster on many occasions, in only one case is his activity specified as witchcraft (Shooting-Ghostway). Ashamed of his name Roamer, he has expressed desire to change it to Holy Young Man. The hero still bears a grudge for the time when Coyote transformed him and tried to steal his wife, and now resents Coyote's presumption in taking a name like his own. Exasperated by the hero's threats, Coyote directs witchery at him which ultimately weakens his "thinking power" and causes sleeplessness and vomiting. Although the form of the witchcraft is not specified, the first attempt to free the hero from it is by the shooting of tree arrows into Coyote's anus. Because the people fear Coyote's ill will and witchery, he is restored. Nevertheless he again bewitches the hero, who is finally restored by a ceremony. In this incident protective supernaturals warn that Coyote is powerful since he is directed in this "meanness" by First Man and First Woman.

The evil father-in-law is presented as an old man, evil by nature, and one evidence of this is his propensity for witchcraft. The symptoms of his witchcraft are said to be incest (Plume, Enemy, Shooting-Ghostway), desire to eat human flesh (Plume), use of parts of the human body in evil magic (Plume, Eagle), and attention to human excrement (Enemy).[115] Since he practices incest with his daughter, jealousy provides the ostensible motive for his attempts on the life of his new son-in-law. The forms of his attacks are diverse: he uses poisoned food and tobacco (Plume, Eagle, Shooting-Ghostway); he attacks in animal forms of snake, bear, cannibal eagle, and mountain lion (Plume, Navaho Wind, Eagle, Shooting-Ghostway), with lightning, thunder or cactus (Plume, Chiricahua Wind, Eagle, Shooting-Ghostway); he tries to trick and strand the hero while hunting or on a raiding party (Plume, Enemy, Shooting-Ghostway). It would seem reasonable that the same taint of witchcraft attaches to other versions of the father-in-law trials which use one or more of these same forms of attack and which characterize the father-in-law as a "tricky old man" (Shooting, Navaho Wind, Chiricahua Wind). The specification of witchcraft in Eagle Way is developed differently. The hero is tested by poisoned food and animal attack (bird, snake, bear). The animal monsters are apparently sent by joint action of his new grandfather-in-law and the chief of the group into which he has married. When he survives these trials and is accepted into the group, it is the chief rather than the grandfather-in-law who tries unsuccessfully to lure him into learning the witchcraft way of trapping eagles. One version of Plume Way (Wc) traces the witchcraft activities of the evil father-in-law Deer Raiser back into pre-emergence times where he is known as He Who Can Change Into Anything and associates with Coyote in seductions and in throwing sticks down the smokehole of a dwelling at night.[116]

It should be noted that in this series of chantway myths witchcraft fears center on the father-in-law. Elsewhere in Navaho myth (e.g., the story of Changing Bear Maiden) and in popular witchcraft anecdotes, it is common to find brother and sister as the actors.[117] The relationship of son-in-law to father-in-law is a potential point of strain inherent in human family organization, and the evil father-in-law motif is of widespread occurrence in North American Indian folklore. As has already been indicated, in the Navaho case the mythological elaboration of tension in this relationship is congruent with expected strains in the formal structure of a matrilineal and matrilocal society in which the basic unit is a relatively isolated extended family.

Although not specified as witchcraft, the activity of the hero in seducing Pueblo maidens by love magic is similar in form to frenzy witchcraft.[118] The hero employs trickery along with his magic, and the act assumes particular overtones of aggression in the context of revenge for his previous maltreatment by the same Pueblo people. However, its malevolent components are mitigated by his subsequent marriage to the maidens. Later he vents his jealousy over Coyote's adultery with his wives by using his love magic to seduce young maidens promiscuously. Although the aggression manifest here infringes on the freedom of others, it does not have the purely destructive intent of witchcraft practiced by Coyote and the evil father-in-law.

Deceit and trickery reach their height in the witchcraft activities of Coyote and the evil father-in-law, and in the love magic of the hero. In the case of the father-in-law and Coyote, witchcraft is presented as evil and the dramatic interest centers on its frustration and the hero's rescue from its effects. It cannot be said, however, that deceit and trickery are characteristics of witchcraft alone. We have seen how they occur in many interpersonal relations and how widespread is suspicion of double-dealing from strangers. The deceit practiced in love magic[119] and in relations with aliens is presented as successful activity on the hero's part. It would seem that deceit and trickery are expected and acceptable modes of dealing with members of the out-group. However, it is difficult to assess the full meaning of this mythological material. It may be that the fantasy character of myth in allowing freer projection of fears, as well as positive wish fulfilments, exaggerates attitudes and actions which in actual life would be tempered by more rational controls. Both the witchcraft material and the general picture of uneasy and deceitful relations with strangers support the Navaho formula for dealing with the dangers of life that advises: "Be wary of non-relatives."[120]

VI. CONCLUSIONS

In this study we set out to examine the content of a substantial portion of Navaho mythology to see what light it could throw on Navaho values. Our first step was an impressionistic survey of the principal themes that appeared in the plot construction of the stories. Then a more systematic approach to story content was undertaken by using certain operational indices to identify value elements. The formalized "explanations" interpolated by the narrator in his account were taken as one index to value elements, and the operation of sanctions in the action of the stories were taken as another. In addition, we watched for the recurrence of action patterns which would give clues to standards of conduct, although in the absence of explicit sanctions we felt the need of collateral evidence confirming the acceptability of these action patterns. Before discussing the theoretical and methodological questions raised by this type of analysis, the findings resulting from use of these various methods will be briefly reviewed.

Review of Findings

The value themes identified in plot construction center in four areas: the maintenance of health; the acquisition of supernatural power; the maintenance of harmony in family relationships; and the process of the young man's attainment of adult status. In reviewing the mythological value data in these four areas, we shall summarize the findings from the thematic analysis, from the examination of "explanatory" statements, and from the operation of sanctions and standards. (See accompanying chart for a summary presentation of these data.)

A large part of the action of the stories focuses on attempts to restore health to the central character. Such concern for health is expectable since these are origin stories of curing rites. It should also be noted that their sizeable bulk in the total body of Navaho mythology reflects a central emphasis of Navaho religion on efforts to maintain health. The Navaho conception of the cause of illness is evident both in the story action and in interpolated explanatory elements; disregard of ritual taboos is pictured as a principal cause of illness or injury. The warning to observe ritual rules tends to be phrased in existential terms, as though based on an automatically functioning "law of nature," particularly when it appears in explanatory or cautionary statements interposed by the narrator. But this injunction has also a prominent interpersonal and normative dimension; the violation is seen as a personal affront to the offended supernatural and his response is phrased as punishment.

The maintenance of health as it appears in the thematic analysis may be viewed as a goal value, and the means of maintaining health — observance of ritual rules — then becomes an important instrumental value in relation to this goal. The systematic examination of story content, for explanatory elements and for evidence of the operation of sanctions, showed that the instrumental value of ritual observance is attached also to other goals — to maintaining agricultural fertility and the game supply. Agricultural fertility does not, however, assume importance in the story content; it is mentioned principally in explanatory statements which link disregard of taboos with drought and damage to crops. On the other hand, concern for the game supply does appear in the action of the stories. Disregard of ritual rules in hunting (including hunting to excess) is punished by supernaturals, and this punishment often takes the form of withholding game. Thus, the value attributed to observance of ritual rules is represented as operating in several areas basic to human welfare.

The second value area identified in the thematic analysis concerns the acquisition of supernatural power. Knowledge is pictured as the key to supernatural power. Knowledge of ritual rules is necessary in the first instance to prevent unwitting transgression of taboos; in many cases the hero's misadventures result from his apparent ignorance of the rules which he is violating. But further than this, knowledge of ceremonial lore furnishes the means of harnessing supernatural power and putting it to work for the benefit of earth people. The hero's trials and misadventures lead to his acquisition of ceremonial knowledge and subsequently to its transmission to his own people.

In addition to knowledge, property is also necessary to obtain access to supernatural power. Offerings are required to gain the attention and help of the gods. The powerful supernatural figures on whom man is dependent are conceived as remote and disinterested but subject to the compulsion of ritual and offerings. The most dramatic illustration of the power of offerings is furnished by the experience of the crippled twins who in their poverty are repeatedly refused supernatural help.

In the analysis of sanctions it was found that the importance of possessing property extends also into the spheres of marriage and relations with aliens. Poverty is cause for shame and the occasion for ridicule and exploitation by aliens. It is associated with physical and sexual unattractiveness. Riches are associated with beauty and sexual conquests. The need for property in undertaking marriage is clearly stated in the injunction that compensation must be made for sexual intercourse (the traditional marriage payment).

The use of ritual knowledge for success in sexual conquests and in dealings with aliens was not so clearly revealed in the thematic analysis, although the ceremony for sexual attraction learned in the Prostitution Way story and the use of war ritual in the Enemy Way story point in this direction. The use of ritual in preparation for war is reported ethnologically, but the use of ritual for "love magic" falls within the realm of witchcraft where actual practice is difficult to determine by ethnological methods. [121]

VALUE ELEMENTS IN NAVAHO CHANTWAY MYTHS

Value Area	Appearance of Value Elements		
	In Thematic Analysis	In Explanatory and Cautionary Statements	In Sanctions and Standards
Health and Illness	Health is represented as a desirable state. Restoration to health is a primary objective of the ceremonies.	Warning that punishment will take the form of illness.	Illness and injury are inflicted as punishments.
Subsistence	-------------	Warning that punishment will take the form of drought or crop failure.	Failure of game supply is imposed as a punishment.
Ritual Knowledge and Power	Knowledge and property provide access to supernatural power. Ritual power thus obtained provides the means of maintaining health.	Warning that violation of ritual rules will bring punishment.	Violation of ritual rules brings punishments. Offerings are required for access to ritual power.
Property	(See Ritual Knowledge and Power, above.)	Stipulation that payment is necessary for sexual rights.	(See Ritual Knowledge and Power, above.) Property is required for the marriage payment. Poverty brings shame, ridicule, and exploitation.
Family Relations	Harmony in family relations is represented as desirable.	Statement of sanctions against improper behavior between specific categories of kin: brother-sister incest taboo; mother-in-law taboo.	Positive family ties are depicted. Brother-sister respect and esteem are depicted. Brother-sister incest is punished.

Sex and Marriage	------------	(See Property, above, for payment for sexual rights.) Justification of sororal polygyny. Statement of traditional punishment for adultery by mutilation of offending woman.	Solidarity between siblings of same sex is depicted. Father-daughter incest is punished. (See Property, above, for marriage payment.) Adultery brings punishment. A woman's unacceptable marriage choice brings punishment. Aberrant unions cause shame. Marriages are depicted as shifting and short-lived. Sororal polygyny occurs frequently.
Self-Assertion and Responsibility	The young hero's assertion of independence is a means to attain adult goals; in this process he becomes transformed into a responsible member of society.	------------	Irresponsibility is disapproved and punished.
Companionship and Loneliness	------------	------------	Ambivalence is indicated in desire for companionship but distrust of strangers; similarly, hospitality is extended to strangers but often with reluctance.
Aggression	------------	Recognition of the existence of aggression in human affairs.	Trickery and deceit occur frequently. War occurs but is limited by disapproval of supernaturals. Witchcraft is punished.

The principle of order and harmony in human relations and in the relation of man to nature has been well attested in Navaho culture.[122] Restoration to health is conceived as part of the process of righting the harmonious balance of natural forces. This conception, although it does appear in the chantway myths, is more clearly spelled out in the ritual poetry and songs which accompany the myths than in the story action itself. The overarching value theme of harmony does, however, receive expression in the area of family relationships. In the thematic analysis the value of maintaining or restoring harmonious family relationships became evident in two typical situations — in the hero's relationship with members of his own parental family and in his newly established marriage. In both instances conflict occurs but is typically resolved. In those cases in which the hero (or heroine) is rejected by his family for unacceptable behavior, he makes reparation by returning to them with the gift of the ceremony he has learned. The situation in his newly contracted marriage is somewhat different; here the hero triumphs over the treacherous attacks of his new father-in-law forcing him to give up his "evil ways" and to become reconciled to the new balance of intra-familial roles. The premium placed on harmony within the family group was seen to be congruent with conditions of actual Navaho life, in which intra-familial cooperation is of crucial importance if the isolated, extended family is to function effectively as an economic and social unit.

The mythological sanctions applied in consanguine and affinal relations again indicate the value of harmony in family relations. There is evidence of disruptive tensions between certain categories of kin, and of the need to keep these tensions under control. In father-daughter and brother-sister relations the disruptive tensions are associated with sexual attraction. Strong sanctions against father-daughter incest are evident (e.g., in community expression of disapproval, in the punishment of the evil father-in-law, and in the abandonment of the offspring of such a union). Sanctions against brother-sister incest are acted out in the Moth Way story, and cautions against such a practice are explicitly stated. Elsewhere in the myths there is indication of esteem and respect between siblings of opposite sex and use of a joking pattern to channel disruptive tendencies. There are little straightforward data showing tension in father-son relations, although the actions of both punishing and protective supernaturals and of the evil father-in-law seem to represent aspects of the young man's father image. In a son's relationship with mother or grandmother, the predominant tone is of mutual support. Similarly the bonds between siblings of the same sex are solidary. Brother heroes or sister heroines support each other through misadventures, and when this standard is violated the offending brothers suffer the internal sanction of remorse.

The tension points which occur in the process of establishing affinal relations in a new marriage were found to be congruent with the Navaho rule of matrilocal residence. Daughters who make a marriage choice unacceptable to their own kin group are threatened with punishment and forced to flee. The hero's trials by his father-in-law were interpreted as having a double reference. On the one hand these trials may be seen as a fantasy representation of the father-in-law's reaction to the entrance of a new son-in-law who will upset the unacknowledged affectional bonds between him and his daughter. On the other hand the father-in-law may also represent to the young man a threatening father figure who will interfere with his claims to an adult position in his new marriage. The adjustment of roles to include the incoming male in the already established extended family was thus seen as a potential point of tension inherent in a matrilineal and matrilocal family structure, such as that of traditional Navaho culture. An explanatory reference to the mother-in-law taboo and evidence of its observance in the story action could also be referred to the need for control of tensions in affinal relations, in accordance with the usual functional interpretation of this custom.

It may be seen from the above that for several kinship relations ambivalent or contradictory attitudes appear in the myths. The presence of such conflicting tendencies is expectable on the basis of our assumptions about the operation of fantasy in myth. We expect the elaboration of fantasy at points of strain and tension, where conflicting impulses occur and must be handled in a socially acceptable fashion. Such fantasy motifs as brother-sister incest and the witch father-in-law can function as a safety valve for the expression of forbidden impulses and at the same time provide a warning against carrying out the forbidden action.

The myths also provide evidence of certain values operating in marriage behavior. While shifting sexual liaisons occur frequently in the stories without evidence of disapproval, the apparent acceptance of such liaisons does not extend to instances of a man's adultery with a married woman. In the story action the hero's misadventures are frequently caused by his witting or unwitting participation in adultery. Retaliation by the offended husband is expected and apparently felt as justified by the community. Sanctions against adultery are specified in an explanatory reference to the traditional punishment whereby women are mutilated for this offense. The existence of sororal polygyny is also "explained" by the narrator.

The value themes associated with the young man's attainment of adult status concern his self-assertion and assumption of responsibility. The hero grows into adulthood by emancipation from his family ties, acquisition of power through ceremonial knowledge, and establishment of new family bonds in marriage. In this process a willful and irresponsible young man at the mercy of malevolent human or supernatural forces in the world about him becomes transformed into a responsible adult with a measure of control over his own destiny and a valued contribution to his people's welfare. The hero's irresponsibility at the opening of the story is typified by his characterization as a "wayward, roving gambler." Cavalier treatment of his own and his family's possessions in gambling is met by their disapproval and threat of

whipping or banishment; disregard of ritual prohibitions in his travels
or on hunting expeditions brings down the punishment of supernaturals;
sexual adventures call forth retaliation by the offended husband. Disapproval of his irresponsible actions is thus evidenced in the negative
sanctions which they provoke. His repeated trials by supernaturals
provide the educative means whereby he learns to heed instructions and
gains power of his own through ritual knowledge. The ability to learn
the complicated details of a ceremony is evidence of his developing
self-discipline, and the communication of this ceremonial knowledge
for the benefit of earth people puts him in a position of community responsibility. At the same time his increasing powers make him better
able to defend himself from attacks. The victory over an evil father-
in-law may be viewed as an expression of this increased self-reliance
and of his ability to establish his adult status in marriage.

The detailed examination of sanctions corroborated the findings of
the thematic analysis with respect to responsibility. In the story action
irresponsible or excessive gambling and impulsive disregard of ritual
prohibitions meet with negative sanctions. Disapproval of laziness and
of aimless wandering "with no purpose in view" is expressed explicitly.

The mythological evidence that responsibility and self-reliance are
valued character traits seems relatively straightforward. Their importance was seen to accord with the ethnological record and to be
consistent with the conditions of subsistence and the social structure
of Navaho life. Evidence for the importance of what we have termed
self-assertion is not so clearcut. Although implicit in the plot construction, it does not become a subject of "explanatory" treatment, nor
does it appear in the operation of sanctions. In identifying this value in
the thematic analysis considerable weight was placed on the accompanying psychological interpretation of the hero's life situation. While
the hero's impulsive disregard of group standards and ritual prohibitions is frowned upon, the actions which express this impulsiveness
contain at the same time another meaning from his own point of view.
He is motivated by curiosity and an adventurous desire to investigate
the unknown; he is restless and dissatisfied without knowing the source
of his dissatisfactions; he pursues his explorations obstinately and persistently. In psychological terms these actions were seen as attempts
to assert his independence from family ties at a time when it becomes
imperative for him to make his own way in the world. These attempts
at independence take the form of flouting authority, and the aggressive
elements in them were interpreted as being directed against forces felt
as constricting. Although the manner of expressing independence may
be disapproved, at the same time its courageous quality and even recklessness seem to hold fascination and to evoke admiration. The persistence and courage demonstrated in these attempts meet with success
in the long run even though many hazards have to be overcome in the
process. This aspect of the hero's adventures is similar to the courage and recklessness shown by the twin war gods of the emergence
myth in undertaking the exploits that freed the world of monsters.

The complex of attitudes represented by the term self-assertion was thus seen to contain both beneficent and aggressive-destructive components. It may be that some of the fascination and admiration attached to the hero's recklessness represents for the audience a desired but disallowed impulse toward expression of these aggressive-destructive components. On the other hand, the positive elements embodied in the courage and persistence of these same actions seem to represent a value in the definition we have used, that is, a mode of action that is deemed desirable.

So far we have summarized findings in which the analysis of explanatory elements and of sanctions supported and filled out the value themes identified in the initial thematic analysis. However, some topics appeared in the examination of sanctions that had not emerged as value themes in the earlier impressionistic approach. These were principally concerned with friendship and hostility in interpersonal relations.

Loneliness and companionship are matters of concern to the mythological characters. The comparatively isolated conditions of Navaho life give a realistic basis for such concern, and in this area there is evidence of some value conflict. One conflict is between the apparent desire to undertake adventures alone and discomfort at the loneliness and homesickness thus induced. This loneliness becomes motivation for travel in search of companions, but here a second conflict becomes apparent in the mistrust of strangers which makes difficult the realization of companionship sought in this way.

In the mythological data mistrust of strangers is linked with beliefs about dishonesty, trickery, and other forms of aggression. Existential beliefs about the nature of aggression furnish some basis for understanding normative standards and their operation in interpersonal relations. The mythological data show a recognition of the existence of aggression in interpersonal relations and an acceptance of its pervasiveness in human affairs. Certain supernaturals are designated as "mean" or illtempered; from them one may expect harm or trickery without provocation. Anger and retaliation for an affront and punishment for violation of personal or supernatural rights are accepted as inevitable. Games and contests lead to hard feelings and anger, and trickery is freely employed in them. The prevalent attitude toward strangers is to expect double dealing and be wary of their proffered hospitality. Aliens are viewed with suspicion; trickery may be expected from them and warfare is an accepted state of affairs. From these conceptions of aggression two trends emerge. On the one hand, there is the assumption that some aggression is unprovoked and springs from an inherent tendency toward meanness. Certain supernaturals are identified as being mean in this way and Coyote stands as the symbol of such unprovoked aggression. On the other hand, some acts of aggression represent a retaliatory response, counter-aggression for harm done to oneself. The mistrust evident in relations with aliens and strangers may reflect something of both of these conceptions.

From the evidence in the myths, the problem of aggression tends to be treated on the basis of a "practical" morality. When it is felt necessary, trickery and deceit are used without apparent compunction in dealings with strangers and aliens, and even with supernaturals. Emphasis seems to be on what the actor can "get away with" in the particular situation rather than on a general moral principle which, as in Christian ethics, is supposed to be uniformly applicable to all situations. Discussions of Navaho ethics have noted the prominence of this "contextual" element in Navaho morality.[123] In judging the value significance of this mythological treatment of aggression, the fantasy quality of myth should again be kept in mind. We have noted that in fantasy there may appear both the disallowed impulses and the sanctions against acting upon them and that it is not always possible to distinguish between these two facets of the mythological expression unless other corroborative types of evidence are at hand.

The myths do, however, indicate some limits to the expression of aggression. Trickery which takes the form of witchcraft practices is considered evil, at least when practiced within the in-group, and the hero's defeat of a witch father-in-law meets with community approval. Warfare when prolonged or carried to excess is stopped by action of supernaturals on the grounds that slaughter should not be allowed to get out of bounds. (The Enemy Way rite is specifically directed at control of the evils resulting from warfare.) These sanctions reflect in yet another life area the desire to maintain balance and harmony in human affairs.

There exists a relatively large body of literature on Navaho culture which has both historical depth and extensive coverage. A substantial portion of this literature deals either implicitly or explicitly with the Navaho philosophy of life and values. Navaho mythology was chosen as the subject of study with this fact in mind. Given the intensive study to which Navaho culture has been subjected, it was not expected that "new" values would be discovered, but rather that some confirmation might be obtained of values already identified from other sources. The picture of value elements resulting from the present analysis was referred at each step to knowledge derived from ethnological investigation. The values identified in the myths were found to be duplicated or to have counterparts in these descriptions of Navaho life as it exists now or is known to have existed in the past. In some cases there were differences in phrasing or emphasis. For example, the term self-assertion as used here covers phenomena that have been dealt with elsewhere under the heading of Navaho individualism. A considerable portion of the ethnological material is devoted to existential ideas on which the Navaho philosophy of life is based — an aspect which has received only minor attention in the present study — and this fact also led to differences in phrasing of materials that were essentially similar.

It should also be noted that not all of the value areas identified in the ethnological literature are represented in the present analysis and that some which assume central importance in the literature may have

received less emphasis or only passing mention here. The present
study has been limited to a selected but homogeneous portion of Navaho
folklore; neither the sacred tribal origin myth nor trickster tales were
included. Some lacunae in this mythological value picture would undoubtedly be filled by reference to these sources.

Discussion of Theoretical Problems

In its theoretical and methodological aspects this study has sought to
extend certain areas of mythological analysis, particularly to explore
some of the connections of mythological data with other aspects of culture and with personality manifestations. We have attempted to make
explicit some of the assumptions underlying the use of mythological
materials for cultural analysis and to test some methods for this use.
Our theoretical approach has employed concepts and formulations that
come from the study of cultural values, from anthropological functional-
ism, and from personality psychology. Values were seen to have both
a socio-cultural and a psychological reference. On the socio-cultural
side, as traditionally defined group standards, they represent a part of
culture and are assumed to be functionally related to other aspects of
the social and cultural system. But cultural values are also linked with
motivations to action within the individual. Because of this psychological reference of value phenomena and because imaginative processes
play an important part in the mythological medium of expression, attention was also given to the psychological dimension of the analysis.
It is, perhaps, in this direction, rather than in the substantive description of values, that the present study can extend our interpretations of
the Navaho myths into new areas.

The theoretical framework here used for viewing cultural values
included a definition of value and some operational methods for identifying values. The intimate relation between existential and normative
ideas in value phenomena was recognized, and areas in which existential
beliefs seem to play an important role in value formulations, as in
health and aggression, were discussed from this point of view. Partly
because of the limits of the mythological materials, but also because of
the magnitude of the problem, no attempt was made to identify a complete system of interrelated values. Some assessment of the usefulness of these value concepts in dealing with the mythological materials,
and of problems arising in their use, is in order.

The thematic analysis and the detailed examination of content have
been viewed as complementary methods of analysis. The identification
of value themes in overall plot construction was frankly impressionistic, and it allowed freedom to explore some of the possible psychological connections of the material. On the other hand, the closer examination of content attempted to use the operation of sanctions more
systematically as an index of values. One had the advantage of freedom
and scope; the other allowed for better methodological controls. By

combining these two methods, it was hoped that some check on the usefulness of this kind of thematic analysis would be obtained. It was found that values identified by the operation of sanctions were in accord with those evident in the thematic analysis, although some areas treated in the former did not appear in the latter and vice versa. The thematic analysis is thus judged useful as an exploratory step to identify crucial value areas and to indicate some of their interrelationships. By more systematic examination of content it has been possible to confirm and amplify these formulations.

Although the thematic analysis is impressionistic, implicit in it is the use of such operational indices of value as sanctions, differential energy expended, and action in "choice" situations. In such value areas as "health" and "power" the differential energy expended by the hero, or by his people for his benefit, undoubtedly entered into the impressionistic estimate of their importance. Likewise his actions in choice situations, such as his decision to embark on a series of adventures, had bearing on the evaluation of such character traits as self-assertion and self-reliance.

Two kinds of mythological data showed the operation of sanctions. Explicit expression of sanctions was found in explanatory elements interpolated in the story action which stated a rule of behavior and the expected penalty for its violation. These explanations often invoked supernatural sanctions against forbidden acts. They have a strong existential component; the punishment is seen as inherent in nature or in man's relation to the supernaturals. Points thus singled out for emphasis by the narrator, particularly if similar "explanations" reappear in different versions or different contexts, were considered to have a special importance; they represent self-conscious formulations by the native raconteur of lessons to be derived from the myth.

Sanctions played out in the dramatic action of the stories constituted the second kind of data. Here it was found that diffuse sanctions played a larger part than organized sanctions in the dramatic action of the stories, but it was sometimes difficult to derive clear evidence from them. Whether a given response represents an individual act of revenge or a retaliation supported by group standards is often indicated by the context, as when the supernaturals assure the hero who has committed adultery that attack by the offended husband is inevitable. The evidence that a given sanction represents group supported retaliation rather than individual revenge was introduced into the discussion of individual cases.

The more detailed analysis of content was extended in another direction. The appearance of recurrent behavior patterns which are not subject to negative sanctions raises the question whether these may be taken as accepted standards for action. This question was viewed as a methodological problem in the analysis of imaginative productions. According to the psychological principles on which the analysis was based, fantasy was taken to include those imaginative productions called into play when the process of need satisfaction is impeded. The

"imagining" process which results may take the form of picturing culturally acceptable actions leading to satisfaction of the need. On the
other hand, if the deprivation occurs in a conflict area, the "imagining"
may take the form of picturing actions that are desired but culturally
disallowed, with or without the accompanying punishment. The thematic analysis did not have to attack this problem directly since it attempted to identify areas which became the subject of fantasy elaboration rather than specific, approved patterns of action within these
areas. (Some exception to this statement should be noted with regard
to the discussion of "self-assertion," where with the help of psychological interpretations it seemed possible to make tentative value de-
ductions.) In the detailed analysis of content the appearance of recurrent action patterns was used to throw light on values operating in
kinship relations and with respect to aggression. However, such materials were taken as suggestive rather than conclusive. For example,
from the pattern of mutual support pictured between brothers, a standard of solidarity may be deduced; this is confirmed by the experience
of the Visionary when the scornful attitudes of his brothers bring negative sanctions into play. Standards indicated in the frequent use of
trickery and deceit do not find such clearcut confirmation from the
operation of sanctions and remain suggestive rather than conclusive.
In general it was found that recurrent action patterns in the myths
could not be used as evidence of specific value standards unless they
were supported by other mythological evidence, such as the operation
of sanctions, by ethnological confirmation, or by psychological interpretations.

The anthropological functionalists have demonstrated ways in which
myth expresses and supports basic aspects of social and religious organization.[124] In the present study certain of the recurrent mythological
situations revealed in the value analysis were interpreted as having
functional connections with the social and cultural conditions of Navaho
life. These were principally situations associated with the young man's
assumption of adult status and those in which he had need for companionship and dependence on others.

The relatively isolated, matrilineal and matrilocal, extended family
group is the basic unit in Navaho society. In a hunting and gathering
economy, such as that pictured in the myths, and to only a slightly
lesser extent in the semi-nomadic sheepherding economy of recent
times, this group must be a relatively self-sufficient economic and
emotional unit. Under the rule of matrilocal residence a woman remains in the extended family into which she was born; a man upon
marriage must find his place in the cooperative economic activities and
the emotional structure of his wife's extended family. The tension
points associated with this family organization are clearly shown in the
dramatic content of the myths. At the opening of the typical chantway
story, the young man is confronted with the problem of breaking his
ties with his parental family and proving his ability to become independent of them, a process that requires self-assertion and the

development of responsibility. Later in his adventures the hero marries and enters a new family group, and here a second tension point becomes apparent. The incoming husband tends to upset the affectional balance of the already existing family and is subjected to attacks by his witch father-in-law. Another side of this tension situation is represented by the young woman who makes a marriage choice that is unacceptable to her people and has to flee to escape their wrath and punishment.

In spelling out the functional relations of the mythological materials, particular attention was paid to the psychological aspects of the young hero's position. The chantway myths were taken as representing various facets of the young man's attempt to establish his adult status — his preoccupation with problems of authority and independence, his emancipation from the domination and safety of the parental family, and his demonstration of ability to undertake adult responsibilities. The hero's separation from his family was seen as ambivalent, containing aggressive elements of rebellion, waywardness, and irresponsibility as well as constructive elements of self-assertion, courage, and persistence. These attitudes are expressed first in relation to familial forces, and then toward relatively impersonal supernatural authority figures. The conflicting elements were seen as resolved in the final outcome by his triumphs, particularly the victory over the evil father-in-law, and by his reconciliation and return to his family with the gift of ceremonial knowledge.

The process of achieving adulthood, with the readjustment of emotional ties and of personal responsibilities inherent in it, constitutes a general human problem, but one that may have a different form and phrasing depending on the social and cultural context in which it takes place.[125] The subsistence conditions and family structure of Navaho life were seen as influencing the particular phrasing of this problem for the Navaho young man. The elaboration of mythological fantasy motifs in the chantway myths reflects the stresses and conflicts arising in this process of achieving adulthood, both in its general human aspects and in its specific cultural phrasing.

These functional and psychological interpretations raise general questions which could best be answered by reference to comparative materials and which remain problems for future investigation. If this type of interpretation is valid, one would expect to find similarities in mythological themes as between societies in which similar social and cultural patterns obtain. Evidence on this problem is not readily at hand. While considerable and rich bodies of folklore have been recorded, in comparatively few cases have they been subjected to the kind of intensive analysis that would reveal recurrent themes. In order to find satisfactory test cases, the social and cultural variables would have to be carefully specified and controlled.

The most pertinent comparative material available is in Benedict's analysis of themes in Zuni myth. Zuni family structure is, like the Navaho, matrilineal and matrilocal. The conditions of subsistence and of community structure are, however, different, and the traditional contrast of Zuni communalism with Navaho individualism reflects these differences. Themes identified in the Zuni myths do not correspond with those of the present Navaho analysis.[126] Among the recurrent Zuni themes are the young man's seduction and attack by threatening female figures and the desertion of children by their families followed by the children's shaming and triumph over the wicked parents.[127] Incidents similar to these occur sporadically in the Navaho myths, for example in the story of the crippled twins and the woman who destroys her lovers, but they do not constitute central themes. It is tempting to relate the apparent Zuni preoccupation with danger emanating from the woman, rather than from the men of the affinal household as in the Navaho stories, with differences within the matrilineal-matrilocal patterns of these two groups. The Zuni matrilineal lineage is more formalized in its functions than is that of the Navaho, and the Zuni woman wields considerable power in familial, economic, and ceremonial spheres. It is possible that the mythological picture of the young man's fear of the woman in sex and marriage could be related to such elements in the social and cultural structure.

    This reference to Zuni material points to one direction for comparative investigation — by controlling the socio-cultural variables and seeing whether similarities appear in mythological themes. The Northern Athabaskans might offer a fruitful field for this type of investigation. The socio-cultural organization in certain of these groups bears some similarity to that of the Navaho (e.g., matrilineal clans, temporary matrilocal residence, a hunting economy[128]). In attempting Pueblo or Northern Athabaskan comparisons with the Navaho, it would be necessary to take account of variables introduced by historical connections. Another direction for comparative investigation would be to work from mythological similarities to their social and cultural correlates. For example, hero tales and the son-in-law test are of widespread occurrence in northwestern North America,[129] and it would be useful to have systematic information on the social and cultural forms associated with various types of these familiar motifs. It is within the larger framework of such comparative studies that the intensive analysis of specific bodies of mythology can best contribute to the identification of cultural values and to the clarification of the general functional and psychological problems associated with this form of cultural expression.

VII. ABSTRACTS OF CHANTWAY MYTHS

Hail Way

Reichard, 1944a, pp. 3-155. The Story of the Hail Chant. (R)

Wheelwright, 1946a, pp. 3-45. Hail Chant Myth. (W)

In the Hail Way story the hero becomes an outcast because of excessive gambling. With supernatural help he escapes punishment by his people. On his wanderings he is seduced by winter thunder's wife, and in retaliation the jealous husband destroys him. He is restored by thunders and winds and, in thus taking his side, they become embroiled in war with winter thunder. In the ritual of peace-making that follows, the hero becomes a patient and learns the ceremony. On a trip to the sky he has additional adventures and acquires further ritual knowledge. He returns to teach the ceremony for the benefit of earth people and finally departs to live with the supernaturals. Among the incidents worked into this story are: a race with frog, with the contestants' bodies and very existence at stake; and the use of a reputedly lazy boy as messenger for the fire dance. A minor incident is the meeting with worm man who controls stinging insects.

This story follows the familiar pattern of rejection of a boy by his family and his subsequent supernatural adventures, in the course of which he learns a ceremony to bring back, without resentment, to his people. After his original misdeed of excessive gambling, the hero is not presented as taking the initiative in courting danger but is drawn into misadventures by the proposals of others, while apparently vaguely aware of his wrongdoing. His seduction by thunder's wife results in the husband's retaliatory attack. He accepts frog's challenge to race in the face of supernatural warning not to venture into danger. In both cases the hero meets bodily harm: he is shattered and his body parts scattered by thunder's attack; and with loss of his body parts and functions he is transformed into a frog. Despite his foolhardiness in thus exposing himself, the supernaturals rescue and restore him physically. His final restoration becomes part of the peace-making between opposing groups of supernaturals; he becomes the patient in the peace ritual. This linkage of personal injury and cure with general warfare and peace-making points up more clearly than in most chantway myths the aggressive and restorative elements that permeate these hero stories.

The two published versions of this legend were given by the same informant, Klah of Newcomb, New Mexico, presumably at different times, although they contain substantially the same material. Reichard's is a text recording; that of Wheelwright is a summary or "retold" version. Since the material of the two versions is so similar, it has been found most convenient to base the abstract on Reichard's complete recording and to indicate in parentheses where the Wheelwright version differs. This detailed comparison of two versions of a single myth by the same informant should provide opportunity for study of individual variations in retelling of myths.

1. Hero Leaves Home

Rainboy lives with his mother, father, an older brother and younger brothers and sisters. He loses his clothing and his father's beads to the Pueblos in gambling games — hoop and stick, dice, ball, kickstick, straddlesticks, racing. His people, including his mother, warn him not to play these games. When he loses his father's token of leadership, the people hold consultation and decide to whip him in public with even the babies as witnesses. He is imprisoned at night to await punishment, and bat woman comes to warn him that on the following day he will be beaten unmercifully, until he has "goose pimples from fear," and to help him escape with her cloak of invisibility. She leads him out magically despite the fastened door. On discovering his escape, the people hunt him angrily with whips. (He lives in a family of five and they tell him he has to leave home because of his gambling. The whipping threat is omitted, as is the help of bat woman. He leaves destitute with only his sister to be sorry at his going. Begochidi[130] comes to hear his story and expresses sympathy for him. W.)

2. Adultery and Attack by Thunder

The hero lives off the countryside, making his own sandals, moccasins, and bow and arrow. He comes upon a house strung with rainbow, and, leaving outside his weapons and poor moccasins of which he is ashamed, he enters to find it beautifully furnished. Within he finds a girl with white face and dark eyes who is painting and who smiles at him tantalizingly. She fetches his moccasins and weapons, whereupon he takes them and leaves, but she draws him back with zigzag lightning, asking if he is indifferent to her. Three times more he departs in shyness, and each time she draws him back, with rainstreamer, forked lightning and rainbow. When her husband winter thunder sees them lying together he sends a hailstorm that shatters Rainboy completely.[131] (He finds a very lovely young girl coloring a blanket. Each time he leaves, he goes farther from the house; each time she draws him back — with lightning, moisture rope, rainbow, and sunray — he comes farther into the room; this is her way of making love to him. Seeing him depart after the fourth time, white thunder[132] grows very jealous and sends a lightning bolt to shatter him. This is specified as the episode at which five ceremonies are connected with each other: Water, Wind, Male Shooting, Feather, and Hail ceremonies. W.)

3. Restoration of Hero

Big fly carries the news of the hero's destruction to the other thunders and winds, who consult with each other and who, with the help of other gods, restore him ritually by placing his bones and flesh between covers and stepping over them. Talking God and Hastse Hogan[133] are given offerings and play a central role in this restoration, as do also the thunder and wind people, ants, bees, cornbeetle, pollen boy, and Begochidi. The last crucial pieces of his body, the "curve of the upper lip" and blood, are gathered by the ants and Begochidi. The gods take him back to the home of thunders, where further ritual is performed and he is then sent back to his family with the admonition not to go near danger. (Begochidi directs the council of thunders and winds. Here the war between the two groups of thunder people, instigated by Begochidi in retaliation for the hero's destruction, follows immediately upon the restoration and before the hero returns home. W.)

4. Race with Frog (Toad)

On the way home Rainboy visits rough frog in his corn patch, who pretends not to pay attention and teases him (by addressing him as "my daughter's child"). As Rainboy notices the peculiarities of frog's appearance — swelling eyes, Adam's apple, rough patches on his skin, and warts from which smoke issues — frog reads his thoughts and agrees with each observation. A little wind monitor warns him not to accept a smoke offered by frog or he will become like him. After three refusals he accepts a challenge to race around a mountain, thinking that frog's running will be erratic. Frog defeats him by shooting hail into his foot, hip, shoulder blade, and occiput. Thus frog wins his body parts and functions — his feet, legs, gait, body, heart, nerves, mind, speech, face, nose, eyes, head — and takes them to his ceremonial altar, where the hero is transformed into a frog. In frog's home he still refuses to smoke, which would have made this transformation permanent. Big fly scolds him for having thus disobeyed but carries news of his mishap to the thunders who assemble to see what can be done. Big fly knows the proper prayerstick and approach to frog. The thunders present the offering, which frog accepts after consultation with his relatives, commenting that only big fly knows the secret of his offering. He hands over Rainboy's body parts which are again restored ritually between covers.

The hero is told to challenge frog to another race and is furnished with magical means of winning — cattail, whirlwind, lightning, hail. Frog tries four times unsuccessfully to persuade Rainboy to touch his magic ax which will kill anyone but its owner. In the race frog at first leads; he blows clouds, rain and fog to confuse Rainboy's course. On the little wind monitor's advice Rainboy does likewise with hail and whirlwind; frog now lagging behind pleads with Rainboy not to take his body parts. In desperation he throws his magic ax at Rainboy asking him to kill him with it because he has nothing left to live for. Little

wind warns Rainboy not to touch the treacherous ax, which will rebound
to destroy the wielder. Still on the advice of little wind Rainboy takes
only the feet, legs, and gait of frog — if he "took everything from him it
would not be good" — and brings them to the gods. After four days they
decide to return them to frog who in return accepts charge of cloud,
rain, and fog for earth people. Here instructions are given not to make
dumplings when planting, or hail will ruin the corn, nor to bring them
into a Hail Chant.

(In W's version the race with toad occurs when the hero is sent
home after the war and peace making ritual of the thunders. Omitted
here are toad's teasing, the thought reading incident, and invitation to
smoke. However, when toad himself smokes, the smoke issues from
all over his body. Here toad wins the hero's legs and shoes, taking the
strength out of his legs and making them crooked like his own. Talking God scolds him for disobedience and warns him not to eat toad's
food. Toad laughs at his gait when he starts home. The gods send big
fly with food, then come to get him, taking the shoes that have been
hidden by toad and leaving kehtahn in their place. In the second race
the hero likewise wins by magic provided by the gods but takes only
toad's shoes and leg tendons, while he is still weak, hot and tired from
the race. Later the people take pity on him and replace the tendons
with lightning and promise that they will be friends and not race any-
more. Here the ax incident is omitted. It is explained that tying a
toad in a garden is thought to bring rain. W.)

5. War between the Thunders

Because winter thunder "has uttered that which is evil," dark thunder organizes a war party against him. Changing Woman and Monster
Slayer are notified. When she enters the council, they all bow their
heads, but she refuses to participate, saying, "Surely I bore my children [to subdue] monsters, not to be in the midst of it," i.e., not to
participate in war. Nor will the war gods join because of her disapproval. They prepare war paraphernalia, including cattail and flint
armor and shields of hot water or ice. The two war parties engage in
a series of four battles with many killed and wounded. For the last
battle measuring worm and woodbeetle join them with "something like
an ice pick" and hot water, whereby they puncture the weapons and ice
shields of winter thunder's forces or spread hot water on them until
they are in retreat. Talking God and Haste Hogan stop the slaughter,
crying, "If you are all killed it will not be good." Both sides retreat.
(Begochidi organizes the war party. Here Changing Woman says that
they must let her do all the fighting: "I do not want either of my sons
to come into battle as they would kill everyone. The other gods can
fight but not my sons. They can be chiefs of the war but must not fight."
In the first battle Changing Woman and the war gods stop the great
slaughter, neither side having won, and Begochidi revives all of the
dead warriors with his song. Begochidi himself halts the next two
battles, and the gods come to intervene in the final battle. W.)

Changing Woman protests that someone ought to make peace, but each side feels that it is too dangerous to make overtures. On big fly's advice dark thunder's people persuade bat to undertake the mission, although he is at first reluctant. Bat and Black God go to the enemy. Bat seizes winter thunder's children and makes them tell where he lives. On their entrance winter thunder greets them with the query, "Since when do Earth People come here." He refuses four times to talk it over, tells them to go away, and threatens to cut them to pieces. Black God in turn threatens to use his firedrill, and, frightened by this, winter thunder summons his people and agrees to negotiate. He accepts the prayerstick, commenting that only big fly knows how to make it. They agree to meet for a ceremony in twelve days.

(W's version is substantially the same except for the following variations. Councils are held on both sides, but no one dares to go as peace emissary. On each of four days Begochidi seeks in vain for someone to go from black thunder's side. A shy stranger, bat, is asked and at first refuses: "No, your great men would not go, so why should I?" Finally on the insistence of Changing Woman and the war gods, he agrees. They find white thunder guarded by a white-billed duck who tries to bar their way but after four questionings directs them to white thunder's abode down "under twenty worlds." In white thunder's hostile reception the comments about earth people and about big fly's knowledge of his prayerstick are omitted. Bat brings the message that they want peace because "many are sick and wounded and all are poor," and they are tired of war. When black thunder in his turn accepts the prayerstick, "their anger against White Thunder was ended." W.)

On the way to the peace ceremony they are puzzled by meeting a boy who, laughing, throws dirt up in the air; he appears first in their rear, then ahead or amongst them in the form of a yellow worm and other transformations. The people want to kill him, exclaiming, "What does he mean laughing at us?" When they catch him, all kinds of stinging insects swarm out of his mouth, ears, face, and nose, attacking and rendering them unconscious. They beg this creature to stop, addressing him as grandfather, and he sucks the insects in, "laughing inordinately he rolled around like a ball." He has gray eyes and red hair and is dressed like a woman. He specifies his prayerstick and says that he is to blame if earth people get sores around the mouth, ears, face, or on the body. He continues with the peace party.[134]

(The boy appears only in the rear. On investigation they find a yellow worm. As they reach to pick it up, it turns into a man who emits bees, as above. This is the first time that they had seen stinging insects. When presented with a kehtahn he sucks back the bees. To their amazement they discover that this is Begochidi, who tells the people he will accompany and watch over them; however, he soon disappears from their midst, presumably to the sky. W.)

6. Peace Ceremony

The peace parties meet and conduct a ceremony in which Rainboy is the patient. Throughout, the two sides exchange ceremonial equipment and perform reciprocal ritual actions, including the extracting of arrows from the wounded of the opposite side. There follows a detailed description of ceremonial procedures. At one point, after the bath, a series of gods enter with various foods — pinyons, god food, wild potatoes, dumplings — all of which are refused, and as they depart the bearers each make prediction that these foods will be scarce, or that when there are many pinyons it will be snowy and cold and people will freeze to death. When more gods gather for the body painting, snake people are refused entrance because they might bite people, and frog enters but complains that the ceremony had not been announced to him. Two boys who are reputedly "lazy, dirty, and pampered by their grandmother" are the runners who invite distant people to the fire dance. Twenty-two acts of the fire dance are described. During this, frog children are trampled on and have to be restored. After the ceremony Rainboy observes the taboos for four days and refuses improper food offered by rat woman. He is instructed that the fire dance henceforth should not be included in the ceremony. Beaver comes to him and they smoke together; although Rainboy disparages his own tobacco, beaver is pleased with it. Beaver reveals further ritual instructions for the use of incense which was withheld because winter thunder was afraid of it.

(When horned toad woman and Changing Woman enter for blessing of the hogan, the people bow their heads.[135] White thunder, with black thunder as assistant, performs the ceremony. He is still angry with the hero and plans to cut him open with his stone knife at the first opportunity. The hero is warned to begin singing before white thunder in the sandpainting ceremony and thus confuse him; he substitutes the line, "We are in great peace," for white thunder's version, "We are in great danger." White thunder is "so startled and ashamed at this change that he did not try to kill the patient that day," realizing that his plan was known; instead he "merely showed his anger by whirling about, still holding in his hand his obsidian knife." Bear and snake people are sent out of the hogan but Coyote manages to sneak in unseen. The sandpaintings are unrolled on cotton. The restoration of toad children is explained: "The Toad is a very sacred person and if we don't cure his young ones who are hurt he will feel badly toward us and we may die." Omitted from this version are: the refusal of food and prediction of scarcity; reputedly lazy boys as messengers; frog's complaint at not being invited; offering of improper food by rat woman. Beaver's instructions occur later in the story; see below. W.)

7. Sky Visit

Returning to the home of the gods as directed, Rainboy finds no one there, starts to sing but instead cries in loneliness.[136] Gopher comforts

and feeds him, and chipmunk first asks him for and then steals some of
measuring worm's tobacco. Talking God takes the hero through door
guards — revolving cross, spotted lion, forked lightning, hail — into dark
thunder's house. They discuss what to do with Rainboy and take him to
the sky on lightnings, rain and sun streamers, and rainbows. Sun offers them something to eat but himself disappears into the distance.
With the help of a little wind monitor, Rainboy passes Talking God's
test of identifying places on earth and in the sky; otherwise he could
never return home. Talking God leads him through the guardians of
spotted thunder's house — revolving cross, winds — where he learns the
Male Shooting Chant.[137] Rainboy is asked if he will take proper charge
of dark clouds, rain, snow, and ice but does not assent until the fifth
query when he is told he cannot return home unless he agrees. Those
present show their pleasure and relief at his assent by putting the right
hand over the left. He is given ceremonial properties but not the rolled
sandpaintings which would wear out with use. The connections between
the Male Shooting Chant and Hail Chant are pointed out; one may be
used if the other fails.

(The hero returns to the gods and is lonely for the boys and girls
who were at the ceremony. He is sent home on a preliminary visit to
his family with warning not to get into trouble again, but on the way he
gets involved in the race with toad [see above] after which he arrives
home, is welcomed by his family and tells them his story. The gods
have given him flowers for his sister. He is lonely at home and after
four days Talking God comes for him. His sister wants to accompany
him to the place where grow such sweet smelling flowers even though
she was not invited. His family cry at the prospect of his departure
and his mother tries to dissuade the sister. The parents are reassured
by Talking God that the gods will do him no harm and that the trip is
important. They travel to the sky on dawnlight. The hero's meeting
with the gods is joyful; his sister feels at first shy, strange, and
frightened but is made to feel at home by the young girls there. They
ascend to spotted thunder's home, meet Sun on the way, and arrive
to participate in a Water ceremony with fire dance. The connections
between Water and Hail Chant are pointed out. Then the Hail ceremony
is held over the hero's sister and he learns it. Afterward she is struck
by lightning without harm. W.)

8. Return Home

Rainboy returns to earth on lightning and his party meets that of the
hero of the Water Chant, who has the same name as his. They smoke
together, note the similarities of their equipment and say that they can
be used interchangeably. Rainboy is sent home to his family. They
embrace him, though they had not recognized him at first, and his father
summons the people to hear his story. In accordance with the gods'
instructions he teaches the ceremony to his older brother, taking
thirty-two days. Both the older brother and he sing over his sister;

they also sing over each other. The hero and his sister depart with
the gods, she carrying pets of dog and ducklings.

(Before returning the hero to earth, Begochidi instructs him that, if
he forgets any part of the ceremony, that part will revert to the gods;
if he makes up any of it or plays with it, he will be punished by spotted
thunder. On the way to earth they meet both the Water and Shooting
Chant people and compare equipment, noting its similarities and what
can be exchanged. The hero and his sister visit and learn various
ceremonies given by the gods, who tell him that he will be punished if
he does not keep this ceremonial knowledge alive. Talking God adds,
"I have saved you many times, now you must behave well and be good
to the people." They are blessed and sent home. On the way they
meet beaver and his wife, who feed them berries from an inexhaustible
bowl and ask to hear his story. Beaver gives more information about
the incense that thunder fears. On his arrival home, the hero teaches
his brother the ceremony — birth order of this brother not specified —
initiates him at another ceremony, holds two more for his father and
mother, and one for all earth people. Again the hero is called back
to the gods to learn how to prepare equipment; here it is specified that
sandpaintings will be used in the future instead of the pictures of cotton
material that are unrolled for use. He returns to give this information
to his brother. Then the hero and his sister depart [as above], he to
have charge of rain and she of plants for the benefit of earth people.
W.)

Water Way

Haile, 1932a, MS., 110 pp. Ceremony in the Water Way. (H)

Wheelwright, 1946a, pp. 55-90. Tohe or Water Chant I. (Wa)

Wheelwright, 1946a, pp. 91-100. Tohe or Water Chant II. (Wb)

The action in the Water Way story concerns principally the rejection or ridicule of the hero and his revenge by successful sexual exploits and other demonstrations of his power. The series of episodes,
which recur in one combination or another in the three versions, includes: rejection by Pueblos (Wa, Wb); ridicule for skin disease (H,
Wb); revenge by adultery or seduction (H, Wa); "downy home man"
(H, Wa, Wb); proof of power through butterfly seduction (H, Wa, Wb)
and through contests with White Butterfly (H, Wb); and trip in hollow
log (Wa, Wb). Three of these episodes seem to come from other chantway legends (the hollow log trip from Plume Way, and butterfly seduction and contests with White Butterfly from Prostitution Way); when
they are introduced here it is usually specified that this is the meeting
of Water Way with these other chantways.[138]

In Water Way these episodes are linked in such a manner as to emphasize the hero's revenge for bad treatment or ridicule by his sexual

conquests. He then goes further to demonstrate his powers by withstanding the offended husband's attack, by killing and/ or reviving his new wives' people, and by successful contests with a powerful adversary. Although women are not central characters in these episodes, it may be noted that they are presented as predominantly helpless, drawn irresistibly by the hero's power or trickery and in the face of their own people's wrath.[139]

The three versions of the Water Way story show considerable difference in plot construction and use of these episodes, and for this reason they will be dealt with separately.

Haile (H)

The principal action of this story is a sexual adventure and the hero's evasion of its disastrous consequences. His adultery is in itself an act of revenge, provoked by the ridicule and rejection that he has suffered when he appears at a ceremony disfigured by "skin disease." although he takes an active role in the seduction, his original involvement in the situation is engineered by two old women, with whom he is sent to live as grandson, and who purposely cause his skin disfigurement and then send him into the public gathering for ridicule. Having taken his revenge by reappearing as a handsome man and seducing thunder's twelve wives, the hero has to flee the angry husband's retaliatory attack. He is able, through his own powers and with supernatural help, to defend himself. In the course of his flight from thunder's attack the hero visits supernaturals in the sky and elsewhere and learns the ceremony.

Woven into this principal action is a second sexual adventure, the butterfly seduction of two non-sunlight-struck Pueblo maidens, which the hero also undertakes with the help of his grandmother; he is transformed into a butterfly and entices them from their underground chamber. The hero then undertakes a contest with a formidable adversary, the Great Gambler (elsewhere known as White Butterfly), in which he bets his newly acquired wives, his possessions, and his own body. He is aided in this race by supernaturals (toad urinates to make his opponent slip near the end of the course) and despatches his adversary by an ax blow on the head. The story concludes with the hero's further visits to supernaturals for more ritual knowledge.[140] Nowhere in this story is it described how the hero teaches his ceremonial knowledge for benefit of earth people.

Wheelwright (Wa)

This version presents a more complicated array of interwoven episodes than that sketched above for the Haile version. In addition to the butterfly seduction, other elements — apparently from Prostitution Way — are introduced, such as ridicule by Pueblo neighbors and learning the ceremony for sexual attraction, which is used in retaliation for this ridicule. The story of the hollow log trip and the hero's subsequent marriage are included from Plume Way. These incidents are woven into a story which, like the Prostitution Way story (see below), emphasizes the hero's poverty and scornful treatment by Pueblos and his retaliation by sexual conquests. In this version also his loneliness and disconsolateness at rejection by women become motivation for further adventures.

The hero, born to a seclusive orphan girl who keeps secret his paternity, is called Beggar and Rough Skin by Pueblos.[141] By supernatural intervention he learns that his father is Sun and is given means of seducing two non-sunlight-struck Pueblo maidens in revenge for Pueblo ridicule. This he accomplishes by the butterfly seduction, later taking his wives with him on a sky visit to protect them from the anger of their people. When his wives' people are later struck by lightning he demonstrates his power by restoring those who had ridiculed him. Subsequently these wives reject him and he returns disconsolate to his mother. In this mood he offends water monster by kicking a rock into the water and is taken to water monster's underwater home to learn the ceremony. Still lonely after his wives' rejection, he dreams repeatedly of a beautiful woman and seeks her in a trip by hollow log, wherein he is aided by supernaturals. To this new wife he brings corn and learns more ritual from his new father-in-law. He returns to teach the ceremony to his people.

In subsequent travels with his mother, they are again badly treated by the Pueblos and the hero is taught the ceremony for sexual attraction whereby he gains riches and retaliates by marrying the Pueblo chief's daughter. Ultimately, however, he departs to his wife of the hollow log trip.

Wheelwright (Wb)

Similar incidents are used in Wheelwright's second version (ridicule for skin disease, hollow log trip, butterfly seduction, and contest with White Butterfly). Here their telling demonstrates the hero's power but not his retaliation for bad treatment as in the previous versions. In fact, the motivation throughout is more obscure. The manner of telling is matter-of-fact and recounts merely the action — the hero's original poor condition, his unexplained action of provoking ridicule by disfigurement, and vindication of the boast that he will marry the non-sunlight-struck maidens.

After the beggar hero has been transformed by Coyote and restored he and his grandmother leave the unfriendly Hopi. The hero decides to take the hollow log trip (motivation not indicated) in which and in the subsequent planting of corn he is aided by supernaturals. He returns to his grandmother but does not tell her of this trip. He brings down ridicule by whipping himself with thistle, poison oak, and other means to make his skin look queer and by his claim that he will marry non-sunlight-struck maidens. This he accomplishes by the butterfly seduction and later, on their petition, destroys and restores his wives' people. He travels with his wives in the sky and on earth demonstrating his powers and meeting with various supernaturals. When his wives are stolen by White Butterfly, supernatural aid is again given him (by spider, frog) for the forthcoming contest. He wins the race by avoiding his adversary's wizardry shooting and kills him with an ax blow. At the conclusion of these events the hero is reunited with his wives. Here there is no mention of teaching ritual to earth people.

The following abstract is based on Haile's manuscript recording, with the corresponding material of Wheelwright's two "retold" versions summarized at the appropriate places. Since the three stories handled here vary considerably in construction, both of Wheelwright's versions are also outlined separately to show their continuity and any elements not included in Haile's version.

1. Ridicule for Skin Disease

Two old women, riverward knoll woman and scabby woman, have wind monitors, one of whom is sent to the sky to consult with Rain Boy and Girl and the thunders about obtaining a boy to help them in their plan for a "different condition (of things)." "Sun's reflected ray, in the form of a boy" (later in the story known as Sunlight Boy) is chosen to go to the two women. He descends on rainbows and first sees their hogan made of beautiful jewels; then when he looks closely it has changed to its original poor condition. The hero and his two grandmothers move, and a new hogan is constructed by willow twigs, flag, and flowers placed tip downward, with the help of bird people in return for offerings.

A Hail Way ceremony is to be held nearby conducted by dark thunder, and the boy's grandmothers sit on the south side of the hogan during the night discussing in whispers their plans for him. Huddled on the north side he cannot overhear their talk, and at dawn he exclaims angrily that they should have been sleeping and asks what could take so long a discussion. He is now ugly in form and is called "the rough one" or "the one who picks up." When they instruct him to race around a certain plant in the morning, he claims that he is lazy and objects to "running back and forth for no reason whatever." However, he is prevailed upon to race by the assurance that what he has been asked to encircle "is in reality horses." On his return scabby woman covers his skin with scabies so that he is an ugly sight and sends him to visit the Hail Way ceremony to test how his appearance will provoke ridicule. At both the hoop and pole ground and the cooking place he is scorned and the people turn away from him in disgust. His grandmother rubs his skin with herbs and flowers so that the sores fall away and he returns to mingle with people at the ceremony unremarked.

This procedure is repeated three subsequent times with the hero

sent to be ridiculed at the ceremony covered with Spanish pock, sores
from the sage plant and from nettle. Each time he protests the whis-
pering of his grandmothers and the command to race, but each time he
accedes when told he is racing in turn for sheep, soft goods, and jewels.
On two visits to the ceremony he enters the ceremonial hogan, where
the twelve wives of the singer, dark thunder, avert their gaze in
disgust.

(In Wb a parallel incident occurs after the hero, who is called
Rough Skin, returns from his trip in the hollow log. He visits a ceremony where he is ridiculed and spurned for his foolish actions. On
each of four days he has whipped himself with thistle, poison oak, and
other means to make his skin itch and look queer. The people laugh at
him when he claims that he will marry non-sunlight-struck Pueblo
girls. In Wb this incident is followed by the successful butterfly seduction. The ridiculing incident is omitted from Wa, although here the
beggar hero is also called Rough Skin and is made fun of by Kisahni
when he wanders naked and poor; see below.)

2. Adultery to Avenge Ridicule

The hero is molded and his hair stretched out by his grandmother.
Resplendent and clothed in jewels, he is again sent to visit the ceremony where he is now welcomed and considered "embarassingly (at-
tractive)." Dark thunder's pretty wives smile on him and are eager to
follow him. On each of four nights he visits thus and in turn commits
adultery with each of the singer's twelve wives in revenge for his earlier treatment. At the end of the ceremony he is warned by his wind
monitor that the singer has seen him and that he must return to his
grandmother before daylight for safety. (Adultery with the singer's
wives does not occur in the two Wheelwright versions, although, as
noted above, the butterfly seduction of non-sunlight-struck Pueblo
maidens follows on the hero's ridicule in Wb.)

3. Downy Home Man

At dawn an attack is expected from the singer and his people with
intent to kill the hero. Although his grandmothers cannot protect him,
they keep watch during the night and in the morning send him to Wide
Lake on a rainbow. His pursuers find only his tracks ending at the
lakeside. The hero has traveled by rainbow to a grass clump in the
center of the lake and pulled in his rainbow bridge after him. When
the pursuers are gone he returns to the lakeside to build himself a
willow hogan. He shoots birds with a bow and arrow given him by his
grandmother and lies in a trench full of their feathers. When warned
by wind of a second attack he again retreats to the center of the lake
and at night when they have gone returns to sleep in his downy bed. He
wakes to see the four winds standing on massed clouds at the four directions; they claim him as their child and say that they will protect him,

that his punishment is inevitable but will only be "on the surface" and not harm him. His grandmothers confirm that punishment for his adultery must take place as ordained.

(In Wb the downy home incident — covering house with feathers and rolling in them to keep warm — occurs after the hero's return from the hollow log trip and before the ridicule for skin disease; it is not combined with escape from pursuers. In Wa it is much attenuated; after teaching the ceremony to his people, the hero feeds on larks by the lakeside until he has a big pile of feathers.)

4. Sky Visit

On his grandmother's instructions the hero again goes to the center of the lake and rises on crossed rainbows through the skyhole. Here he finds a Water Way ceremony in progress with water monster old man as singer. After being greeted with, "Around here earth surface people are not allowed," he explains his presence. As he observes the sandpainting, prayersticks, and singing, he is learning the ceremony without realizing it. During the proceedings his grandmothers enter, now turned to young maidens; water monster old man is their mother's father's brother. Bird, reptile and water animal people participate in the ceremony, as do Talking God and House God[142] who give songs although not invited. The door guards and big fly are warned against the thunders and spotted wind who are called "no good." At the close of the ceremony the hero applies to his grandmothers for aid in obtaining non-sunlight-struck maidens.

(In Wa and Wb the hero's sky trip occurs after he has married the non-sunlight-struck Pueblo maidens. In Wa the hero and his wives are taken into the sky to avoid the wrath of the wives' people, as recounted in the Prostitution Way abstract of the butterfly seduction. In Wb the sky trip occurs after his wives' people have attacked them, been slain, and restored. They meet Sun, find a ceremony in progress and avoid a lightning attack by giving offerings [Wa, Wb]. The women want to catch two baby lightning people but are persuaded not to for fear of the parent lightnings, and give the babies offerings instead [Wb]. The hero discusses his powers with lightning man and water monster woman; at one point he demonstrates his power by shooting an arrow which returns to him with eagle feathers and corn ears [Wb]. The hero sings an Awl Way song to cure reptiles and fish who have been stepped on in the dancing [Wa]. "The travelers were told that women who are going to have babies must not see people that are hurt, or dead people, or animals, and this was the first time that men knew this" [Wa]. The party returns to earth in a black cloud, where upon follows the theft of wives and contest with White Butterfly to regain them [Wb]. In Wa the wives are sent down from the sky and there follows the attempt of wives' people to punish them.)

5. Butterfly Seduction

Seduction of non-sunlight-struck Pueblo maidens occurs in all versions of the Water Way legend. For variations in presentation of this episode, see Prostitution Way abstract.

6. Attack by Thunder

What is presumably the attempted retaliation by thunder for the hero's adultery with his wives takes place during the hero's journey for contests with the Gambler. He sends his new non-sunlight-struck Pueblo wives ahead and visits with horned toad, who enlarges his home by blowing to admit him. Since the hero has "bothered a mighty one" who is "without mercy," horned toad gives him the protection of a dark flint; he is to put this in his mouth and blow upward when in danger. After the hero overtakes his wives, a thunderstorm arises, but on the advice of wind the hero uses the flint to blow the lightning away and thus protect himself from thunder's attack. (The attack by thunder is omitted in Wa and Wb.)

7. Contests with White Butterfly (Gambler)

For this episode as it appears in Haile's version and in Wb, see Prostitution Way abstract. It is omitted from Wa.

8. Visits to Supernaturals

After conquest of the Gambler the hero visits various supernaturals gathering further knowledge and equipment of the Water Way ceremony. At each of these visits he is greeted with, "Earth people are not allowed," but with the proper offerings he gains access. Thunder people thus give him songs and instructions for offerings. Bird people give him instructions for offerings and equipment. After testing his identification of door guards, which the hero accomplishes successfully with the help of his wind monitor, water monster gives him instructions for prayersticks.

(Learning of the ceremony from water monster takes place in Wa after the hero has lost his wives and returned to tell his mother of his wanderings. The next morning he leaves without telling her where he is going. He kicks a rock into the lake and Talking God comes to warn that this action was wrong and to put him on guard. The rock has turned into water monster who emerges in a water spout and drags him in. Water monster lives under the water with his wife, son, and daughter. They serve him corn balls which he cannot finish; water monster comments on his small appetite and swallows one at a mouthful. The hero learns the ceremony from water monster.

Outline of Wa[143]

1. Sun Father. An orphan girl of the Kisahni clan[144] lives alone and refuses suitors. She pays the chief of her clan with turquoise and in return he protects her, providing food and covering. After each of four nightly visits from a strange man she measures his footprints to make sure she has each time had the same visitor. It is Sun; they have intercourse during the day and she gives birth to a boy. When questioned she insists that she doesn't know who the father is and tells her son that his father is cactus. He is called Beggar and Rough Skin, wanders naked and poor, and is ridiculed by the Kisahni (cf. Ridicule for Skin Disease, above). Horned toad tells the boy his true father, who comes to help him; Sun admonishes his mother for not telling the boy who his father is. Sun gives him songs as means of seducing non-sunlight-struck Pueblo maidens and Talking God gives him beautiful clothes; thus he will avenge himself for Pueblo ridicule.

2. Butterfly Seduction. See Prostitution Way abstract.

3. Wives Punished by Their Own People. See Prostitution Way abstract.

4. Sky Trip. This takes place while the hero is protecting his wives from the anger of their people, see above.

5. Wives Stolen. See Prostitution Way abstract.

6. Visit to Supernaturals. See above.

7. Hollow Log Trip. See abstract of Plume Way legend. The hollow log episode is here prefaced by the hero's loneliness after losing his two wives and his repeated dreams of a beautiful woman.

8. Reception by Father-in-law. See abstract of Plume Way. Here the father-in-law of the family into which the hero marries does not try to harm him. The hero performs the Water Way ceremony over him and receives more ceremonial equipment.

9. Return to Mother. The hero returns to tell his mother of his adventures. He teaches the ceremony to two Kisahni. The performance with them as patients is described. In choosing messengers for the corral dance a grandmother offers her reputedly lazy grandson; he has practiced in secret and the people are astonished at his handsome appearance. The runners bring back tokens (warm cooked corn and yucca bud) with news that the Apache will come; the White Mountain Apache arrive on time but the Jicarilla are late because they have been gambling (hoop and pole) on the way. The runner to the east has returned with a joke, that five old people will also come; the deaf one says he will listen, the blind that they will watch, the crippled that they will dance or walk all the way. During the performance in the brush circle, four sisters who have been mutilated by their husband for adultery (nose or ear cut off) enter with sharp knives planning to kill him in revenge. On finding that he has hidden from them, they sing a curse instead: "In four days the Deer will strip your body with his hoofs." They depart to the north with the warning that when they turn their faces south there will be drought.

10. Downy Home Man. See above.

11. Travels with Mother. This concluding section duplicates in summary form the opening events of Kluckhohn's version of Prostitution Way legend. The hero suggests to his mother that they travel west because the Kisahni are unfriendly. They make offerings and meet various holy people, naming places where they stop on the way. During the winter the Kisahni feed them but when they refuse to continue this in spring, Talking God cares for them and takes the hero away for a ceremony. He is bathed to take away his human smell and given 'chewing berries" and bow and arrow. On his return he kills antelope and on wind's advice leaves them in payment for the ceremony. Wind also advises him to refuse a smoke offered by squirrel people; he accepts tobacco to please them but later throws it away. He tells his mother that he has learned the ceremony of sexual attraction. While she is out he chews the berries given him and blows around the hogan, transforming it with beautiful furnishings. Now the Pueblos admire their riches. The hero marries the chief's daughter and twins are born. The twins and their mother are placed in their future abode. The hero's mother is instructed to join the corn clan of the Pueblos, while the hero returns to his beautiful wife at the end of the rivers.

Outline of Wb

1. Coyote Transformation. The hero, who is a beggar-wanderer, lives with his grandmother and is called Rough Skin by the Hopi. While hunting with a deer mask he is transformed by Coyote, who takes his deer mask for himself. In this form he can make only coyote noises in answer to questions but is restored by being passed through hoops. He is made to vomit the coyote food he has eaten. The Hopi are unfriendly to the hero and his grandmother, who escape with the help of a wind monitor and continue their wanderings; he hunts and she prepares the food for him.

2. Hollow Log Trip. See abstract of Plume Way legend.

3. Downy Home Man. The hero returns but refuses to tell his grandmother about his Hollow Log Trip. He traps birds and rolls in feathers; see above. In his travels he meets Monster Slayer, who tells him how he slew the monsters.

4. Ridicule for Skin Disease. See above.

5. Butterfly Seduction. See abstract of Prostitution Way legend.

6. Wives Punished by Their Own People. See abstract of Prostitution Way legend.

7. Sky Visit. See above.

8. Travels on Earth. The hero and his wives attend a ceremony like that performed in the sky. They meet people on their travels — hail people; ducks, whose offer to give them a ride is refused as dangerous; water horses; bear, against whom their magic arrow will not be effective. Finally they return home where the hero leaves his wives for further wanderings.

9. *Wives Stolen by White Butterfly*. See abstract of Prostitution Way legend.

10. *Contest with White Butterfly*. See abstract of Prostitution Way legend.

Male Shooting Way

Newcomb and Reichard, 1937, pp. 32-41. Myth of Male Shooting Chant. (N&R)

Reichard, 1939, pp. 38-73. Legend of Male Shooting Chant. (Ra)

Reichard, 1934, pp. 194-195. Portion of Shooting Way Legend. (Rb)

The story of Male Shooting Way[145] tells of the travels and adventures of twin brothers and their acquisition of ceremonial powers by contacts with supernaturals. The two principal versions (N&R, Ra) begin with familiar portions of the war god story from the general origin myth, but the sequence of incidents following upon this varies somewhat in the two versions. One story (N&R) first recounts visits to Changing Woman, two adventures of Monster Slayer (involving bullroarer and rattlesnake), a visit to Sun for ritual knowledge, and encounters with whirling-tail-feather, arrow people, and water ox; at several points these events are connected with previous material of the general origin myth. The other (Ra) tells of pulling down the sun and moon and of the hero's adventures with snake people. The central portions of both versions are more similar than these opening events; in both cases they include a hunting transgression, swallowed by fish, and encounter with buffalo people. Again the concluding events show variation: The N&R account adds encounter with translucent rock people, dogs and bears, porcupine, and weasel; the Ra version ends with a journey with ant people and the teaching of the ceremony for earth people. The hunting transgression and swallowed by fish are repeated in the third fragmentary version (Rb). After these adventures have been completed, the ceremonial knowledge thus gained is taught to earth people and the participants depart to live with the supernaturals (Ra).

This story as a whole deals with the adventures of twin heroes provoked by their inadvertent or intentional venturing into strange circumstances or forbidden territory and with the usual acquisition of ritual power consequent upon such encounters. Throughout the complicated and often confusing array of detail runs the theme of their courageous or foolhardy courting of danger. The heroes repeatedly undertake, wittingly or unwittingly, forbidden or dangerous adventures. From the resulting catastrophes they are protected or restored by supernatural aid, and gradually, as a sort of immunity is gained through the resulting accumulation of sacred power, they are better able to withstand and combat these dangers by their own efforts.

Courting of danger may take the form of venturing into forbidden territory, as when the older twin overcomes rattler, approaches the whirling-tail-feather, hunts in forbidden territory, or out of curiosity visits snake people despite his host's warnings. In each case he meets with some difficulty or danger but eventually emerges safe and wiser with ceremonial knowledge. As stated in one version (N&R) the hero takes pride in venturing into forbidden spots, "for he reasoned that he always came back restored and richer in lore for Earth People." His precarious situation may result from transgression of a taboo, as when the older twin ventures forth without his talking prayerstick or uses arrow feathers from the sacred grebe without permission. Accident may befall without the hero's knowledge of transgression, as when the younger brother reaches for a feathered cornstalk and falls into the water to be swallowed by fish. Or the hero may be attacked without apparent offense on his part, as when the older brother is torn up by dogs and bears or when he is shot by weasel. The rescue or restoration from these mishaps is usually by intervention and ritual treatment by supernaturals, in the course of which the hero gains ceremonial knowledge.

Two of the hero's adventures involve his marriage, first to a snake wife and later to buffalo women. In his snake marriage there is intimation of his father-in-law's trickery, and ultimately Coyote takes the hero's form and transforms him to a coyote in hopes of stealing his snake wife. From this accident he is, however, restored. Likewise, when the hero marries two buffalo women, he again meets difficulties, this time an attack by the offended buffalo husband. With his own power he is able not only to withstand this attack successfully but after the slaughter to restore the buffalo people for his wives.

Reichard has summarized two versions of the legend, one informant giving the form according-to-holiness (N&R), the other, a pupil of the former, giving a story that combines both holiness and evil-chasing elements (Ra). She characterizes these stories as not differing in essentials, the latter being "in almost all respects supplementary and complementary to" the former.[146] Her third version (Rb) is a fragmentary summary. The following abstract will handle these stories separately except in the central portion where incidents are duplicated in the three versions.[147]

1. Adventures of Holy Man and Holy Boy.[148]

a) N&R

Holy Man and Holy Boy are sent by the war gods to visit Changing Woman since she had forbidden the war gods themselves to return; she accepts them lovingly. They attend a council of holy ones for the purpose of deciding what chant should come first; Coyote says that the Shooting Chant has already been so designated. Sacrifices are stipulated as necessary for ceremonial treatment and ritual functions are apportioned to those present.

Slayer of Alien Gods is overcome by lightning for drawing a man's figure on his bullroarer. Child of Water sees that his brother's prayerstick has turned red and hastens to his aid. He is restored by the holy people and big fly, who is designated as his guardian, and told how to construct the bullroarer properly.

Slayer of Alien Gods insists on going into places forbidden by big fly, who nevertheless accompanies him as guardian. He overcomes rattler with his tobacco and restores him, receiving as reward bows, arrows, abalone, and rattler's skin. After traveling to various places to learn sandpaintings, Slayer of Alien Gods returns to his brother; together they go to Hanging Cloud where are found their two sets of counterparts, Holy Man and Holy Boy, and Changing Grandchild and Reared Within the Earth. At Sun's request Slayer of Alien Gods poses the problem of persuading Changing Woman to go to a new home in the west. These four without the war gods easily persuade Salt Woman to go to her new home but Changing Woman is adamant in her refusal in the face of both enticements and anger. The counterpart of Slayer of Alien Gods (Holy Man) speaks to her disrespectfully: "You certainly have little sense. What do you mean? Over there whatever you say will be done. All you need do is speak and from the tip of your speech rain will start to fall and the tip of your speech will see beautiful flowers blooming everywhere." She finally accedes to a new delegation of gods but bemoans her lonesome fate.

Holy Man seeks out forbidden territory where the whirling-tail-feather is located. This whirling object is described as about the size of a wagon wheel with a painted face, mouth, eyes, and tail feathers spreading out in four directions. "As it revolved it blew water three miles in every direction. Its force was so strong that it first laid prostrate, then killed anyone who came within its range ... it makes the heart sink, the head spin, and the ear curtained (deaf)." After four unsuccessful attempts to dissuade Holy Man from approaching, turtle-dove deceives the whirling wheel by telling it no one is present. When it stops spinning Holy Man lays his bow and arrows on it ritually and enters to find a person just like himself who gives him a sandpainting.

Holy Man and his brother travel with Holy Woman and Holy Girl to Dawn Mountain; because the women are with them they go by rainbow hidden in a dark fog so the holy people won't see them. They leave the women for a visit to Sun, who gives them ritual information and equipment. During recital of this information on their return, Holy Girl "has a fit" (given as the origin of fits and spells) but is restored by the ritual obtained from Sun. These four visit Changing Woman in her home in the west and see how she changes her age and form as she passes through doors at each of the directions. She decrees her gifts to earth people — cloud, rain, pollen, dew — and gives them prayersticks. She tells them that now "there is no meanness left" in her; however, First Man and First Woman who went east are mean, and from them will come epidemics, colds, and coughs to be cured by offerings of white corn.

On the way home this party visits the apparently deserted home of arrow people. They are threatened by the arrow people, who emerge from empty quivers hanging at the four directions, and save themselves with the talking prayersticks given by Changing Woman. Here a sandpainting is learned and Coyote gives songs which help overcome their injuries.

In a series of visits to places where ceremonies are being conducted, Holy Man and Holy Boy obtain further ritual information and equipment. On this trip Holy Man gets into difficulties with water ox man because he ventures forth without his talking prayerstick; a party of gods brings it and intimidates water ox man; thus is acquired ritual for people injured by water.

Holy Man and Holy Boy set out with the women again in a similar journey for ceremonial powers. At one place they trace singing to an old and cracked kernel of corn. "It was singing because of its great thirst," and they bring rain with a prayer. At another place they learn the corn sandpainting.

b) Ra

Holy Man and Holy Boy, sons of Changing Woman, visit their father, Sun, in the same manner as did the war gods. They return from the sky with a final trial still to be completed. As they are recounting their experiences, Coyote complains at the absence of Holy Woman and Holy Girl, who are also children of Changing Woman. While they are being brought from the arrow people, a painting of whirling feathers is made. The twins pull down the sun and moon; at the same time Holy Woman and Holy Girl pull down the black and yellow winds. They each throw an arrow or wand at the painting of the sun, and when it refuses to swallow these arrows, they do so themselves, an act which causes the assembled people to "scream with horror." Sun accepts this as proof of their power and assures that no harm has been done. Holy Man and Holy Boy remain on earth with the powers acquired from their visit with Sun and he returns to the sky with offerings that he has requested from them.

Changing Woman and her two sons and daughters return to the emergence place where they see paintings of the arrow people. Holy Man makes the arrow chief angry by stealing feathers from his sacred grebe to use on ordinary arrows. The family returns home.

2. Marriage to Snake (Ra)

On a hunting trip Holy Man and Holy Boy approach habitations, and Holy Man sends his brother home so that he may investigate them alone. Holy Man enters the home of big snake where he is greeted as son-in-law. When asked for tobacco he refuses three times but on the fourth request gives some of his poisonous tobacco which renders big snake unconscious. At his wife's pleading, Holy Man revives big snake in return for all of his treasures (repeated four times). Big snake then

bargains to get back some of his valuables; he gives Holy Man five
paintings and asks him to become his son-in-law. Curiosity and desire
for more ceremonial knowledge take Holy Man away on visits to other
snake people despite big snake's warnings of danger. On the first such
expedition to the head of all the snake people at sky-reaching-rock he
is given another painting and led to understand that big snake is a
"tricky old fellow" who hasn't told him much. From this and two subsequent visits (to grinding and endless snakes, snakes with striped
bodies) he obtains paintings and other knowledge of the Shooting Chant.
On his return each time big snake scolds him for disobeying and repeats his request that Holy Man marry his daughter.

3. Coyote Transformation (Ra)

On the fourth expedition to visit red people Holy Man is transformed
into a coyote. Red Coyote had planned this because he wanted to marry
big snake's daughter, but warned by wind she recognizes him by his
smell even though he is in Holy Man's form. Both his own family and
his new snake family track and restore Holy Man by pushing him through
hoops. The snakes and red people complete restoration of his senses —
speech, hearing, sight — and health. At the conclusion of this episode
Holy Man leaves his snake wife and her people.

4. Sky Visit (Ra, Rb, N&R)[149]

Holy Man and Holy Boy separate in hunting. While eating the fat of
a mountain sheep he has killed, Holy Man is picked up by lightning and
transported to the home of thunders in the sky. He had offended his sun
father and the sky people by using without permission arrow feathers
from the sacred grebe of the arrow people. (The Rb and N&R versions
give a somewhat different reason for the intervention of sky people —
because he hunts on forbidden territory. In N&R the thunders entice
Holy Man with a mountain sheep. In Rb he guesses that the mountain
sheep is the reason for the prohibition to hunt and kills it.)
The sky people propose to teach Holy Man more thoroughly how to
use his power. He is shown a sandpainting of the home of thunder
people which disappears to reveal the entrance to big thunder's home.
At first big thunder is angry at the intrusion of earth people, but is
pacified when his big fly explains who Holy Man is. He informs Holy
Man that he has been brought here because he disobeyed Sun's instructions. Together with representatives from other chants Holy Man
learns about equipment and ritual and then is brought back to earth.
During his absence Changing Woman and Monster Slayer had prayed
for his safety; Holy Man recounts his adventures to them. (In N&R
Holy Man is taught sandpaintings by the thunder people who have enticed him with the mountain sheep. In Rb it is not clearly stated that
the older brother is taken to the sky, although the desire of thunders to
teach ceremonial knowledge to earth people is specified. Here, after

he is struck by lightning, a bear discovers him, exclaims that he will nevertheless "return without harm," and while singing songs rubs his back successively against four trees; with bear's help and that of big fly and otter the older brother is saved.

5. Swallowed by Fish (Ra, Rb, N&R)[150]

With the help of the gods they search for Holy Boy. After missing the rendezvous with Holy Man on their hunting expedition, Holy Boy had wandered in search of him and stopped to visit various people, snakes, and ants. In the center of an expanding and receding pool he sees a cornstalk with two eagle feathers. While reaching for the feathers he falls in and is swallowed by a huge fish which takes him through four habitations of water people. Holy Boy uses a flint point to cut his way out of the fish and then heals the cut. Meanwhile, the search party has found only his footprints at the edge of the pool. The holy people of the waters at first object to the presence of an earth person, but on learning from big fly who he is, they give him sandpaintings and other ritual knowledge. He is sent back to earth and welcomed with a ceremony of thanks for his return. (N&R state only that with the help of various holy ones, Holy Man rescues his brother from the fish. In Rb the younger twin has been warned against the place of the large cornstalk; nevertheless he breaks off an ear and is swallowed by fish.)

Because both brothers are thin and tired after their adventures a Shooting Chant ceremony is held for them. Runners are sent to invite all earth and sky people to participate in the fire dance of the last night. Later a similar ceremony is held for Holy Woman and Holy Girl.

6. Trip with Buffaloes

For this episode see abstract of legend of Flint Way.

7. Concluding Adventures of Holy Man and Holy Boy

a) N&R

After returning from his encounter with buffalo people, Holy Man is joined by his brother in a search for earth people who had previously gone north. They come to the home of translucent rock people who teach them songs and two of whom join them. At night they visit people who cannot see their faces but who smell that strangers are present. While Holy Man is recounting his adventures one of their translucent rock companions commits adultery with the wife of the highest chief, and they are sent away with a curse. After this, on the fourth night of their travels, Holy Man is torn up by two dogs and eight bears. After he is restored by ants, sun, moon, and wind people (said to be part of the now extinct Ant Chant), his companions won't let him rejoin them until the fourth night.

Holy Man again goes hunting and finds porcupine in the form of a little old man. Porcupine reads his guest's thoughts about his appearance — small eyes, rough skin — and feeds him magically from spruce and pinyon trees growing from the same root; procupine tells Holy Man not to look, and the inner bark becomes jerky, the pitch fat.

In his last encounter Holy Man is shot in the heart by shell arrows of white weasel. With blood flowing from his mouth he tries to sing songs for himself. His younger brother carries him to the cactus people who restore him and pull out the arrows. They meet the holy people of the Female Shooting Chant and agree that the bundle contents shall be the same for both Male and Female branches. Holy Man's last act in this story is to go on a long trip spending a night on the summit of each of twelve mountains; he reports to his brother that he "found all holy and beautiful."

b) Ra

After the buffalo encounter Holy Man returns to Holy Boy. Ant people accuse Holy Boy of never having paid for medicines they gave him, and in anger they shoot the two brothers and take them east as captives in the direction of the buffalo people. On the trip the two revive. When Talking God appears (as in the buffalo encounter) to warn them against going farther, they pay the ant people with unwounded buckskins and are released. On Coyote's suggestion they take four days for the return trip, completing the cure of Holy Man's and Holy Boy's wounds on the way.

Holy Man and the holy people teach all of the ceremonial knowledge gained in these adventures to earth people and then ascend to the sky with all of the sandpaintings and sacred paraphernalia, leaving various insect and animal people to represent them on earth. Several reasons are given by the holy people for taking back to the sky the sandpaintings and equipment and for relying instead on man's memory to reproduce them: to prevent quarreling over them as material possessions; to ensure the perpetuation of what would otherwise be perishable objects; and to guarantee knowledge and use of them to any who have sufficient interest to learn the sacred lore.

Big Star Way

Wheelwright, 1940, 13 pp. Myth of Sontso (Big Star).

The Wheelwright story for Big Star Way is a comparatively brief "retold" summary[151] which, however, clearly reveals the usual chantway pattern both in the themes emphasized and in its manner of combining episodes, some of which are familiar from other contexts, into a loosely constructed, continuous narrative. The story falls into three parts in which different members of one family play the principal roles.

The first portion of the story (incidents 1-3) concerns the marriage of the sister to a son of great snake and her child's transformation to and restoration from snake form. A poor family welcomes a snake son-in-law who knows hunting magic and can help them find food. The child born of this marriage is stolen by snakes and taken to their subterranean home. With supernatural aid the child is rescued and restored from snake to human form, and in their visit with snake people the family learns ritual and taboos.

The taboo against eating deer intestines thus learned from the snakes figures in the second part of the story (incidents 4-5), which deals with the older brother's adventures. Three times he intentionally disregards food taboos and falls sick or is transformed into a snake. From these predicaments he has to be cured or restored by supernatural help. However, after his final impetuous act of shooting whirlwind boy, he is able to defend himself from the angry father by his own ritual power. He learns the Wind ceremony and teaches it to his people.

The last and longest section (incidents 6-11) recounts the younger brother's adventures. Coyote tricks him onto sky-reaching-rock and steals his wife. In the sky he meets with adventures as a result of his disobedience in wandering. From one of these (attacked by rock wren) he has to be rescued, but in a second (war with stinging insects) he is victorious through his own powers. He learns the Big Star ceremony and returns to earth to take revenge on Coyote. After teaching the ceremony to his own people, both he and his brother depart to live with supernaturals.

Events in the first two portions duplicate several of the episodes from the Navaho Wind Way story and are properly a portion of that legend.[152] The younger brother's encounters in the third portion constitute the events from which the Big Star ceremony derives.

This narrative presents in three different settings the theme of mishap to the hero and his rescue, with the resultant accrual of ritual knowledge to the hero and his people. Some of these adventures are suffered passively, as when the child is stolen by snakes and the younger brother is tricked by Coyote. Others are provoked, as by the ritual transgression in disregard of food taboos. Still others seem to be a less premeditated but impulsive flouting of danger, as in the shooting of whirlwind boy and disobedience of warnings not to wander. Both heroes have to be rescued by supernaturals but in later adventures are able to withstand danger or overcome enemies by their own powers.

1. Downy Home People

A family of a sister, two brothers, and their father and mother live in a cave in poor conditions. They trap birds for food and at night moisten their bodies and roll in feathers to keep warm.

2. Marriage to Snake

The parents offer their daughter to a stranger who knows hunting magic and helps them find food; he shows them how to make buckskin clothing and to trade with the Pueblos for pottery so they can boil their food. He is the son of great snake. After a son is born the new husband departs for his home, telling his wife and her family to follow him.

3. Snake Transformation (child)

The family loses the trail and camps near a lake. For four days they play games leaving the baby by the lake, and each day when they return for him they find that he has been moved nearer the lake until finally he disappears. The messenger fly tells them that great snake has taken the baby. The sister and older brother are taken down into the lake by Talking God where they find fields of flowers and birds. In response to offerings, the four winds pass a snake through four hoops, splitting off the skin and revealing the lost baby grown to adult size. The sister and brother learn medicines and various taboos — against eating intestines, heart or lungs of deer, against sleeping in an arroyo, against lying with head close to a tree — and return to earth.

4. Snake Transformation (hunter)

On the hunt the older brother disregards the taboo against eating deer intestines and becomes sick; his younger brother makes offerings to a wind who performs a curing ceremony. Disregarding his brother's plea, the older brother then kills and eats of a snake and is himself transformed into one. His sister's son with help of supernaturals — wind monitor, messenger fly, Talking God, Fire God, Water God — comes to his rescue and he is restored by being passed through three hoops. Again the older brother disregards a food taboo and has to be cured by a wind ceremony.

5. Killing of Whirlwind Boy

In anger the older brother shoots at a little whirlwind that crosses his path, and the son of cyclone falls injured. The older brother runs home frightened at what he has done, but he is told that nothing can help him now, nothing can face the cyclone. However, he is able to demonstrate that his ritual power is greater than that of cyclone. To do this he builds a hogan of prickly cactus, with a coal from the fire marks a crescent around his heart called "shield of fire," sticks arrows in the earth to the four directions outside his hogan, and marks four zigzag and four straight lines across cyclone's path. At cyclone's request he restores whirlwind boy. Later this same older brother has the wind ceremony performed over him and becomes a singer of it.

6. Coyote Strands Hero on Sky-Reaching-Rock

Meanwhile the younger brother has married and two sons have been born to him. While he is away preparing a ceremony for his older brother, Coyote visits his wife. Coyote offers to help with the ceremony and leads the younger brother to a high rock where he has painted a nest of crows to look like eagles. When the younger brother climbs after them, Coyote blows to make the rock grow up into the sky and, leaving his victim stranded, goes away laughing to steal his wife.

7. Sky Visit: Hero Disobeys Instructions

From the rock the younger brother emerges into the sky, where are ranged the houses of eagle and hawk people at the four directions. He finds himself surrounded by angry people who cannot understand his language but breaks through them and finds in an outer circle of houses black star people who are friendly and offer to help him go back to earth. The hero disobeys his host's warning not to go near the eagles and hawks nor to the hole through which he entered the sky. Homesick, he wanders to the sky hole and looks down at the earth; a rock wren attacks him and hides him under a rock. The star people promise for him that he will learn three of the wren's songs and he is released.

8. War with Stinging Insects

On the following days, in defiance of warnings, he visits the eagles and hawks, helping them in successive encounters with bees, wasps, rock wrens, and prickly plants. Each time the birds are forced to retreat; then the hero advances among the enemy and kills them with his medicine. He heals the injured birds, takes some of their downy feathers for his medicine, and brings back from each encounter in turn a bee, wasp, stone, and prickly plant as trophy. He shows his bird friends that each of these is now harmless. The bee and wasp he sends to earth with instructions to be useful to men in ceremonies. The prickly plant he burns before the eagles to prove his conquest. The hero advises the birds not to attack these people any more; the rock wren has claimed, "It is because I am attacked that I am fierce."

9. Further Adventures in the Sky

The great star teaches the hero his ceremonial knowledge. He tells him also the significance of dreams and omens. The wind monitor that had accompanied him in the sky will henceforth only speak to him in dreams; the omens of ringing ears or twitching nerves are warnings to be still and wait for a message, "for usually our minds prevent the message coming through." The hero then performs ceremonies in the sky and is sent through the sky hole back to earth on clouds.

10. Retaliation for Coyote's Adultery

He finds his old home deserted. After the warning of his ears' ringing. the fire poker three times directs him to his family. His wife is ashamed and will not speak when he enters because their home smells of Coyote. In the distance Coyote's voice is heard summoning the hero's two sons to bring in his kill; he calls them by the contemptuous name "gland-eaters." When Coyote enters the hero accuses him of having made him suffer. In return he feeds him a star wrapped in fat, which the greedy Coyote swallows; then he rushes out in agony and drops dead. The hero also kills Coyote's two children.

11. Performance and Teaching of Ceremony

The hero holds his ceremony to cleanse his wife and sons of the pollution of Coyote; at the same time he is teaching it to them. The star people and also the members of the hero's family, his mother, father, older brother, sister, and her son, appear to help with the ceremony. Coyote, apparently revived, tricks the hero into learning his songs but refuses to tell "why he had been so mean." Big Star makes peace between them with instructions that neither should return to the wife and the admonition that there will always be different kinds of people in the world — snake, coyote, star people — and that "they must make the best of it." The hero's older son is taught one form of the ceremony (Male), his wife another (Female), and his younger son a third (Evil Chasing). They travel with the hero and the star people to learn more songs, prayers and medicine. The hero thus gives the Big Star ceremony to his people as his older brother has the Wind ceremony; then they are both taken away by supernaturals.

Mountaintop Way

Coolidges, 1930, pp. 202-209. The Myth (Cub Mountain Chant). (C)

Matthews, 1887, 387-417. Myth of the Origin of Dsilyidje Qacal. (M)

Wheelwright, 1951, pp. 1-16. Myth of Mountain Chant. (W)

The parallel legends of Mountaintop and Beauty Way continue the stories respectively of the two sisters who, at the conclusion of Enemy Way, have been seduced by bear man and snake man. The Beauty Way legend describes the younger sister's attempted flight from her snake husband and her adventures in his snake home.[153] The Mountaintop Way legend gives the parallel adventures of the older sister in her flight from bear man. Wheelwright's "retold" version begins with these adventures but shifts to episodes with other central characters — dangerous women; boy raised by bear who is guided by firepoker to his own people; death pretended to accomplish marriage; boy raised by owl who becomes dangerous to his own people — and culminates in the super-naturally aided escape from Ute captors and return of the hero to teach the powers thus acquired. Matthew's version begins with this latter episode of the hunter captured by Utes and his subsequent escape. In the Coolidges' brief version of the Cub Branch story two sisters are handed over to the Utes by their father. In all three the events of escape and return from Ute captors are similar.[154]

In these episodes recounted for Mountaintop Way both female and male characters play central parts. In undergoing misadventures and emerging with ritual power their experiences follow a similar pattern, but the motivation that brings them into these difficulties differs somewhat as between the heroes and heroines.

The female characters become involved in danger by events apparently beyond their own control. Two sisters have been seduced by the magic smoke of old men, bear and snake, with premonition of their wrongdoing but helpless to prevent it (see Enemy Way). The first portion of Mountaintop Way tells of the older sister's flight from her bear husband, how she ultimately finds herself among her husband's people but is protected there by them and other supernaturals, her visits to supernaturals for ritual power and final return to her own people. The remainder of the story concerns adventures of her son and grandsons, one of whom escapes from Ute captors. Another version substitutes two sisters as heroines in this escape from Utes. Their father hands them over to the Utes ostensibly to pacify the enemy and prevent their continued raids. It later develops that he has power to recall the girls when he wishes and he claims that he sent them for the ceremonial equipment and power that they steal from the Utes. This planned adventure, engineered and controlled so to speak by the father, is somewhat unusual in the chant myths, and may be related to the fact that in this version we have heroines instead of the typical venturesome male hero.[155]

The principal male hero of Mountaintop Way takes a more active part in the misadventures that befall him. Like the heroines just referred to, he is captured by Utes. In one version this follows on his commission of a single forbidden act; against his father's instructions he hunts to the south and is captured by the Ute enemy. In the other version the hero becomes "troublesome" as he grows up, the implication being that he is dangerous with bow and arrow as was his owl boy brother; after capture by Utes he is adopted and becomes a chief, but in this position his (unwitting?) act of using his feather tent decorations for his arrows brings down on him punishment of his captors. Supernaturals help these heroes to escape and hide them from their Ute pursuers. They then visit various supernaturals, accumulating ceremonial knowledge, and return to teach it to their own people. In all versions the fugitives, whether male or female, meet a succession of apparently impassible obstacles and narrowly escape their Ute pursuers, but in each predicament they are delivered from disaster by supernaturals or magical aid.

Wheelwright's version includes two incidents — the boy raised by bear and the boy raised by owl — in which a baby is deserted by his family. In the first case the family is frightened away in famine by a starving mother bear, and in the second the child of a questionable marriage is abandoned in shame. Both of these boys return to their own people, the bear boy with knowledge of the bears' secrets and the owl boy with dangerous power to kill. Although holding some resemblance to other chantway figures in their desertion and return with power, the characters in these episodes present a different picture in the use to which they put their powers. The owl boy becomes destructive to his people and has to flee from their anger. The bear boy by pretending death acquires a new wife in a manner which, by its association with the similar incident when Coyote marries his daughter, suggests incest or at least forbidden sexual practices.

The following abstract is based on Wheelwright's version up to the Ute capture. After this, Matthews' fuller version is used with parallel material from the Wheelwright and Coolidge stories summarized in parentheses at the appropriate places.

1. Flight from Bear (W)[156]

The older sister of the Enemy Way story who has been drawn into marriage with bear old man escapes from him and from the anger of her people. She flees to the mountains, eating berries to keep alive, and travels exhausted and almost naked. When passing a bear's cave she hears birds comment, "There goes our sister-in-law," and cries in shame. Chipmunk leads her into a cave where, protected by Talking God, she is brought past guards to the "First Earth" people who are sorry to see her suffering. Here she is bathed and dressed and remains a long time, giving birth to a bear baby girl which has fur on its limbs, breast, and back of its ears, but has a white face.

2. Travels (W)

The heroine sees the first Mountaintop ceremony and is taken by gods on a long series of visits to supernaturals where she learns further ritual. Among those whom she meets on the journey are: Mountain Goddess (or Hunger); rock man; water monster; chief of birds; holy young men and women; Changing Bear Maiden, who is married to Coyote; turquoise, prairie dog, porcupine, bear, blackbird, water, mirage, swallow, and otter clans; bluebird, deer, mountain sheep, white swan, sun, mountain jay, and squirrel people; and beavers, bears, antelope, and rats.

3. Dangerous Women (W)

The heroine observes a spring ceremony in which bird maidens and others grind corn to the music of flutes and the songs of squirrels.

Changing Bear Maiden and Hunger (Thin Woman) are the prettiest maidens grinding. They play a game in which the woman tosses a cornmeal ball to the man of her choice. If it does not break she marries him. Changing Bear Maiden and Thin Woman alone are successful in this marriage test, but they prove harmful to their lovers. The man taken by Changing Bear Maiden gets boils and sores; Thin Woman starves her man to death.

4. Return Home (W)

The heroine returns to the bears' home, where she is frightened to learn of the presence of her bear husband. He tries to seize her but is prevented by the chief because he does not know her name ("which would give him power over her"). The supernaturals take her to her own people but her bear daughter remains with the bear people.

5. Raised by Bear (W)

Back with her own people the heroine marries and has a son. During a long drought the parents are frightened away by a starving mother bear, leaving the boy in his cradle. Instead of eating him, however, the bear takes him home and brings him up in the way of the bears, teaching him their secrets and especially to listen to the voice of the wind. When he is twelve another famine strikes and, warned by wind that the mother bear now intends to eat him, he escapes north. On the advice of wind he takes refuge from the pursuing bear in a cave with fire at the entrance (two nights) and by hiding in cactus (two nights). On the fourth day she gives up the chase and tells him where he can find the tents of his own family. She gives him a prayerstick and wand for his return.

6. Marriage to Wife's Sister (W)

The boy finds and embraces his family who do not recognize him until after his story has been told in council. At eighteen he marries and two baby girls are born to him. His people decide to move back to their old home from which the bears had driven them. Meanwhile the hero has "fallen in love" with his wife's younger sister who lives with them. He pretends illness, tells his family to leave him behind on a platform to die, and advises them that the wife's sister should marry so that she will have food and protection. He jumps down from the platform and after a year of hunting approaches his starving family. He brings them deer meat, and they show shame at their poor clothes. His former wife gives him her sister in marriage, but he is not recognized until he oversleeps, allowing his new wife to see him by daylight. She tells her sister, who is at first very angry but becomes reconciled to the new situation. In shame the new wife abandons the baby boy born of this marriage.

7. Boy Raised by Owl (W)[157]

The boy raised by owl is given a bow and arrow when four years old and by the time he is twelve is a great hunter. Owl grows afraid of him and sends him to find his own parents. In the search he is guided by firepoker, pestle, potsherd, his own hiccough, hand twitching, and ringing in nose and ear to a series of their deserted camping places. When he finds his people near Mesa Verde, his mother does not recognize his embrace but his father and brothers do. Here the owl boy becomes dangerous to people, shooting first an old man, then an old woman, a boy and girl. Warned by wind he flees his people's anger. On the trail he cuts a series of paired wands; at each spot where he has made these, his pursuers find an increasing number of paths. Discouraged by this evidence that he now has company, they turn back, and owl boy goes to join the Utes. It is one of owl boy's younger brothers who is captured by the Utes and now becomes the hero of the remainder of the story.

8. Capture by Utes (M,C,W)

A family of mother, father, two sons, and two daughters live a nomadic existence in a barren land, the men trapping small animals and the women gathering seeds. The daily routine, division of labor, and living conditions of a former time are described. When the family comes to big game country, the sons are at first unsuccessful in hunting but the father instructs them in the proper ritual and helps them prepare a mask for stalking deer.[158] The three men take a ritual sweat bath in silence, followed by a yucca bath. The sons dream of killing deer. Certain portions of the first quarry go to the father as gifts for his services. The father has the elder brother shoot at the buck ritually and is told that after this whenever he shoots at a mountain mahogany he will find a dead buck, at a cliff rose a dead doe. The two brothers hunt together, the older using the stalking outfit, the younger driving the deer toward him; or the older brother hunts alone and afterward sends his younger brother out for the meat.

The older brother disobeys his father's instructions not to hunt to the south. He goes out to the east, circles to the south and crosses the San Juan river; from a hilltop he looks out northward over the country of his people and is overcome with sadness at its beauty and sings a song. Here it is specified that had he looked south in the direction of his journey instead of gazing to the north, later events might have been different. However, the supernaturals hear his song and protect him during his succeeding adventures. On descending from the hilltop he is surrounded by Utes on horseback and, after discussion in which one of their old men persuades them not to kill him, is taken as captive back to their main camp. The hero prays to his deer mask for protection.

(The Coolidge story has a similar family group, but here the two sisters are heroines. Nearby live five crippled warriors who shoot from loopholes in their hogan and who are feared by the Utes. Ute war parties try repeatedly to capture the two girls, and their father, who is a "great medicine man," finally hands them over so that the Utes will leave the family alone. All except the father weep for the departing girls.

In the Wheelwright version, both of owl boy's younger brothers become troublesome as they grow up. The elder of these two brothers is first captured by the Hopi and has to be rescued. Later, when he is twelve, he is captured by the Utes.)

9. Escape from Utes (M, W, C)

The Utes persuade the hero to teach them how to use the deer stalking outfit. When they go hunting he is warned by an old woman to save himself; the next evening when he goes for water he is similarly warned by an owl man and told to follow owl's voice when he next hears it. Preparations for a ceremony are under way and the hero is tied by hands and feet to two Utes while a council discussion takes place. Talking God appears and likewise warns him that he must do something to save himself, that the council has decided to whip him to death in the morning. A bird (*goccoci*) brings sleep upon his captors. According to Talking God's instructions the hero takes up the tent stakes and slips out while the Utes sleep, taking with him "bags filled with embroideries" and "tobacco from the pouches near the fire." During the subsequent pursuit he is aided by supernaturals and helpful animals. He follows the owl's hoot to a canyon rim where Talking God tells him to slide down a spruce tree to the bottom of the canyon floor with a rainbow to travel on and hides the hero in a hole in the cliff, blown large for him, until the pursuing Utes have departed. Talking God laughs at the hero's first unsuccessful attempts to walk on the soft rainbow and enter the tiny hole, but in both cases finally gives magical aid. After traveling some distance he again hears his pursuers; this time a mountain sheep blows a cleft in a rock spire to hide him. Next bushrat likewise enlarges his hole to protect him. When bushrat's wife offers food, wind monitor advises the hero not to eat it there or he will become one of them. In their search, the Utes push a stick into the hole but none of the bushrat family is harmed. He is hidden in a rock wall by another small animal, *kleyatcini*. Talking God takes the weary fugitive magically to a mountain top from which he looks down on his pursuers. After crossing the San Juan he hears the Utes drawing near again. Whirlwind digs a hole in the ground as a retreat for the hero during the ensuing hail storm. The four twigs gathered from the spruce tree in his descent are pierced through four mud balls and pointed toward the enemy; when blown in this direction they cause a hail storm which destroys many of the Utes and disperses the remainder who return home.

(In Wheelwright's version the hero is adopted by a Ute chief and when twenty-four years old is made a chief himself. He takes some feathers from the decorations of his tent to use in hunting. Angered by this action, the Utes decide in council to whip him to death. Now treated as a slave, he is warned of his danger by holy mountain man while getting water and is given a basket and prayerstick. His captors are rendered impotent by a snowstorm, although it is summer, and by sleep brought by a dove who frees the hero from his bonds. He escapes with the Ute treasure which is magically reduced in size to be carried. From this treasure he pays the supernaturals who aid him in his flight — Talking God, wind, packrat, whose food he refuses to eat until she offers cornmeal and yucca, and spider. The Coolidge version continues with the escape of the sister heroines. At the end of a year their mother again weeps for their return; their father performs ritual on a mountain top, praying and throwing pollen toward the north so that "the spirits of his daughters were moved" and they plan to escape. He assures the mother that they will return. Talking God in the form of an owl comes to the girls where they are kept prisoner in a tepee in the middle of the encampment and instructs them that he will send little sleepy owl to cast a sleep spell over their guards and that he will untie the tepee lacing. They secrete strips of beaver and otter skin, beaded moccasins, and a Ute war bonnet to take with them. In this version the flight of the girls is similar in general plan to that of Matthews' hero, but details of their protection differ. They are to flee south to a big eddy in the San Juan where someone will await them. Finding no one there, they weep and the elder sister sings a song about going home. When their salt tears fall into the water, beaver appears and enlarges his hole so that they can hide from the Utes. He teaches them a song which carries them across the river on a rainbow. A mountain sheep bars their way and with his horn makes a deep canyon which they cannot cross. They sleep but dream of the Utes chasing them and wake. Little holy wind shows them how to step into baskets with prayersticks and song and they are thus transported across the canyon. Mountain sheep is angry and smoothes out the canyon so that their pursuers can cross. Woodrat now enlarges his hole to hide them, gives them food, a song and "four wild potatoes strung together on a piece of spruce" which will bring on thunderstorm and hail. When the Utes appear again, the older sister chews the potatoes and sprays them to the four directions with singing, and a great storm of hail and lightning disperses them. Ahead they see a man, who turns to a stump as they approach but is again transformed into a man when they have passed. The stump man massages their sore and swollen feet and draws out the pain with a prayerstick.)

10. Visits to Supernaturals (M, W, C)

The hero descends another precipice by a spruce tree and Talking God directs him to a distant fire. When he protests that he is too weary, Talking God takes him there by lightning. Here in the bottom of a valley he finds four bears in an underground cave who ask for tobacco. When given some that he has stolen from the Utes, they fall unconscious, but the hero revives them by rubbing the pipe on their bodies.

He sleeps there and learns to make bear prayersticks and a sandpainting but is warned not to accept their food. In succession he meets four weasel men who emerge from a tornado, the great serpent, lightning, Holy Woman, four bear maidens, squirrels, skunks, porcupines, snakes, and rock crystal young woman, from each of whom he learns prayersticks. In these encounters he is sometimes protected by wind and may allay the supernatural's anger by calling out his own name, Reared Within the Mountains. One of the four bear maidens, part human and part bear in form, had learned from Coyote how to change herself into a bear; she is an invulnerable warrior who hides her vital organs when she goes into battle. The hero refuses to eat the food of squirrels and porcupines so as not to be turned into one of them. During these travels he also visits butterfly man and woman; the latter bathes, molds, and dresses him in fine clothes to look like the four gods called Reared Within the Mountains. He meets holy young men who demonstrate the warrior stance with arrows in their extended right hands or who hold saplings above their mouths ready to swallow them as in the fire dance. In the course of these travels he has also learned sandpaintings. Talking God has joined in the last of these visits and keeps the hero with him for four nights before showing him from a hilltop how to return to his family.

(In the Wheelwright version the hero grows lame in these travels and is carried by porcupine. Squirrels help him down a canyon trail. He meets various persons, including holy mountain man, and they move by rainbow over a lake to Shiprock. Later, packrat helps him find the trail, and he meets a man with a pigtail hiding behind a rock. Talking God guides him to the home of bears for the night, where he is warned not to eat until offered cornmeal and salt. He pays the bears from the Ute treasure and becomes a patient in a series of ceremonies which he learns. During the ritual he is frightened by the croaking of frogs and is restored by the singer. At one point in these travels his homesickness is indicated; "... he looked back to his old home where he'd been Chief and felt very sad, but kept on down the mountain...." At the conclusion of the ceremony he is "absolutely cured of all evil and his old evil dreams" and now has "new thoughts in a new body." He is warned that the ceremony must not be forgotten and is told that sand is to be used for the paintings.

The sisters of the Coolidge story do not visit with supernaturals in this manner to obtain ritual equipment. It is merely stated that Talking God teaches them a song and gives them a rainbow on which to return home.)

11. Return Home (M, W, C)

Before receiving the hero, his family has a ceremony performed over him to remove the alien influences of his captivity. They welcome him with embraces and tears and he tells of his adventures. But the odors of the lodge are now intolerable to him and it is decided that a "great dance" must be held over him. This is to be the "dark corral" ceremony as it has been improved and enlarged by the knowledge gained by the hero in his supernatural adventures. To invite the Apache and other alien tribes runners are sent out, one of whom is a reputedly lazy boy offered by his grandmother. She is ridiculed for suggesting him, but he and a friend appear as beautiful and courageous young men. When they return quickly from their mission with the guests' promise to attend, the people no longer ridicule but accept the young men into their games. Dancing is held in a huge circle of branches with a great crowd of aliens contributing their dances. The Jicarillas arrive late after stopping to play nanzoz on the way.

The people are not fully convinced of the racing power of their new-found runners. The grandmother explains that her grandson has prac-ticed running around a mountain each morning before sunrise. A race between the two runners is proposed, one runner representing the Nava-ho, the other the alien tribes. Valuables are wagered — jewels, shells, embroidered buckskin, skin armor — and the reputedly lazy boy wins for the Navaho; this is why the Navaho have ever since been richer than their neighbors.[159] Later the dissatisfied aliens challenge him to an-other race and win back part of their goods.

Although the hero has been cured by the ceremony so that his peo-ple's lodge no longer smells unpleasant to him, he is troubled by dreams in which the holy people beg him to return to them. On a hunt-ing trip with his brother he is taken by them, saying as he leaves that he will be seen in showers, thunder, birds, etc. His family mourns for him as for one dead.

(The hero of the Wheelwright version returns to tell his family the story of his travels. During five years he teaches his younger brother his ceremonies, and after their successful performance he is taken away by the gods. In the Coolidge story the father's prediction that the girls will return when the sun shines on his basket of corn pollen placed under the smokehole is fulfilled. Before entering, they are bathed to take away the influence of Ute ghosts. When they give their father the equipment stolen from the Utes, he tells them that it was for these and their medicine power that he had given them to the enemy. A ceremony is performed over the girls. For the fire dance, runners are sent out. As in the Matthews story, one of these is a reputedly lazy boy who later wins valuables for the Navaho in races against aliens. The Jicarillas are delayed because they have stopped to play the hoop and pole game.)

Prostitution Way

Haile, 1931a, MS., 94 pp. Prostituting Way. (Ha)

Haile, 1932a, MS., pp. 36-68. Portion of Water Way (Hb)

Kluckhohn, 1944, pp. 96-108. Prostitution Way Chant Legend. (K)

Pepper, 1908, pp. 178-183. Ah-Jih-Lee-Hah-Neh. (P)

Wheelwright, 1946a, pp. 55-67. Portion of Legend of Water Chant I. (Wa)

Wheelwright, 1946a, pp. 95-100. Portion of Legend of Water Chant II. (Wb)

The Prostitution Way story has been recorded in considerable detail and with an apparent continuity of structure not always found in the chant myths. The two full length versions recorded by Kluckhohn and Haile give a substantially similar series of events woven together by somewhat different narrative treatment. Following the introduction of the hero and his grandmother, the principal events are: flirtation with and ridicule by Pueblo women; ceremony of gods conferring powers of "love and game magic" on the hero; marriage to non-sunlight-struck Pueblo maidens and payment of marriage gift for them; "downy home man"; butterfly seduction of non-sunlight-struck Pueblo maidens; theft of wives by White Butterfly and the hero's retaliation for this by overcoming him in a contest. These events are not all presented in the same sequence in the two principal versions, although the final episodes appear to be more stable and recur in similar form in the Water Way story.

The story as a whole emphasizes sexual conquests, principally as means of the hero's self-justification and revenge for insults suffered. His power is acquired as usual from supernaturals, in this case by their offer to teach ritual for love and hunting magic which he is then able to employ for his own ends. At the opening of the story the beggar hero and his grandmother live near Pueblo peoples upon whom they are partially dependent for their poor livelihood. In the Haile version the Pueblo women use him sexually, at the same time ridiculing and tormenting him, and with his newly learned love magic he retaliates by seducing and marrying two of their sequestered non-sunlight-struck maidens. Later when Coyote tricks the hero, exchanging forms with him and committing adultery with his wives, the hero takes out his anger and chagrin by leaving them, commanding the plants and holy people to sexual excess and seducing pretty maidens wherever he travels. In the Kluckhohn version, although the hero and his grandmother have been treated poorly by the Pueblos, there has been no sexual rejection before the hero learns his love magic; however, the first use of this new power is for seduction of a series of Pueblo women and young men by the hero and his grandmother, of which the climax is his trickery of the non-sunlight-struck maidens into marriage.

Through these sexual exploits runs a closely linked theme of payment for sexual rights. At the same time that the hero acquires love magic, he also learns hunting magic and is given hunting equipment. In payment to supernaturals for this power he gives his first kill. When he finally marries the non-sunlight-struck maidens he pays their people

prodigally with antelope killed by his hunting power.[160] It should also
be noted that sexual power is here linked with power to command property. One of the powers given the hero with his love magic is that of
chewing and blowing on a gum substance whereby he is able to transform poor surroundings into a home with beautiful furnishings. Likewise, he himself is transformed to a "resplendent" appearance by
learning the ceremony.[161]

The further events of the Prostitution Way legend — butterfly seduction and contest with White Butterfly — have already been discussed as
they appear in the Water Way story. Here they seem primarily to extend the theme of sexual conquests rather than to introduce new elements. The seduction of non-sunlight-struck Pueblo maidens by taking
the form of a butterfly and enticing them from their underground chamber is undertaken simply on the hero's own desire, or to make good a
boast that has been ridiculed by the gods. When these wives are stolen
by White Butterfly, he is impelled to their rescue by jealousy or anger
at being ridiculed. For this contest he is given supernatural aid (by
spider, frog, mouse, snake, and worm). In both of the Prostitution Way
versions of the contest, despite victory over his formidable opponent,
the hero then rejects these non-sunlight-struck wives, in one case
sending them home and in the other killing them by forcing them into a
spring. This rejection of his wives after he has avenged himself for
their theft is similar to his previous rejection of the non-sunlight-
struck wives stolen by Coyote.

The role of women in these events should be noted. In one version
they first appear as tormentors of the hero, getting him to work for
them and using him sexually. Predominantly, however, they are presented as helpless to withstand his love charms; they are drawn irresistibly by these charms even while partially aware of their wrongdoing. Both types of feminine role recur in other chantway stories
where women play a significant part.

It is interesting that in no version is mention made of teaching this
love and hunting ritual to earth people. This may be related to the fact
that the powers gained here are not for public performance in curing
illness but for private and even secret use.

The following abstract will summarize in parallel fashion the events
of the legend as they appear in Kluckhohn and in Haile. After the establishment of the setting for the story and introduction of the hero and
his grandmother, the first two incidents — ceremonial conferring magical powers on the hero and his flirtation with Pueblo women — appear
in reverse order in the two versions. The first marriage to non-sunlight-struck Pueblo maidens and payment of the marriage gift are substantially similar in both. Haile's version includes, in addition, a
coyote transformation to terminate this marriage. For the final episodes four additional versions are available; three form a part of Water
Way (Hb, Wa, Wb) and the fourth is an early recording of an unidentified chant legend (P).[162] The principal events of this portion of the
legend will be summarized, followed by indication of the way in which
each of the six versions departs from or supplements this outline.[163]

1. The Hero Travels with His Grandmother

a) Kluckhohn (K)

A boy who has been hidden away and abandoned by his parents at birth is taken by wind people to the holy people. Unable to nurse him, they find a woman who takes the baby right away and raises him on soup of rats and rabbits. She and the boy go everywhere together. When he is twelve they settle near Jemez and stay there for eight years until he is full grown. They are hungry and poor; the boy hunts rats and rabbits, while the grandmother finds corn and cooks for him.

The boy unwittingly arouses the Pueblos' anger by breaking the prayersticks that he finds in his wanderings, thinking that "whoever had put those prayersticks away was bad." To escape their wrath the boy and his grandmother flee westward taking care to hide their trail. The grandmother is tired, and they lie over a day in hiding. By the third day the Pueblos give up the pursuit. The fugitives continue their journey, with enumeration of some fifty-seven places to which their travels take them. From one of their camps the boy tries to climb a mountain alone but is blown back by wind. Three times they come across caves from which issue strange noises or lights; on two such occasions these are holy people holding a ceremony. Twice they see or hear a dog barking; on the second occasion the boy wants to catch it and chases it to a lake. When the dog jumps into the water, a spout rises up in the center of the lake and the boy understands this as a sign that the water is angry and runs away. The water falls on him as he hides behind a rock but finally subsides; later during their travels they again see the water spout. After four years of these travels they settle near Walpi. The boy hunts for food in the daytime and the grandmother grinds for the Hopi and brings back a little corn meal and berries.

b) Haile (Ha)

The hero is born from a plant made pregnant by sun; his brothers and sisters are similarly born to various butterflies. His grandmother is vegetation woman who feeds him on the milky juice of flowers, birds' eggs, and mustard seed cakes. When grown he traps birds and field rats. Occasionally they are given scraps of food. His grandmother fashions feather clothes for him.

2. Hero Acquires Magical Powers

a) Kluckhohn (K)

After staying at Walpi for four years the hero tires of walking around in this one place and decides to take a circle trip by himself and visit on the way. "He thinks that he might see some people and if he does, stay one night with them." Talking God appears to him and communicating by signs finds that the boy has the proper shell, pollen, and rock offerings. He takes the boy to the home of Cone Towards Water

Man, his wife and seven children, who object to the smell of the new-comer. His host wants this guest thrown out immediately but his wife intercedes to see what the hero wants. After paying his host the proper offerings of shell, pollen, and rock, the hero is bathed five times to get rid of the smell; after the third bath it is not so heavy and remains only at the hair line of his neck, but the smell is not entirely eliminated until in the fifth bath a tiny rabbit emerges from his neck and is killed. It is the rabbit that has made the smell. Cone Towards Water Man performs further ritual — bathing, songs, shaping — over the hero, at the conclusion of which he is loaned a bow and arrow with instructions to shoot two buck and two doe antelopes, each time leaving the arrow on the body. This will be in payment for the ceremony. The hero carries out these instructions on his way home.

His grandmother is still at the Hopi village grinding; she has been missing him but from the evidence of her fresh tracks he knows that she is all right. With the magic of blue and black gum given him by Cone Towards Water Man he creates a new hogan with proper furnishings. If he chews and blows on the gum it will turn into whatever he needs. By means of wind monitors given him during the ceremony, he finds his grandmother working "down underneath the village." They return home, where in the following days the hero entertains a succession of Hopi women and his grandmother a series of young boys. The Hopi women come for breakfast; then when he accompanies them into the woods to help at woodcutting, he has intercourse with each one. The women are reluctant to leave but he sends them home and each day others come in increasing numbers. "He finally cleaned up all the women in Walpi and his grandmother all the young boys."

b) Haile (Ha)[164]

While his grandmother is busy gathering green hedge mustard, the hero flirts with maidens who are grinding corn. The grandmother and boy continue their travels because she is dissatisfied with his behavior but unable to stop him. Arriving at a Hopi village in pitiful condition, they are given scraps of food and poor lodgings. Even these small portions are decreased, and the grandmother continues her search for hedge mustard while the hero earns the names "boy that goes around picking (food scraps)" and "the one that looks on in expectation." The Pueblo women riducule him, saying that his expectant look is not for food but for women; they tease one another by calling him "your husband." He helps the women get water and wood on promise of food. On the fuel collecting parties the women wrestle with one another over whom he is to work for first; they strike and abuse him as they urge him to hurry. At first he plays freely about the village with the children, who later stone him and call their mothers names when they defend and protect him. He is angry and ashamed of his own crying at this treatment.

Twice while he is away with the Pueblo women a resplendent stranger appears before his grandmother to ask for him and is surprised when she does not know his whereabouts. She reports that the stranger eats her cakes of hedge mustard seed with enjoyment. The hero jokes with her that this visitor must be her husband and she protests that he must not say such things (given as origin of grandmother-grandchild joking relationwhip). The stranger has given instructions to clean up the home and have the boy there for his next visit. He takes the hero away with him on sunray and rainbow to be "straightened and fixed up" by his brothers and sisters, meanwhile admonishing the grandmother not to grieve because he will return. A ceremony with bathing, prayers, songs, and pollen painting is held for him. His sisters press his limbs and shape him to look like themselves, then joke about how ugly he was before, addressing him as younger brother. He is dressed in beautiful garments except for his feet, which were forgotten in the shaping process and are now covered with carelessly sewn buckskin. Through doors to the four directions he is shown beautiful vistas of flowers, birds, and game: "Rainbows too hovered about the place and zigzag lightnings were flashing opposite each other, he-rains there were falling and from the corn in that place pollens were dropping, hearty laughter was heard on all sides." A deer is killed, from which a stalking outfit (antler and cane) are made for him; he is instructed that when he similarly kills an antelope this one that was killed for him will return to the gods. He is given marshplant pollen for love magic, also jimson weed, yellow thistle, and loco weed. The secret names of men and maidens are revealed to him as a means of calling them in love magic.

The origin of the differences between male and female genitalia is given. It is said that the genitalia would not be satisfied with valuables; they desired only each other. It is proposed, "Suppose the two of you stand side by side and begin to think with it! ... The thoughts of the man at the time continued on from there as a black object, but the thinking of the woman, instead of turning upward, dropped back into her crotch.... They were also told to give a call with their generative organs. On the man's side his organ gave a beautiful call like that of a corn beetle, (while) the organ of the woman's side gave its call without any order. Even though it be so, if nothing be paid me in exchange something bad will be the outcome. If he (man) do it to me without a compensation he shall fall just below it, she said...." Thus is the sanction for the marriage gift stated. The hero has been given love magic for acquiring a woman and also the means of making payment for her in the stalking outfit for deer. He is now sent home on his new means of travel, by lightning, rainbow, sunray, and sun side spots, and appears to his grandmother resplendent as was her former visitor.

3. Marriage to Non-Sunlight-Struck Maidens

a) Kluckhohn (K)

The hero wants to use his love magic on two non-sunlight-struck maidens who live underground in Walpi and come out only in the early

morning for water. He waits for them at the water hole and blows the
water out of their jars. As one starts to refill hers, he takes the other
aside and has intercourse with her; he repeats this with the second
maiden. They report the strange man to their father, who thinks they
have taken too long at the water hole. Although he too is non-sunlight-
struck and never goes outside, the father searches for the strange man
by comparing measurements of his footprint at the water hole with the
size of all the men's feet in the Hopi towns. Finally he hears of the
hero and his grandmother who live outside the village. The hero does
not try to escape. When his foot is found to have the correct measurements, the father addresses him as son-in-law and invites him to Walpi
"to come overnight and make it sure." The hero stays with his two
wives and next day kills twelve antelope by drawing them to him with
sunbeams as payment for his wives. On succeeding days he kills more
antelope — fourteen, thirty, and finally fifty — and each day his father-in-
law gives him a new girl until he has six wives. "That's the reason we
call this story Prostitution Way."

b) Haile (Ha)

During his flirtation with Hopi women and play with their children,
the hero had learned about the not-light-struck girls and their walled-
in water source. During his ceremony their names had been revealed
and he had been assured that they were now his. On his way to the
Hopi village he uses incantations and sings about his marsh plant and
jimson weed power; he draws the maidens' foot prints, mentioning their
names. He approaches them at the water hole unseen and jars the dip-
ping gourd of one so that she spills the water. The other maiden sees
him and throws water on him. In the ensuing scuffle he "bothers" both
of the maidens and then gets water for them and sends them home.
Their father inquires why they have taken so long. When questioned
four times whether some man had come to them, they finally assent but
protest ignorance of who he is. The father searches all the men and
even the holy ones but can find no one to match the large footprint at
the water hole.
Meanwhile the hero has gone hunting with his stalking outfit. To
entice the game he uses prostituting songs, similar to those used previously for the girls, and calls their names. From his first kill he
makes a stalking outfit of his own and leaves the one given him by the
gods with the vension. Now he sings of power, thus causing the father
to remember him and try the foot measurements. The father is pleased
at success in the long search for his son-in-law, and the hero promises
to come to their home. The hero dresses in his resplendent costume
furnished by the gods, rolls his valuable possessions into a ball of blue
pitch and goes to his wives. The father-in-law has prepared their bedding. They give him food and he spends part of the night with each one.
Next day with proper ritual he kills antelope sufficient to furnish one to
each home in the village, and on the succeeding days kills two, three,
and four for each home, thus paying all of his marriage obligation.

From this originated the saying, "If a person marries he goes in debt."
His wives are well pleased with him; on his return home each night
they show their satisfaction by laughter; "Very much they were in love
with one another." He too is "perfectly satisfied with the place" and by
his magic of chewing blue pitch makes the room "beautiful beyond description" with new furnishings. After the four days of hunting to pay
the marriage gift, his wives go to their mother's home and from there
bring him food.

4. Parting from Wives

a) Kluckhohn (K)

While the hero has been occupied with his new wives, his grandmother has continued entertaining all the young boys. The hero now
wants her to leave with him; he blows the new hogan that he created for
her back into his mouth. With grandmother and two wives he travels
by sunbeam and rainbow to Canyon de Chelly. Each day the Hopi men
come in search of the girls but the hero hides them by lifting them out
of sight on sunbeam and rainbow. It is explained that this is "where
the people started getting two wives — two sisters. The sun also had
two wives. That's why policemen can't stop it — it is something written
down back there." However, the hero decides that it doesn't "look very
well — his having two wives and sleeping with them right there," so he
sends them back home with a live feather and cattail for protection.
Their people gather to whip them and the girls save themselves by
throwing down the cattail to form a cloud of fluff and ascending into the
air on the feather. They return to their husband, and the party of four
travels east. On the way the hero leaves his wives and grandmother.
First he tries to leave his grandmother at one place but finds it owned
by inhospitable bear people. The hero continues east stopping at Pueblo
villages and making conquests of their girls with the plant pollen given
by Cone Towards Water Man. However, he does not bring them home
with him. On this trip he moves camp by using his magic blue gum.

b) Haile (Ha)

Separation from his wives is effected by a different chain of events
in Haile's version. While hunting Coyote blows his hide against the
hero, transforming him into a coyote. Dressed in the hero's clothes,
Coyote eats and sleeps with his two wives for four nights, "crawling
from one to the other woman just as he desired." The younger sister
suspects that something is wrong but the older senses nothing amiss.
During the day Coyote can only raise dust in his hunting. Meanwhile
the gods come to rescue the transformed hero who has been crawling
about aimlessly eating berries and fruits. He is restored by being
passed through four hoops which strip off the coyote skin and is then revived ritually. The coyote skin is saved, and the hero blows it onto Coyote to change him back into his proper form, cursing and admonishing

him with angry words, "Because of your cruelty many hardships came to me!..."

On the way home with an antelope he has killed, the hero is invited into ground squirrel's home. Although impatient to get home, he enters the hole that has been enlarged for him. Squirrel man gives him secret tobacco to complete his magic. His previously acquired powers enable him to conquer in love making so that all people "will laugh out (aloud) at your bidding." However, this tobacco "will not laugh out, it will not lose its mind," and even the holy ones who taught him avoid and dread it. Squirrel man teaches him the smoking ceremony and requires a buckskin in payment. While teaching the songs of the blessing part of Prostitution Way, squirrel man is angered by a voice from outside interrupting with the word "gola." After futile attempts to discover who is thus ridiculing him, porcupine and horned toad appear and protest that they were singing from inside the fuel pile not to ridicule him but to contribute a new conclusion to the song in place of the usual "ni-yo-o." This substitution is accepted.

Before departing with his grandmother, the hero visits his wives, who weep and plead with him not to leave. The younger sister insists now that she was correct in suspecting the coyote man. They are about to give birth to children of Coyote. The hero exonerates them from blame since Coyote had come to them in his shape, saying that he too has "suffered much on his account." Nevertheless, he cannot be dissuaded from his intention to leave. The wives try vainly to follow him and his grandmother to Canyon de Chelly. In his jealousy about Coyote he commands the plants and holy people to sexual excess. "Immediately laughters, sure enough, sounded in those places and there were no uncertain sounds of much gladness among them. This, I suppose he said because that feeling was still in him against that coyote who had committed adultery with his wives in the past." Later he hears that his Hopi wives have given birth to a hairy monster with snout and wide lips which is thrown away in a bowl of hot ashes.

The hero travels with his grandmother wherever a ceremony is being held and seduces the prettiest maidens as he wishes. "The thing that had worried him before when coyote did this to him, not once did it come to his memory again." On these travels they meet big toad woman who tells them of a ceremony and warns not to go near the home of Big God, "who is very mean,... and never allows visits to be made to him." At one place they exchange prayers with bear people, who take off their hides and use them to furnish their homes with a fluffy interior. The hero makes a hogan and plants a cornfield for his grandmother, tending it with the help of holy people.

5. Downy Home Man (K, Ha, P, Hb, Wa, Wb)

The hero makes his home beside a lake where he traps birds and collects their feathers. Before going to bed at night he wets his body and rolls in a trench or bed of feathers which stick to him and keep him warm. Thus he earns his new name Downy Home Man. (In two versions this incident is attenuated: it is stated merely that the hero lives in a feather house, is very poor and eats only birds [P] or that he goes to a lake where he feeds on larks until he has a big pile of feathers [Wa].)

6. Butterfly Seduction (K, Ha, P, Hb, Wa, Wb)

The hero undertakes to entice two non-sunlight-struck Pueblo maidens from their subterranean chamber where they are not allowed to see the light of day. (He either boasts that he can obtain the maidens [K, Wb], is aided by gods [P, Wa] or his grandmother [Hb] in attempting the feat, or simply undertakes it on his own desire [Ha]. The boast is made during attendance at a ceremony where he has drawn ridicule for his strange actions and skin disease [Wb], or he claims that he can get the girls for the gods who have been unable to obtain them even with the help of the famous gambler Earth Winner [K]. They do not believe his boast and ridicule him [K]. These maidens do not want to marry; they are guarded by neighboring bird villages [P]. The hero feels that he is unworthy to attempt this feat but is persuaded on the fourth insistence of the gods [P].)

To accomplish this feat he transforms himself successively into different bird forms in order to approach their home undetected and finally into a butterfly which flutters into their chamber and attracts their notice by its beauty. The non-sunlight-struck sisters attempt to catch the butterfly to copy its pattern in their weaving, and in their pursuit are unwittingly drawn out of their chamber into the light of day. (In one version the hero performs his love magic, uses only the butterfly transformation, and there is no mention that the girls want its pattern for weaving [Ha]. In another version he first goes to the girls' home in his own form in a preliminary attempt to win them; the butterfly transformation is resorted to after their refusal [Wa]. Three versions indicate that the younger or both sisters are aware of wrong doing but helpless to resist. The older sister takes the initiative in suggesting that they follow the butterfly, the younger protests against this but joins in the chase [K]; she suspects that this may be someone using the butterfly transformation intentionally for their undoing but is finally persuaded to help catch it [P]. The older sister is so distracted by the butterfly that she uses an incorrect term of address to her sister, calling her "older sister," to which the younger replies that this is an "ugly way of calling me relative"; as the butterfly leads them outside they remark on their disobedience, and the younger sister now admits, "In vain I try not to want it, in vain it dissatisfies me" [Hb].)

When safely away from the village the butterfly changes to a corn-beetle, whose call the girls follow, and finally appears as a man. At first he pretends not to understand why they are following him. Now that they have come so far, the sisters decide that they want to stay under his protection to avoid punishment by their own people. (In two versions the cornbeetle transformation is omitted [K, P], although in K it has been used in the approach to the girls. Those to whom the hero had boasted now do not want the maidens; they claim to have no way to care for them [K]. In only one version is permission of their people obtained; the hero tells his story and with their permission to take the girls he hunts antelope for the marriage payment [Ha]. As soon as they are drawn into the sunlight in the excitement of the chase the girls fear that they will be put to death for disobedience [P]. The girls accuse the hero of taking advantage of them, that "only a bad man would do such a thing"; he protests that he wants them to enjoy the beauties of the world [P]. He urges them to go back, knowing that they cannot, and is gratified when they implore him to save them [P].)

The hero brings the maidens to his home, which is poor compared with their former abode. They have difficulty adjusting to the diet of bird meat but finally accept it. Later the hero enlarges and beautifies his house by use of his magic blue gum. The women live with him as his wives. (Details of the return home are omitted from two versions [Hb, Wa]. In another the diet of bird meat is not mentioned but the hero explains to them the origin of his name and how the birds laugh at it; the girls sack the down and store it in the hogan [Ha]. The hero and his home have been transformed to beauty when they first arrive but on the morning after the marriage ceremony both he and the house return to their poor condition to the disgust of his new wives [P]. All versions except Hb state explicitly that the hero marries the women; here, how- ever, he embraces them saying that they have become his for good; they indulge in love making, whipping each other with flowers, "thus creating affection for one another" [Hb]. In one version the marriage is not consummated for a year; wind warns him that he has done too much singing on the way to get the girls and that if he now overdoes he will get sick and go crazy [K]. Nevertheless, the girls keep house for him while he travels to Pueblo villages, and at the end of a year he takes them as wives [K]. In this same version when the girls wake to find the house transformed, they scratch the blanket and to their sur- prise stripes of fire come from it [K].)

7. Wives Attempt to Return Home (P, Wa, Wb)

At this point in the story three versions give an incident similar to the punishment of the hero's first non-sunlight-struck wives; however, the details of the retaliation show considerable variation as between these three versions.

a) Pepper (P)

The wives want to return home because they do not like their hus- band's poor home and food. He consents to their making a visit home and with the help of the gods provides them with hail, cloud, rain, and thunder with which "to annihilate the people of the village should they offer violence." On their approach the girls are recognized and their people start to beat them to death for their violation of the "sacred

laws of the city." The girls resort to their hail powers but are overcome with grief and pity when they see the bodies of their people slain
by the storm. Those who escape are forgiven, and the girls visit for a
time.

This version does not continue with the theft of the wives by White
Butterfly. The sisters return to their husband contented for a while
with his home and food. Soon, however, they depart in search of a
better home, but they quarrel. Distressed at "this new phase of their
married life" and not wanting to continue in this manner, one sister
disappears into a spring, calling to her husband to look at her for the
last time, and the other follows. Their husband wanders about sad and
disconsolate at their loss.

b) Wheelwright (Wa)

On warning from a Pueblo woman that his wives' people are coming
to whip them, the hero flees with them and takes them with him into the
sky (see Water Way legend for sky trip). After traveling there the
wives are sent back to earth hidden in a black cloud and with a bullrush
for protection. Their people whip them and they use the bullrush and
fog to escape and return to their husband in the sky. Lightning strikes
twelve of the Pueblo people and the hero restores them, thus demonstrating his power to those who had ridiculed him. This time the women
stay on earth, although still afraid to return to their people.

c) Wheelwright (Wb)

The hero sends his wives home with bullrush and breath feather for
protection, which they use when their people whip them. Now angry at
their own people they enlist their husband's aid to destroy their thirty-
two brothers. He sends an arrow wand and basket into the village which
cause a flood, destroying the village and all the crops and leaving only
the girls' father and mother alive. On their petition with offerings, he
restores the people and crops on condition that the father and mother
not watch while this is being done. The hero and his wives then ascend
for travels in the sky.

8. Marriage to Three-Ear (Mush) Woman (Ha)

With his wives the hero visits his grandmother and finds that she is
well taken care of by her grandchildren, the vegetation people. He
leaves his wives on a trip to his birthplace and hears from arrow snakes
about people who do not yet have a son-in-law because none has been
able to pass their test. He approaches their home performing the usual
preparatory love magic — drawing footprints with marshplant pollen and
singing. He is greeted as son-in-law, and the daughter serves him
mush made from a special three-eared corn plant. On advice from
wind he picks out jewels from the center and the four directions of the
dish, which action is received joyously by his host; he is the first suitor
to pass the test. The hero lives for a long time with this woman until
he remembers his two wives.

9. Wives Stolen by White Butterfly (K, Ha, Hb, Wa, Wb)

In his absence his two non-sunlight-struck wives have been stolen
by White Butterfly. He tracks them in the face of ridicule or warning
of his adversary's great powers. On the way he meets helpful animals,
spider and/or frog, who give him magical means of overcoming his
opponent. (The wives are stolen by two butterfly boys and turned into
birds; they reject their husband, one saying that he was not kind and
that she no longer wants him, the other that she has now become different and in any case he must become one of the holy people; the hero
is sad and lonely at this rejection [Wa]. In this version there is no
contest with White Butterfly [Wa]. The hero traces his wives by his
flute and blowing smoke which point in the proper direction [K] or by
evidences of where the women and their seducer have played along the
way [Ha]. He is angered by these sights [Ha] or by the ridicule of
birds [K]. In two versions help is given by spider, who enlarges his
hole and invites the hero in [K, Wb]. In one case this is spider woman
who offers to loan him her twelve daughters to bet against White Butterfly's wives; she warns them not to laugh because White Butterfly
might not be pleased with their teeth, which are set far apart and not
very good [K]. In the other case it is a spider man who tells the hero
of dangers on the way — cutting reeds, mountain like a bear's open
mouth — and gives him means of protection from these — eagle feather
to fly over the cutting reeds, holy plant for protection from the bear's
mouth [Wb]. In two versions frog gives help [Ha, Wb]. The hero comes
upon a strange old man hoeing; when he notices peculiarities of his
appearance — blistered skin, webbed feet, bloated skin, bulging eyes,
smoke issuing from his ears — the old man reads his thoughts and
agrees; they smoke together and the hero is given the mud hoe to use
as an ax in his encounter with White Butterfly [Ha]. In the second version frog is mowing a field and reads the hero's thoughts; he gives the
hero a ceremony in return for offerings [Wb].)

(The Haile version of Water Way [Hb] follows a somewhat different
pattern. There is no theft of the wives; as soon as the hero has obtained the non-sunlight-struck maidens he starts out with them to seek
the Great Gambler [equivalent of White Butterfly]. On this journey
horned toad gives him a dark flint to put in his mouth and blow upward
with, which the hero uses to protect himself from lightning [see Water
Way abstract]. They meet bird people who in exchange for offerings
give him "mind and thought" and the name of the Gambler's home.
They warn his wives not to smile at the Gambler or their husband's
strength will fail in combat; on the other hand the Gambler will be
weakened by sex jealousy if his wives can be made to smile at the hero.
Old man toad is hoeing his garden and reads the hero's thoughts in the
usual fashion; when they smoke together the hero prepares the first
smoke on wind's advice to prevent toad from slipping in something
poisonous; toad tells him how the Gambler cheats at games and that he
will have to bet his wives. The hero's last visit is with spider man,

who enlarges his home and says the holy people will gather to help him; as he leaves the hero uses his dark flint to blow away the webs at the entrance but restores them on spider's plea.)

10. Contest with White Butterfly (K, Ha, Hb, Wb)

The hero evades White Butterfly's guards and catches him unawares. In a contest for the wives the hero is victorious despite White Butterfly's witchcraft shooting. When White Butterfly realizes his defeat he tries to trick his adversary into striking him with his own magic ax which will rebound and kill the wielder. The hero, however, successfully dispatches him, and butterflies emerge from his slain opponent's head. By this victory over White Butterfly the hero regains his wives. The hero gains entrance to White Butterfly by some trick: his hawk and hummingbird guards are frightened by a hail storm sent by spider and the hero (K); whipporwill shakes scale from his wings to make him sleepy (Hb); or a windstorm puts the lightning and bear guards to sleep (Wb). Either White Butterfly or the hero temporarily pretends friendship — hero (K); White Butterfly (Ha, Hb, Wb). White Butterfly proposes a contest of games, racing, or wrestling (K, Ha, Hb, Wb); the wives and the contestants' possessions and even their own bodies are the stakes (K, Hb). In one version there is a series of games — hitting ball through hole in house, hoop and pole, pushing posts — which the hero wins by help of animal trickery, e.g., using a mouse to guide his ball through the hole, a snake in his hoop, worms to eat through his post (K). In these contests White Butterfly admits defeat only after an argument, and the story teller points the moral: "That is the way it always is when people play together, one gets beat and then they get mad at each other." The final contest in this version (K), and the only contest in two other versions (Wb, Hb), is a footrace which the hero wins by avoiding (Wb) or by throwing back the wizardry shooting intended for him (in foot, hip, shoulder, back of head) (K), or when his opponent slips where toad has urinated near the end of the course (Hb). In this race the hero is advised by a wind monitor and taunts his opponent (K). In all four versions White Butterfly is finally killed with an ax. In three cases, with nothing left to live for after the racing defeat, he asks the hero to kill him with his own ax (K, Hb, Wb). Already warned of White Butterfly's deceit and that this magic ax will rebound on the wielder, the hero substitutes his own (K, Wb). In one case this is the only contest and the hero substitutes White Butterfly's ax for the mud hoe provided by toad (no mention of its rebounding on wielder) (Ha). When White Butterfly is struck on the head, a flock of butterflies fly up in a cloud (K, Ha, Hb).

After these heroic attempts to regain his wives the hero may be reunited with them (Hb, Wb) or he may reject them (K, Ha). (Note that these latter two versions are both of Prostitution Way.) His wives are afraid to stay with him in his downy home by the lakeside so they agree to be taken back to their Pueblo home; he tells them "not to feel badly about it"; he himself rejoins his first two wives, the non-sunlight-struck maidens from Walpi (K). He repays spider woman with cloth won from White Butterfly and returns her twelve daughters (K). In the other Prostitution Way legend the wives follow the hero despite his rejection (Ha). When they all chance to drink from the same spring, he tells the two wives to look carefully at their reflection and kills them by forcing them into the water (Ha). After this conclusion to his marriage the hero collects his earthly belongings and leaves for good; before doing so he sees that the moths that emerged from White Butterfly's head are returned from the sky in rain and he makes the prediction: "Everywhere on the earth there shall be prostitution" (Ha).

Moth Way

Haile, 1931b, MS., pp. 94-104, notes pp. 117-119.

Like the Prostitution Way legend, to which it is appended, the brief story of Moth Way deals with a sexual theme. It tells of the berdache's sexual approaches to both men and women butterfly people, refusal to let them marry, and solution of the dilemma by brother-sister marriage which is punished by destruction in the fire. Principal concern in this story is with the dramatic and disastrous consequences of brother-sister incest.[165]

The decision to try brother-sister marriage results from the barrier raised against marriage with aliens, a ban which is doubly determined. In the first place marriage has been forbidden by the berdache protector Begochidi, who has paid sexual attentions to both the young boys and young girls. In addition, their parents are reluctant to let the children whom they have raised with such care and love be taken from them in marriage. But the solution to this predicament by instituting brother-sister marriage results in the participants' self destruction by rushing madly into the fire.[166] The moth or butterfly which flies into the fire thus becomes the symbol for "craziness" resulting from incest.[167]

This origin story for Moth Way differs considerably from the usual pattern of chantway myths and, except for the final ritual instructions, has the flavor of a simple moral tale. There is no single hero who gains knowledge and power through his exploits and no resort to supernatural aid. Punishment or retaliation for the hero's transgressions is in most chantway stories visited upon him from external sources. Here the impulsive, self-destructive act of rushing into the fire presumably represents, in psychological terms, the internal sanction of guilt resulting from incest. It should also be noted that brother-sister rather than parent-child incest is chosen as subject for this moral tale. The latter appears in the myths only as father-daughter incest and, although associated with witchcraft, does not have these dire results.

1. Marriage Refused

Begochidi lives with the butterfly (moth) people. He raises and takes care of them, never letting them out of his sight. As a berdache, he is in the habit of putting his hand to the crotches of the butterfly boys and girls saying, "Bego, bego,"[168] but he will not let them marry. Begochidi leaves for country where there is game. The butterfly people hold a discussion and appoint chiefs who check each night to see if all have returned, thus maintaining his rules in his absence. When the butterfly boys and girls are asked in marriage by aliens, the chiefs refer these requests to the parents, who are reluctant to give their children in marriage. "As for me when I think of this, is it for a man who has been raised in some other place that a person is nursing his baby here? And after having raised it what an awful thing it would be should one give her to a man elsewhere!" They move camp several times for pollen gathering, and each time there are more fruitless marriage proposals from aliens.

2. Brother-Sister Marriage

A council of all the people is called. The method of recognizing someone who wants to speak in council is specified, that the speaker must stand rather than sit while talking. A chief presents the problem for consideration — what is to be done about marriage. He reviews their relationship with Begochidi, that he had great love for both the men and women and they in turn for him, that he had forbidden them to marry, and that now in his absence they are still guided by his wishes in refusing marriage. On the other hand, the butterfly parents have not wanted their children to marry aliens and thus be taken from them. The possessiveness of parental love and responsibility is emphasized again: "...at the time you became pregnant with those children, no help came to you in any way" from the people who are now asking for these children in marriage. If their offers are accepted, "...your daughter would be one place somewhere and your son would be another place, but you would be crying for them." To solve the difficulty and keep the families together the chief proposes that brothers and sisters shall marry each other. "So this coming evening you children, some of whom are boys, some girls, those that love each other shall prepare their bedding for one another, they shall lie together, everyone of them you must place under one another's cover. That alone will be a good thing in my opinion, because you love your children and they themselves love one another." The other chiefs agree to this proposal and it is carried out.

3. Rushing into Fire

"On the following morning everybody (seemed) happy as moving again began, and brothers and sisters had their arms around each other." They start traveling again and at one stopping place four fires are built some distance apart. "Then it seems they rushed into those fires one on top of the other, burning themselves up. They simply tramped over each other from all sides in a mad rush to get into the fire." Finally the chiefs extinguish the fires, but the people are wild as though they have drunk whisky. A rock ledge is made to separate them so that they cannot see one another (presumably the men and women), and both sides quiet down. Since no cure is known for such a condition, "Therefore there is absolutely a mutual fear of their lower parts between brothers and sisters, the mere thought of such a thing is to be feared."

4. Ceremony Performed

However, it is claimed that medicine from the generative organs of one litter (of the same parents) of coyotes, blue fox, badger, or bear may be used ritually to take away the effects of such incest. For this the brother and sister patients are seated with buttocks touching and vomit up butterflies in opposite directions. The butterflies, which are "sort of out of their minds, staggering about any old way" are driven by wind people around the fire and out the smokehole.

Beauty Way

Haile, 1932b, (MS.), pp. 17-108. Beauty Way. (H)

Wheelwright, 1951, pp. 17-22. Myth of Beauty Way. (W)

The Beauty Way story is one of the few chant myths having a woman rather than a man as central character. The story, together with its antecedents in the Enemy Way legend, shows some interesting similarities in motivation as well as some differences from the male hero stories. This story and that of Mountaintop Way continue the experiences of the two sisters who have been seduced by the magic of old bear man and old snake man at the conclusion of the Enemy Way story. As is usual in such incidents of seduction, the women have been drawn irresistibly and reluctantly against their better judgment into the liaison and for this bring down on themselves the wrath of their own people (cf. the Prostitution Way story). In this case they wake in the morning to find their handsome lovers transformed into disgusting old men. With return to their own people now blocked by their anger, the two women take frantic flight, their new husbands in pursuit. Thus the events leading up to the story of Beauty Way show the sisters as drawn helplessly and with only slight protest into their unfortunate situation.

The opening of Beauty Way finds the younger sister in this frantic attempt at escape from her snake husband. Although given supernatural help in her flight she ultimately finds herself in the subterranean home of her husband's people. Here the tone shifts, as it were, and the emphasis changes from her involuntary involvement in difficulties to a more intentional disobedience that brings upon her a series of disasters. In the latter role her actions are similar to the usual chant hero's impulsive flouting of danger (several of these typical incidents being duplicated here), and, like the hero, she is rescued from these mishaps by her supernatural protectors. In disobedience of instructions she lights the fire at night, to find to her horror that she is surrounded by snakes; in curiosity she opens forbidden water jars letting loose a series of storms; and finally in lonesomeness she strays in forbidden directions, each time meeting disaster (captured by squash plants, shot by toad, buried in play with rock wrens) from which the snakes restore her. Although her hosts complain at her stupidity or wilfulness and criticize her for "going about aimlessly," she justifies her actions, to herself, as satisfying her curiosity, or as defense against loneliness, or finally that she has always emerged safely and can thus risk another adventure. Here the motivation for disobedience or seeking adventure is more explicitly stated than in most of the chantway stories of heroes. At the same time her protectors' complaints at her disobedience and their disapproval of her "aimless wandering" are also explicitly voiced.

The sisters return to teach the ceremony they have learned to their own people and then depart to live with the supernaturals. Here, as in the hero stories, neither anger nor resentment are harbored on either side for the original rejection and the sisters are welcomed with their new ritual knowledge.

The following abstract is taken principally from Haile. Parallel material from Wheelwright's retold summary is included in parentheses. [169]

1. Flight from Snake Husband (H, W)

The sisters flee over slopes and mountains with no definite objective except escape. On one ascent five endless snakes lie across their path and, despite their pleas, rear up to bar the way until Talking God intervenes to subdue them, giving the sacred names of the snakes and instructions to sprinkle pollen and step over them. They follow a stream and where it forks separate with tears and hopes that they will meet again. It is here that the legends of Beauty Way and Mountaintop Way branch. Their husbands follow with torches; they have been able to track the sisters even in the stream bed by smoking and following the direction in which the smoke floats. Trying to hide her footprints, the younger sister continues the desperate flight through thunder and rain. By this time she makes a strange sight, still decorated with jewels but with her lower clothing all torn away. She comes upon a black rock with a pool on its surface. As she kneels to drink in her thirst she is halted by the voice, heard four times, of a resplendently dressed young man. He advises her that this is not a place for earth surface people and warns that "a person should not eat." She tells her story of trying to escape from the old man. The rock is an entrance guard which tilts to reveal a ladder when the stranger taps it with his weasel pouch. He assures her that the old man cannot follow her here, and she descends.

(In Wheelwright's version two racer snake people open the lake entrance for the heroine.)

2. Reception by Snake People (H, W)

In the country below, the heroine finds mountain sheep, ruins, and gardens. In her hunger she tries to pick melons, which move away from her; she gathers corn and borrows a knife from a nearby hogan to cut off the kernels. Despite the assurances given by the strange young man, this turns out to be the home of her husband's people. She grinds green corn, makes gruel and serves it (eaten with fingers) to them. The old man who has been pursuing her arrives, his "lips all parched and covered with dust," and passes into the rear room without noticing her. Thunder people indulge in target practice, shattering trees with lightning, rainbow and arrowsnake arrows.

Before going to sleep her hosts warn her that they are "just ugly in shape" and under no circumstances is she to relight the fire during the night. However, waking from an exhausted sleep with sore feet, swollen ankles, knees, and waist, she builds up the fire to find herself surrounded by snakes. She tries vainly to escape. Finally throwing dirt on the fire, she lies down again but can no longer sleep. Next morning her hosts, again in human form, complain how their new daughter-in-law "showed no regard for anyone" and they exhibit the bruises she made by stepping on various part of their bodies (arm, neck, legs, back).

She is left alone for the day with directions to prepare beans and corn while the others go out for food. She prepares the food as she has been accustomed to at home, but the portion increases magically in size to overflow all the bowls she can find and fill the whole house. On their return the snake people admonish her that she should have known that two kernels of corn and two beans were sufficient to put into the pot. They "slap together" the disorderly heaps and by midnight have reduced it to the original quantity.

(Below the lake she finds a pleasant land where she eats from the many cornfields. At the snake village, which is like a pueblo, she is told that earth surface people are not allowed but, on telling her story, is accepted. She is fed pollen mush from an inexhaustible bowl, and in turn cooks corn for her hosts on the instructions of her husband's niece. Although she has been advised that her husband doesn't come here, he enters and passes into an inner room unnoticed. In this version her trials and disobedience in the home of the snakes are omitted. W.)

3. Disobedience of Instructions (H)

On each of the next five days she is warned, but without explanation, not to touch certain water jugs. Curiosity gets the better of her; she opens them and lets loose successively storms of dust, hail, he-rain, she-rain, and mist. On their return the snake people scold her for

disobeying, exclaiming that she "certainly is a great one," no wonder
that she "goes about aimlessly," that she visits "everywhere with no
aim in view." Didn't she know that the jug contained wind! They complain of the suffering she has caused them; they have been able to return only with great difficulty through the storms, and in the mist some
of them lost their bearings and stayed out all night. A digression explains that if anyone stays out over four nights it is concluded that "he
must not have done anything good."

On three successive days she is forbidden to go to the east, south,
and north. Again she disobeys these instructions protesting, "Why
should I be lonesome! Why should I stay in one place for no reason
whatsoever!" On each excursion she falls into some trouble from
which the snake people have to rescue her. First (to the east) she
walks among the squash plants which draw together and roll her up inside a ball; directed by big fly, rescuers cut her out with a flint point.
(This is why one should not lie down in a [corn] field; sickness will result.) Next (to the south) she finds a pool of water; small toads jump in
from the edges to warn their father of her approach. Toad denounces
angrily that an earth surface person should be going about here and
shoots mudballs at various parts of her body (soles, hip joint, small of
back, meeting of shoulder blades, hollow of head); she is lamed and
felled by this witchery. Big fly advises the snake people what has happened. They decide that only toad himself can cure her but do not know
the proper offering. Big fly warns that toad cannot be trusted, he may
merely make her condition worse than ever. They are advised to hire
big snake man, who removes the toad's darts and shoots them back into his hip (this is why toads squat and merely hop about). Her final
disobedience (to the north) is an attempt to join the rock wrens in play;
she admires the way they are rolling themselves on stones, but when
she tries it herself the rock tips and falls upon her. The wrens dis-
claim knowledge of what has happened to her; big fly advises that she
must be buried under the stone. The "smelling and digging" people
(wolf, mountain lion, wildcat, badger) dig out her bones which are restored ritually, and when wind enters her body, she breathes again.
After each of these catastrophes the snake people scold her for disobedience, for causing unnecessary labor; they ask can she not hear,
and again exclaim that it is no wonder she goes about aimlessly. On
her last trip, however, she reasons to herself that when she "visited
here and there" she always returned safely and why should this be an
exception.

4. Learning the Ceremony (H, W)

The heroine spends four winters with the snake people, learning the
songs of Beauty Way, prayersticks, sandpaintings, foot liniments, incense, and other ritual procedures. The complete ceremony with bough
circle is performed over her by the old man who was once her snake
husband, although she does not recognize him during the performance,

and because of this they can no longer live as husband and wife. This would be improper; however, there is also a prayerstick and sandpainting for this. Instructions are given for her trip home. She is to bring the ceremony to earth people, except for the bough circle protion. At the same time a ceremony (Mountaintop Way) has been held for her older sister, whom she will meet at home.

(Her husband appears as a hansome young man. She is happy to see him and they eat together laughing. He admonishes her for running away, and she stays for two years while he teaches her the Beauty Way ceremony. During this time she grows lonesome and asks to go home. She is allowed to go on condition that she will return when she has taught the ceremony to her brother. W.)

On her departure she is accosted four times by a voice and pleasant song (representing singing while corn grinding) which, on wind monitor's directions to look in the rear of the room, turns out to be yellow and white corn, and she takes a kernel of each. "On that account, I suppose, leaving is not hurriedly done." (Haile notes: " 'leaving a wife' is meant, although the connection does not seem clear.")

On the first and second nights of her trip home a hoot owl man comes to her as she sits smoking. He makes the usual greeting, "earth surface people are not allowed here," and questions her closely. They address each other as grandchild and granduncle. At first she answers evasively, "... long ago I left for any old place, therefore I still go about this aimless way." He protests that she doesn't look like "one that wanders about with no purpose in view." She finally tells her story and he gives her additional herbs and incense, saying that this information has been left out because her teachers fear these substances, "this kills them." (In Wheelwright's version also owl does not believe her evasive reply. He gives her more medicine and incense.)

As she approaches her home after four nights on the journey her older sister appears and they embrace, weeping with joy to find each other alive. They fear to enter the hogan because of their family's former threats to kill them for their marriage choice. The older sister consults the younger who puts the decision back on her, "whatever you think (is well)"; they decide to risk it since the supernaturals have told them to return home. They enter unnoticed by their family of mother, father, and two brothers, are questioned as strangers, but when recognized by their story are welcomed and embraced. The father prepares a bath, and ritual is performed over them. The sisters teach their ceremonies to the youngest brother, one sitting on either side alternately teaching songs, prayersticks, and other ritual. When the instruction is complete, with no part of the ceremony withheld, the sisters depart for the homes of snake and bear people, where the younger sister is to be in charge of cloud, rain, mist, and vegetation for the service of people on earth.

(Wheelwright's version makes no mention of the older sister's return. The heroine is welcomed by her people and tells of her adventures. Her mother, who had thought she was dead, cries over her. In teaching the ceremony to her brother, she cannot remember the songs. She sets out corn kernels in rows to represent the songs and next morning grinds these kernels and feeds them to her brother as mush; thus he learns the songs by eating them. After completing his instruction she returns to live at the snake home under the lake.)

Night Way

Two separate stories are given for the Night Way ceremony. "The Visionary," apparently the principal myth for this ceremony, appears in six versions, while for the story of "The Stricken Twins" only one version is available.[170] Both stories embody a similar theme — rejection of the hero by his family and his ultimate vindication by supernatural aid — which is, however, in both instances elaborated by different materials.

The principal plot elements of "The Visionary" are as follows: The hero's visionary experiences are scoffed at by his brothers until he is able to validate a prediction of their hunting luck. The hero is enticed by gods in animal form and taken to witness their performance of the ceremony; while with the supernaturals he undergoes further adventures. He returns to teach the ceremony thus learned to his people and then departs to live with the gods.

The Visionary is a hero who undergoes rather than seeks out supernatural adventure. Although his claim to visions may represent a form of self-assertion, he does not voluntarily court danger or adventure by disobedience.[171] While he is hunting, the gods withhold his arrow and come to claim him; in the visit with them he is stolen and has to be rescued. In the face of his family's scorn he does, however, hold stubbornly to his vision claims. When these are vindicated by the supernaturals, his triumph is reflected in the brothers' abject remorse.

The story of "The Stricken Twins" opens with seduction of a maiden by a supernatural. The twins born of this union are apparently difficult to control, and when they wander from home they are unaccountably crippled by a rock fall. Because of poverty their family feels unable to support them and abandons them. Through their tedious search for cure the gods refuse help for lack of offerings until their supernatural kinship is finally established. During the cure, they impulsively break the taboo on speaking and are again cast out by the gods. This time, however, they are furnished with magical means of obtaining Pueblo valuables whereby they pay for cure. They return to teach the ceremony to their own people.

Here, as in "The Visionary," overt courting of danger and wilful disobedience are at a minimum. The twins submit passively, almost masochistically, to the indignities and scorn of the supernaturals and of the Pueblos. In the face of this suffering they seek a cure with dogged determination and tenacity. Underlying this facade are hints of a more active participation: the accident which cripples them occurs while they are asserting childhood independence and curiosity in wandering from home; and they use magic to trick the Pueblos out of their valuables.

In the twin story the importance of the heroes' kinship with supernaturals is stressed. Although such a relationship occurs in other chantway myths, it does not assume such central importance for the plot. The insistence on payment for curing also becomes of paramount importance, whereas usually it is treated merely as a detail.

In these Night Way stories the hero returns to teach the ceremony to his people. It is somewhat unusual to find in both cases explicit evidence of shaming the families concerned for their initial rejection. In "The Visionary" this is seen in the brothers abject remorse when the hero is vindicated. Before their final cure the crippled twins return to give their family another chance to help them but are still rejected.

The Visionary

Stevenson, 1891, pp. 280-284.   The Brothers.   (S)

Matthews, 1902, pp. 159-171.   The Visionary.   (Ma)

Matthews, 1902, pp. 197-212.   So, a Variant of the "Visionary."   (Mb)

Curtis, 1907, pp. 111-116.   Legend of the Night Chant.   (C)

Wheelwright, 1938, pp. 1-13.   Tleji or Yehbechai Myth.   (W)

Sapir and Hoijer, 1942, pp. 137-259.   The Visionary.   (S&H)

The six versions of this myth, published over a fifty year period from 1891 to 1942, are almost identical in plot construction and show remarkable similarity of detail.[172] One of these (S) is merely a plot summary but is included here because of its early date. In the following abstract, material from all six versions is summarized event by event. The opening episodes, in which the hero's visions are proved true and he is taken by supernaturals, and the concluding events of his return home are substantially similar throughout all versions. The hero's visit with supernaturals shows greater variation, and in this central portion of the story events which occur in only one or a few versions are dealt with separately.

1. Report of Visions not Credited (S, Ma, Mb, C, W, S&H)

The Visionary is the youngest (W, S&H) or next to youngest (Ma, Mb, C) of several brothers. His elder brother is described as rich, while the hero himself is a "wayward, roving gambler" who in his wanderings stakes the property of his brothers on gambling (C). His reports of visionary experiences are not believed by the brothers, who ridicule and scorn him. In four versions a sister's husband is part of the family group (S, Ma, C, S&H); this brother-in-law is sympathetic to the hero, believes his reports of visions, and in one case remonstrates with the brothers for thus dismissing his reports (S&H). The brothers go hunting without the Visionary. This may be stated or implied as an attempt to evade him (C, S&H) or to leave him at home to take care of the hogan (Ma), and in one such case the sister confirms his guess as to where the brothers have gone (S&H). The hero follows but is unable to overtake them before nightfall. He suspects that they have intentionally evaded him but he hopes to help them carry their game and "be rewarded with a pelt or two" (C).

During the night the hero has a vision; he sees the fires and hears the voices of the holy ones (crows — Ma) who are holding a ceremony. They recount how a crow and magpie have been killed by the hunters. It is specified that this happened when the birds were in search of meat (C) or when they lighted on the carcass of a slain deer (S, Mb). The killing of the birds may be treated as their own fault; "That is what must be expected if you will go to such places you must expect to be killed" [sic] (S). "They ought to be killed. Whenever they see red meat they go thither" (Mb). Since they did not heed warnings to be careful, it is now too late to help them (C).[173] The holy ones are apparently considering whether their ceremony should be stopped in view of these deaths (S, W, S&H), but in only one case is this action taken (W). Later in this same version Talking God lays down the rule that if anyone dies the ceremony must stop at once (W). Twelve deer have already been killed by the hunters, and the holy people consider that this number is enough (Ma) or that the hunters should be punished for killing the magpie and crow by not being able to kill more game (Ma, S&H). When the hero overtakes his brothers the next day, he is able, on the basis of this information, to tell them what has already transpired in their hunting and/or to predict that they will have no more luck. At first only the brother-in-law believes him (S, Ma, C, S&H), but after repeated failure in hunting (Ma, S&H) or simply because the hero has been able to tell what they had previously killed (S, W), his brothers also begin to credit his visions. The holy people (crows) control game but the brothers are reluctant to admit this (Ma). In one version the brother-in-law tells him that these were also hunters disguised as birds in search of meat for the holy people (C).

2. Game Decoy (S, Ma, Mb, C, W, S&H)

On the way home from this hunting trip (S, Ma, Mb, C, S&H) or a few days later (W), the hero ambushes four mountain sheep but at each attempt to shoot them he either becomes paralyzed, is seized with spasms and trembling, or is somehow unable to release his arrow. After four or five such attempts the sheep reveal themselves as gods. They transform the hero into, or dress him as a mountain sheep, resume this form themselves and depart with him. In two versions the hero faints when

he beholds the gods but is revived by them (S, S&H). The brothers follow his trail (S&H) and find his discarded clothing or the tracks of what
are by now five mountain sheep (Ma, Mb, C). Now they believe his
visionary powers (Ma, C).[174] They weep for him (S&H) or blame themselves for his disappearance (S, Mb); they make offerings (Ma, S&H)
and pray for his return (Ma, Mb, S&H). "The eldest brother cried in
his remorse, for he saw that his brother was holy, and he had always
treated him with scorn" (C). The brothers are assured by wind that he
will return (Ma). In one version, when they try to follow his trail, the
hero appears to them from a height on a cliff, chiding them for not
having believed his tales and telling them that he is being taught by the
gods and that they should return home (S&H). In another, the sacred
offerings made by the brothers serve to pay the gods for the ceremony
the hero is to learn (Ma).

3. Visits with Supernaturals (Ma, Mb, C, W, S&H)[175]

The accounts of the hero's adventures with supernaturals vary more
from version to version than have the events so far; nevertheless, certain uniformities run through them. The hero travels magically with
the gods on rainbows or sunbeams and is advised in his actions by a
spirit monitor. He visits ceremonies, usually held in a cave, and is
shown the sandpaintings and ritual as performed by the gods; he sees
the prayersticks and other sacred objects of the chant. At some point
the hero is stolen and taken to the sky or underground, from which
predicament he has to be rescued. After learning the ritual, he wants
to return to his own people, but must pass certain tests before this is
granted.

3a. Hero Stolen

Stealing of the hero by the wind gods, Hastseayuhi or Coyote appears
in four versions (Ma, Mb, W, S&H). This may be in retaliation for their
exclusion from the ceremony (S&H). In two versions it occurs when the
hero's protector, Talking God, forgets his responsibilities and participates in the dancing (W, S&H). Talking God alone (Ma, Mb), or together
with Hastse Hogan[176] (W, S&H), ascends into the sky in search of the
hero and brings him back to the ceremony. In one version the rescue
party passes four sets of obstacles (sweat houses that cause blindness;
spinning tops that cause distraction; distaffs that cause bodily distor-
tion; people who chop up their victims) by using magic words (W). In
Mb the hero is stolen twice; first, he is taken underground by the wind
gods, who cast a spell so that he loses his reason, from which predicament he is rescued and restored by Talking God; later, during the
ceremony he is taken up into the sky by Hastseayuhi and again rescued
by Talking God. In both incidents Talking God divines by means of his
"magic strings" to discover what has happened to him.

3b. Supernaturals Excluded from Ceremony

Anger and revenge on the part of those gods who are excluded from the ceremony are hinted at in one version of the foregoing incident. When the wind gods and owls want to gain entrance to the ceremony, the other gods are frightened and try to pacify them with offerings; immediately after this they steal the hero (S&H). Later in the same version Coyote wants to participate and asks to perform the blessings for the patient; at first he is refused, but when he retaliates by taking away the voices of the gods they are forced to give him his way. This exclusion and retaliation occur in other versions (Mb, C). Water sprinkler, angry because he had not been apprised of the dance beforehand, sends rain, thunder, and lightning and has to be appeased by a smoke (C). Or, as the gods are gathered for the ceremony a succession of thunders is heard and a series of gods apply for entrance and have to be pacified with a smoke (Mb). The great serpent crawls around the room four times asking why they have not invited him and complaining that they always leave him out when they have a merry time. Coyote and other intruders enter unobserved and have to be driven out. Coyote is expelled with the admonition, "... You have no right here and no interest in our ceremonies..." Later it is discovered that Coyote has stolen the singers' voices in revenge. He is first approached with peaceful words and an invitation to enter. When he refuses four times, Monster Slayer becomes angry and wants to have him dragged in; but his youngest brother, Born for Water admonishes, "It will avail nothing to be angry with Coyote, wrathy words and loud commands will not influence him" (MB). He is propitiated with offerings and the promise that he will be made "god of the darkness, of the daylight, of the herain, of the she-rain, of the corn, of all vegetation, of the thunder and of the rainbow." Even then he is loathe to enter and perform his cure to restore their voices for fear people may laugh at him.

3c. Tests to Return Home

Throughout these adventures Talking God has acted as the hero's guardian and protector. When he expresses desire to return to his people, permission for his departure is given on condition that he pass one or more tests: to identify the Talking God who has been his protector and who rescued him from the wind gods (Ma, S&H); to perform correctly a portion of the ritual he has observed (Ma); to accept only the food offered by his god protector, who feeds him from an inexhaustible bowl (Mb). An air spirit or wind monitor gives the warning or advice that enables the hero to pass these tests successfully. In addition to portrayal of Talking God in this protective role, there is indication of his dangerous qualities: on first hearing Talking God's call the hero is paralyzed until revived by the gods' magic (W); Talking God cautions the hero that when his voice is heard in the future it will be an ominous sign, that something will happen to him or to his people on that day (Mb).

3d. Further Adventures with Supernaturals

A few miscellaneous elements appear only once among the different versions of the visit with the gods. Instructions are given that prayer-sticks will not be acceptable to the gods if a menstruating woman enters where there is a ceremony (S&H). The gods' sandpaintings are kept on deerskin (C) or on sheets of sky (Mb) or naska ("it may have been cotton") (Ma) rather than being made new in sand each time. The picture cannot be given in this form to men who are not as "good" as the gods; "They might quarrel over the picture and tear it, and that would bring misfortune; the black cloud would not come again, the rain would not fall; the corn would not grow" (Ma). When the hero is first brought into the gathering of the gods, they complain about his "earthly odor" and he has to be bathed to get rid of it (C). Or Monster Slayer protests that the gods should not have brought him because, "The Indians are a bad people. We do not want them among us" (Mb). In this same version Monster Slayer administers witch medicine to participants in the ceremony; snake is naked and has no place to put the medicine so he puts it in his mouth for safe keeping, and that is why snakes are poisonous (Mb).

Two accounts allow the hero to return to his people for a visit, but before teaching them the ceremony he is brought back for additional adventures with the gods (Mb, W). These versions elaborate in greater detail the incidents of travel with the gods, the ceremonies and ritual paraphernalia observed, but they add few plot elements. In one the hero is crippled by contact with mountain sheep and antelope which necessitates ceremonial cure in which the principal ritual technique is sweating (Mb).[177] Among the further adventures in the second elaborated version (W) are: 1) Sending of the dog to Acoma as messenger of the ceremonies; in a coyote-like trick he undertakes a test of eating thirty-two kinds of food and runs off with the presents given in reward for his success. 2) An encounter with spider, who captures the visiting party of gods when they enter without permission a rock where girls are grinding corn; spider is pacified by a gift of string and teaches the hero figures of the string game. 3) Tests to see if the hero knows the names of all the prayersticks. 4) Visit to "some bad people who are struck by lightning during their ceremony." This version also emphasizes the necessity for humans to obey the ceremonial rules and keep ritual objects holy in order to keep well and happy. In a final gathering of the gods the hero is instructed in the evil results of negligence, which the gods will punish by sending disease and plagues (locusts, grasshoppers).

4. Return Home (S, Ma, Mb, C, W, S&H)

When the hero is sent home to teach the ceremony to his own people, sorrow is expressed at the parting. The gods are sorry and expect him to return, but they recognize that his family must long to see him (Ma).

The hero weeps; he is lonely and wants to return to live with them (Mb). When he is sad and lonely for the gods, they appear once more to him with final instructions about preparation of a particular prayerstick (S&H). On the way home he has become "twisted" due to his great sadness at leaving the gods and has to be "straightened out" and made "entirely human" by performance of this new ceremony over him (S&H). On the way home owl gives him further ritual instructions (Ma, Mb, W, S&H).

His family, who now recognize his visions, express joy at his return and receive him with affection and rejoicing (Mb). They build a separate house for him (Mb). In all versions the hero teaches the newly learned ceremony to his people, but the manner of teaching and the person to whom it is taught vary from version to version. In two cases no details are specified; it is stated merely that he teaches the ceremony to his people (S), or that in the course of six years he teaches his brothers all that he has learned (W). In another, he teaches the ceremony to his older brother who then performs it over him to cure his "twisted" condition; the knowledge is passed on in turn to each of the two next younger brothers and finally to an outsider, leaving all four brothers free to depart to live with the gods (S&H). In the three remaining versions the ceremony is taught to the youngest brother (Ma, Mb, C).[178] The hero performs the ceremony over his younger brother (C), warning him to learn it exactly or he will become blind, warped, and twisted(Mb). The hero performs for his people the new ritual which cures disease of the eyes, but the elder brothers are not able to learn the songs; the hero suggests that they pay him a fee to ensure being able to remember them (Ma). However, the youngest brother, who is considered stupid, is able to learn the ceremony: he has been memorizing the songs while pretending to sleep; his grandmother protests that the "elder brothers have better minds than he," that he can't be expected to learn where they failed, but she nevertheless urges him to arise from his sleep and try (Ma). Heretofore this younger brother had looked ugly and stupid and never combed his hair, but after learning the ritual he took more care of his personal appearance (Ma).

After teaching the ceremony the hero departs to dwell with the gods (Ma, Mb, C, W, S&H). In one case all four brothers disappear together (S&H). Assurance may be given that he will continue to watch over performances of the ceremony (W), or that he will return to give more instruction. He warns his younger brother that he will meet him once more (which occurs in another myth of Night Way) (Ma), or he is offered a wife and home among the gods but does not accept them immediately because he must return to teach his brother one more sandpainting (Mb).

The Stricken Twins

Matthews, 1902, pp. 216-165.   The Stricken Twins.

1. Supernatural Father

A poor family consisting of a woman, her mother, her husband, and
their son and daughter, live in Canyon de Chelly. They do not have
corn nor sheep but live on wood rats, seeds, and wild fruits. The adolescent daughter hears a strange voice while gathering yucca alone;
her family pays no attention to her tale. The hearing of voices is repeated four times, and on the fourth day Talking God appears and asks
her in marriage. The girl is shy in his presence and does not answer
his questions until the fourth repetition. She fears to ask permission
of her family because he is "too fine a man." When he proposes marriage in secret, she is afraid of not being able to keep the secret.
After the fourth repetition of his request, she agrees, They meet on
each of four successive days and not again. She is remorseful and
fears to face her parents lest they learn her secret and kill her. When
four months later she feels motions within her, she still does not talk
to her family; twin boys are born at the end of nine months. Her family
asks whether this happened when she heard voices. She protests that
she doesn't know who the father is, that it must have happened in her
sleep. Her brother takes her side saying that she knows no more than
she tells, that perhaps the holy ones are responsible and that in any
case it is good to have their number increased.

2. Crippled Children Deserted

As the twins grow to boyhood, they wander often from home and
their family has difficulty keeping track of them. When about nine
years old, they leave home and their tracks end mysteriously. The
possibility of their kinship to the holy ones is remembered and their
mother thinks they may have gone in search of their father. After five
days, the twins reappear; the elder is blind and carries the younger,
who is lame. They tell their story — how they wandered a short way and
rested in a rock shelter; how its roof closed over and trapped them;
how they were finally let out by the squeaking god only to find themselves thus maimed.

The lame and blind twins become a burden to their family and are
asked to leave. For four days they travel in a circle near their home
in hopes that their family will take pity on them. During this time
Talking God provides them with food and covering: each morning they
find food beside them and on the fifth morning an inexhaustible bowl
of mush; each night they are kept warm with a "blanket of darkness."
They finally decide that their family has really abandoned them and
start in search of the residence of the gods. Talking God appears,

listens to their story and instructs them how to gain entrance to the home of the gods but does not reveal his own identity.

3. Visits to Supernaturals

In the home of the gods at Tse'intyel, Hastse Hogan asks how the twins have gained entrance, since earth people have never before been there. All the gods, including Talking God, deny having given them the secret. The twins tell their story and say that they are looking for a cure. The gods deny ability to cure them, although they are lying, and send them on to other holy ones who may be able to cure them. Here the gods again deny that they can help the twins and send them on to yet another dwelling of the holy ones, where they are asked if they have brought the sacred offerings that are required as payment for a cure. Since they have not, they are again refused and sent on to other holy ones. The twins' search is continued through thirteen similar refusals on the part of the gods because they lack the necessary of-ferings. During this search Talking God protects them without directly admitting his relationship to them: he admonishes the other gods for not curing the twins and for mocking them, because "perhaps they are your kindred"; when asked directly, rather than denying cure, he evades the question by not responding; he continues to provide them with food and instructions. Once the twins return to see if their family will ac-cept them and are again rejected. Toward the end of this tedious search the twins are not asked for offerings but are sent from one dwelling of the gods to the next and are finally directed to return to Tse'intyel.

4. Kinship Recognized

Here a council of the gods is reconsidering the children's plea. They wonder why Talking God hinted that the twins might be their kin-folk. A test in which the twins choose Talking God's poor bow and arrow in preference to others because it is suitable to their poor es-tate is taken as proof of his kinship relation to them. Talking God is reprimanded by the other gods for not having told this so that the twins could have been cured sooner; he protests that he indicated as plainly as possible that they were his children. The other gods magically provide food (sheep and inexhaustible food bowl) for the twins and, after they have eaten, give instructions to put the remaining meat back in the skin so that the sheep will come back to life. Talking God reveals himself to them as their father, saying that he had not done so sooner because of his promise of secrecy to their mother. The gods greet them as kindred and prepare the curing ceremony.

During this ceremony the children cry out in joy as they realize that the cure is taking effect, thus breaking the taboo on talking in the sweathouse. Everything vanishes and they are left blind and lame as before. Now they cannot be cured without payment (given as the reason

why the Navaho today have to pay for curing). As they depart in sadness, they cry and their crying turns to song. The gods call them back
to hear the song and resolve never again to turn away their own
children.

5. Pueblo Valuables Won by Trickery

In order to secure sacred offerings the gods send the twins to
Pueblo towns (Moki) with plagues for their crops (kangaroo rat, worm,
talisman to produce wind, grasshoppers), which will be let loose in
the fields and for the riddance of which the twins will be paid. The
twins travel to the Pueblo towns on a rainbow. They are refused food
and shelter, mocked and teased by the Pueblos. They let loose the first
pest and the Pueblo's finally offer valuables as payment for their help
in getting rid of it. Soon the Pueblos treat them badly again. This
procedure is repeated three more times, and each time the twins acquire more valuables. By the fourth time the Pueblos begin to suspect
that the twins have sent the plagues as revenge for their bad treatment.
They plot to kill them and regain their valuables, but the twins escape
miraculously on a rainbow with the sacred offerings.

6. Ceremony and Return Home

Before the curing ceremony proceeds, the twins are sent to see if
their family will accept them but are driven off again. Two of the gods
are angry at not being invited when they hear of the division of the
valuables but are pacified with their share of the gifts. After the curing the twins are shaped by the daughters of Hastse Hogan to look as
beautiful as their brothers. Then the girls point to them saying, "Behold our ugly brothers!" (This is given as explanation of fact that a
girl will speak of her younger brother as ugly no matter how beautiful
he is.) During the singing the twins are "seized with hypnotic convulsions" and are cured of this before the ceremony proceeds (given as
explanation for patient's falling into trance today). After completion
of the ceremony the twins return to teach it to earth people and then
depart to become guardians respectively of the thunder storm and of
animals.

Plume Way

Matthews, 1897, pp. 160-194. Natinesthani (story of Feather Chant).
(Ma)

Matthews, 1902, pp. 171-197. The Whirling Logs (Night Chant). (Mb)

Goddard, 1933, pp. 161-163. Game story. (G)

Stevenson, 1891, pp. 278-279. The Floating Logs (Night Chant). (S)

Sapir and Hoijer, 1942, pp. 25-37. A Legend of the Hollow Floating Log. (S&H)

Wheelwright, 1946, pp. 69-78. Portion of "Tohe or Water Chant I." (Wa)

Wheelwright, 1946a, pp. 92-94. Portion of "Tohe or Water Chant II." (Wb)

Wheelwright, 1946b, pp. 9-15. Feather Chant. (Wc)

Wetherill, 1952, pp. 88-89. Plumeway. (Weth)

     The hollow log trip is one of the most popular episodes among Navaho chantway legends. The hero leaves his people and travels down a river in a hollow log attended by supernaturals and meets with various adventures along the way; on arrival at his destination he plants and raises corn, again usually with the help of supernaturals and a pet turkey who has accompanied him. In four versions (Mb, S, G, Wb) the hero thereupon returns to his own people, bringing them ritual and/or the corn that he has learned to raise (Mb, S, G).[179] Four other versions continue instead with the hero's marriage in his new home (Ma, S&H, Wa, Weth) which introduces a series of trials in which the hero outwits his witch father-in-law (Ma, S&H, Weth). After these adventures he returns to teach his people the ceremony.
     The two principal episodes of Plume Way — hollow log trip and witch father-in-law — show the hero as gaining in power through his supernatural adventures. In the hollow log trip a rejected, lonely, or restless hero conceives of a solitary escape which will take him to new lands. To ward against the dangers thus incurred, supernaturals come to his aid, and from them he gains ritual power. In the second episode the hero is able to withstand the trials imposed by a witch father-in-law by his own courage, with only nominal aid (warnings of his wind monitor) from supernaturals. These two episodes result respectively in the hero's acquiring knowledge of agriculture and power over game. At the end of the hollow log trip he plants a garden with the help of supernaturals and brings the corn thus raised to his own people or to his new wife's family. In the principal version of Plume Way (Ma) the hero acquires power over game from his witch father-in-law.[180]
     The variation in motivation for the hollow log trip, as between different versions of this episode, presents a familiar range for the chantway myths. In three versions the hero has been rejected by his family for excessive gambling and his departure has the quality of a resentful escape. In another version he leaves in similar mood but his offense is not specified. On the other hand, four versions (two each of Night Way and Water Way) present him as seeking further ritual knowledge or a wife by this trip. His obstinate insistence on making the trip despite warnings of supernaturals and/or concern of his own people is emphasized. Once this persistence is recognized by the supernaturals,

they help him in launching his hollow log, protect him from dangers during the trip, and provide his pet turkey with seeds for his garden to be planted at the end of the journey. During the trip and at its conclusion he gains ritual knowledge.

The witch father-in-law episode is presented principally as a series of treacherous trials or attacks which the hero is able to evade or turn against the evil father-in-law. The gods play a lesser role here, although in several cases the hero is warned of the father-in-law's trickery by his supernatural monitor. However, the hero has powers of his own, and even in his first meeting with the new father-in-law shows them by giving him tobacco or corn that renders him unconscious, as though the battle between them is to begin even before the father-in-law reveals his evil designs. The elements that enter into the witch father-in-law situation, here as well as elsewhere, are: sexual jealousy over the daughter, use of witchcraft, attempted food poisoning, attacks on the hero by animals or other natural phenomena. The hero flouts his father-in-law's warnings not to venture in certain directions and by this disobedience meets people who confirm his suspicions of the old man's witchcraft.

Only three of the nine published versions of the hollow log story are given as the origin myth of Plume Way (Feather Chant). Of these the early account given by Matthews (Ma) is the most detailed and complete. Wetherill's story is similar in outline,[181] but the story summarized by Wheelwright (Wc) is so divergent that it will be dealt with separately. Two briefer versions are given as portions of the Night Way legend (Mb, S) and two for Water Way (Wa, Wb).[182] Two versions give substantially the same story but show no indication of their chantway source (G, S&H). Material from all of these nine versions has been used in the following abstract.

The Wheelwright version of Plume Way (Wc) includes reference to the above discussed episodes, but they are here subordinated to other events. This story is introduced by a portion of the general origin myth: separation of the sexes, emergence, placing of heavenly bodies and other natural phenomena, and slaying of monsters by war gods. An account is given of the witch father-in-law's evil activities in pre-emergence times. The story of Plume Way proper apparently begins with the birth of the hero, who seeks his sun father through dangers and trials in which he has supernatural aid. He is finally acknowledged by Sun and given game power. He is unsuccessful in hunting, however, until after completion of episodes similar to the hollow log trip, planting with help of turkey and marriage to daughter of the guardian of game (all of which are here attenuated). With the help of his new father-in-law he indulges in excess of hunting and becomes paralyzed, "crazy," and finally transformed into an antelope. Restored from this condition, he drinks at a pool, is swallowed by fish, and later restored by his father-in-law. He returns to his people with ritual knowledge. The material of this version is not clear enough for satisfactory comparison with other versions. Throughout the hero apparently takes more

initiative in exposing himself to danger and violating taboos. Although
the father-in-law was formerly a witch, his relations with his new son-
in-law are here apparently benevolent.

1. Hero Leaves Home (Ma, Mb, G, S, S&H, Wa, Wb, Weth)

In three versions the hero is rejected by his family for excessive
gambling in which he loses his own and his relatives' property (Ma,
G, Weth). His brothers threaten to kill him (Ma, G).[183] He lives with
his grandmother and niece in poorer conditions than the other members of his family (Ma). Disturbed by the realization that his family is
"tired of him," he hunts wood rats alone to the four directions trying
to decide on a course of action; he is torn between running away and
his responsibility for providing his niece with food (Wa). In the Goddard story also there is evidence of the hero's special relationship
with his niece; she gives him a necklace to wager at gambling, and it
is to her that he returns with corn after his hollow log trip (G); see
below.

The hero's motive for leaving home is in other versions his desire
for further ritual knowledge (Mb, S, Wa), and to seek out a beautiful
woman who has appeared repeatedly in his dreams as his wife (Wa).
In the latter story the hero has returned to his mother restless, sad,
and lonely after the loss of his two non-sunlight-struck Pueblo wives,
which he keeps secret from her as well as his plans for the hollow log
trip (Wa). In two cases his motive is not clear: he has been brooding
because of having "committed a fault on himself" (nature of fault not
specified) (S&H); or while he and his grandmother are wandering as
vagrants, he simply decides to undertake the trip (Wb).

2. Preparation of Hollow Log (Ma, Mb, G, S, S&H, Wa, Wb, Weth)

The hero prepares the log in which he plans to float down the river
(Ma, Mb, G, S&H, Wa, Wb), taking several days to fell and hollow it out
with fire (Ma, Mb, S&H, Wa). When he is about to embark, Talking God
and other supernaturals intervene and warn him against using the log
(Ma, Wa), or when once in the water the log sinks and they come to
rescue him (Mb, S&H). The supernaturals magically construct the log
boat for him (Ma, Mb, S, Wa, Wb, Weth), hollowing it out by means of
lightning, wind, or rainbow (Ma, S, Wa), furnishing it with windows of
rock crystal (Ma, Mb, Wa, Wb), and plugging the ends with cloud (Ma,
S). On this trip his own (Mb, S&H, Wb, Weth) or his niece's (Ma) pet
turkey accompanies him, following the log along the river bank. Unknown to the hero, the supernaturals provide the turkey with all kinds
of seeds (Ma). During the preparations the turkey is troubled, restless,
and refuses to eat because he knows the thoughts in his master's mind
(Mb). The hero instructs the turkey to follow the log (S&H).

Two versions give detailed description of obtaining the help of
supernaturals. After discovering the hero's plans they send him home

to his grandmother with instructions for ritual conduct and to await
their visitation (Ma, Mb). He claims that he can furnish the proper offerings when in reality he owns nothing but his own rags; he has his
niece steal the sacred objects from their neighbors (Ma). His grandmother is skeptical that the supernaturals would visit "such poor people
as we are," but when Talking God and Hastse Hogan[184] arrive, she is
convinced, bids the hero to go with them, and asks for his return (Ma).
The supernaturals take him by rainbow to their rock home, where he
is fed from an inexhaustible bowl which Talking God can empty with
one sweep of his finger (Ma). When the assembled holy ones find that
he cannot be dissuaded from this venture, they construct the log for him
and provide food and water for his journey (Ma). In Matthews' Night
Way version the hero has already launched himself unsuccessfully in
his hollow log when the supernaturals come to rescue him (Mb). His
preparations have been made secretly for fear of his grandmother's
displeasure; on each of twelve days he approaches his work of burning
the log by a roundabout path and does not answer her questions truth-
fully. After his departure two brothers follow his tracks and are able
to reconstruct what has happened to him (Mb). It is they who make
offerings to the holy ones to free his log from the river bottom (Mb).
The hero still cannot be dissuaded from his intent, so the gods send
him home to await their help (Mb). There he tries to pacify his grandmother's anger at his deception; he protests fear that she would have
prevented him from carrying out his design (Mb). He promises to
bring back more ritual knowledge for his younger brother whom he
instructs to perform ritual for him each morning until his return (Mb).

3. Hollow Log Trip (Ma, Mb, G, S, S&H, Wa, Wb, Weth)

While floating down the river the hollow log is intercepted and/or
the hero captured and detained by the Pueblos (Ma, Wa, Wb), water
monster (Ma, Mb, S&H, Wb), frog (Ma, Mb, Wa), and others. The supernaturals who have launched the hero guide and protect him on this journey (Ma, Mb, S, Wa, Wb, Weth). He evades the Pueblos when they try
to catch the log with ropes (Wa), or a storm is sent to drive them off
(Ma, Wb). He is stopped by water monster and makes offerings to be
released (Mb), or he is captured and released only when Black God
threatens to set fire to water monster's under water abode (Ma, S&H,
Wb). Water people pull the log under water and take the hero through
water monster's guards and down through four chambers of his house;
here Black God and water sprinkler come to rescue him (Ma). In a
similar incident frog hides the hero in his under water home; he wraps
him in water slime, puts him on a shelf in the back room, and denies
his presence until threatened by Black God's fire; when frog yields the
hero, water sprinkler puts out the fire (Wa). In other versions the hero
also meets frog, who warns him of disease contracted by those who
enter the water and the proper offerings for its counteraction (Ma), or
when passing the dam of turtle and frog people with the proper offerings

frog reads his thoughts about his ugliness, big eyes, rough skin, swollen throat, thin legs, and the smoke issuing from his warts (Mb). Elsewhere on the trip the log becomes stuck and is pried loose by fringe mouths (Mb); it is stopped by various water people who demand offerings (beaver, otter, fish, water coyote, turtle and frog people) (Mb); or even the supernaturals who are accompanying the hero mischievously detain him by trees planted close to the water's edge and will not free the log until they receive offerings (Mb). When the log sinks into mud, water sprinkler sends a too generous rainstorm to float it and has to be stopped by other supernaturals (Mb).

During this trip the hero feels lonely in his log and sings a song of grief (Wa). His turkey follows the log down the river (Ma), running along beside it on the bank (Mb, Wb) and helping in the search when it is drawn under water (S&H).

Two versions omit the adventures of the trip. In one of these the hero takes corn, specular iron ore, and pollen with him (G); in the other the hero floats in one arm of a Jerusalem cross while male and female supernaturals sit on the ends of the cross arm (S).

The objective of this journey is variously identified as a large whirlpool at the end of the San Juan River (Ma), crossing waters (Wb), the junction with the Colorado River (G), whirling waters or whirling logs (Mb), a big lake surrounded by mountains (Wa), the ocean (S&H), or a place described as having shore on one side only (S). Here the log is drawn to the bank (Wa), pulled out (S&H), or it spins in gradually wider circles until beached and the supernaturals release the plugged ends (Ma, Mb). The log returns upstream (Ma, Wa). At this point the hero is given another name, He Who Floats (Ma). He is directed to go to a nearby hill by the supernaturals (Ma) or spider (Wa). Three versions give ceremonial procedures at the end of this journey: the hero finds here a whirling cross of logs on which holy people are seated, and he learns songs, ritual, and sandpaintings (Mb, S); or he emerges from the log paralyzed and covered with green slime, and restoration ceremonies are performed to enable him to talk again and shut his eyes (Wb). In Mb the hero has also gained ritual knowledge in the course of his trip: on two occasions he is shown sandpaintings and hears songs and prayers; on the first such occasion when learning from fringe mouths he falls "upon the ground in a fit" and has to be restored ritually, but in the second exposure to ceremonial knowledge these convulsions do not occur (Mb). The sandpaintings he sees are unrolled as on a cloud, but he is told that imitations in sand must serve for earth people (Mb).

4. Corn Planted (Ma, Mb, G, S&H, Wa, Wb, Weth)

The hero is lonely in this new place (Ma, G) but is comforted by the presence of his turkey pet (Ma, Mb, S&H). The turkey appears unexpectedly and is welcomed with joy (Ma, Mb) or his presence is accepted without comment (S&H, Wb). He covers the hero with his wing or

feathers to keep him warm (Ma, Mb, S&H). The turkey and/or supernaturals help the hero plant and raise a garden (Ma, Mb, S&H, Wa, Wb,
Weth). The turkey shakes seeds out from his wings (Ma, Mb, S&H) —
beans, pumpkin, corn, squash, melon, tobacco. The supernaturals plant
for him at night (Wa, Wb), or the hero himself plants (Ma, Mb, G, S&H),
and the crops mature magically in a short time (Ma, Mb, S&H, Wb,
Weth).

Four out of the eight versions end with this episode and the hero's
return to his own people (Mb, S, G, Wb) to bring back to them the knowledge of gardening thus acquired (Mb, S) or to relieve famine (G). In
the four versions that continue with the hero's marriage, he introduces
corn to his new wife's family (Ma, S&H, Wa, Weth). In these versions
also his turkey pet may be lonely and angered at his desertion and
disappear (Ma) or return to his own country (S&H). The hero is sad
to lose his pet (Ma, S&H).

5. Return Home (Mb, G, S, Wb)

In the versions that do not continue with the hero's marriage, his
return home is variously interpreted. After the corn planting he simply
returns to his grandmother but does not tell her of his adventures (Wb).
He brings back to his people knowledge of corn raising (Mb, S). Or he
relieves the famine that had commenced with his departure by magical
increase of the corn thus brought back (G). This demonstration of
power is affected through the niece (see *Hero Leaves Home,* above)
who on the hero's insistence goes to the storage pits and finds them
replenished; the family who had rejected him for gambling now welcome
him back with promises not to speak evil of him henceforth (G). The
hero here addresses his niece as "my little mother" (G).

In Matthews' Night Way version (Mb) the hero learns ritual for corn
raising and preparation of corn and other foods. Instructions are given
for the ritual plucking of leaves and tassels during lightning storms.
Squash and beans should be cooked in a pot; melons eaten raw. The
supernaturals also warn him of taboos connected with use of corn. It
should not be cooked until it is ripe nor eaten before it is fully cooked,
or frost and floods will damage the crop. In the "vigil of the corn"
ceremony the corn is fed with dried meat; if it were to be fed with corn
it would thus consume itself, just as feeding meat to the masks would
cause men to eat each other. When giving this warning Talking God
refers to the time that ugly woman fed corn to the corn with the result
that "the people starved and men ate the flesh of other men." During
the hero's instruction in ritual the children of Talking God and Hastse
Hogan play outside and one boy falls asleep after plucking cornsilk and
is rendered unconscious; the hero cures him with Night Way ritual, in
return for which Talking God shows how his offerings are made. The
holy people send a messenger to bring the hero home; although lonely,
he is loathe to leave his stores of corn. The messenger confers with
Talking God and Hastse Hogan, who see that the crops are transported,

with magical decrease in size, to his old home. When bidding goodbye
the supernaturals tell him that had he stayed to plant another year he
would have become slave to the holy people of this place by gambling
away his possessions to them. The hero is welcomed home by his
family but admonished for the absence of his turkey who they claim
used to bring rain. In the midst of this complaint the turkey appears
and they laugh with joy. The hero holds a ceremony to teach what he
has learned to his younger brother; Talking God and Hastsezini
(Black God) participate in this ceremony together with their two
virgin children who grind the medicine. From the vegetables brought
back at this time the Navaho first acquired seeds of corn and pumpkin.

6. Hero Acquires a Wife (Ma, S&H, Wa, Weth)

In four versions the hollow log and corn planting episodes are followed by the hero's discovery of a family dwelling nearby into which
he marries. He sees a distant fire at night and locates it by means of
sighting through a forked stick (Ma, S&H, Wa). Only after the fourth
day of searching is he able to find its source (Ma, S&H). As he approaches the hogan he feels shy and ashamed (Wa) and, thinking that
wealthy people must live here, takes off his poor clothes to enter in
only his breech cloth (Ma). Here he finds a young woman alone engaged
in decorating a buckskin shirt with fringe and shells; her father and
mother live in a hut nearby (Ma). The father enters, immediately referring to the hero as son-in-law, and asks his daughter why she does
not bring in his possessions and spread a skin for him to sit on; to each
of her father's questions she only "looked sideways and smiled" (Ma).
The father invites the shy visitor to sit beside his daughter (Ma). Or
the hero is welcomed and fed by the family of father, mother, daughter,
and son; at first he is addressed as grandson but the father soon suggests that he marry the daughter, who is just like the woman of his
dreams, and they live in a hogan apart (Wa). In a third version the
hero finds an old man with whom he spends four nights despite the inhospitable reception of being warned that "earth people are not to wander
about;" here it is not until the hero returns from a visit to his farm that
he is addressed as son-in-law (S&H).

The new father-in-law is rendered unconscious by poisoned smoke
(Ma) or by corn (S&H) given by the hero. The old man's request for a
smoke is refused until after the fourth repetition; then the hero gives
him poisoned tobacco, different from what he himself smokes, which
causes the father-in-law to perspire and swoon (Ma). The daughter
runs to tell her mother, who sends presents for the hero to revive her
husband; he does this by fumigation, infusion, and rubbing the patient's
body (Ma). This incident is repeated four times, and the father-in-law
praises the tobacco and says that he had never felt so happy as when
smoking it (Ma). When the old man in turn offers his tobacco, the hero
refuses it on warning from wind that it will kill him; instead he smokes
his own regular tobacco and this time offers it to the father-in-law (Ma).

In answer to the father-in-law's inquiries why the first mixture made him swoon, the hero lies and tells him it must be because he is sick, naming four diseases any one of which may be the cause (Ma). In the Sapir-Hoijer version a similar incident occurs when the hero brings corn from his garden and roasts it; this is a new food for his father-in-law, who faints when he tastes it but revives (S&H). In Wetherill's version, offer of smoking concludes the hero's trials and proves to the father-in-law that he has learned to heed warnings. The hero is warned by wind that his father-in-law's tobacco will kill him; although the father-in-law has switched their pouches, the hero takes from his own (Weth).

7. Showing of Corn and Game (Ma, S&H, Wa, Weth)

The hero has brought corn to his new relatives-in-law (S&H). In other versions he takes his wife to see his garden (Ma, Wa, Weth), which pleases her greatly (Ma, Wa). He has already brought her some corn and told her how it can be cooked in four different ways, but she wants to see the plants from which it comes (Ma). In cooking, the corn increases magically (Ma). In gratitude for the gift of corn the father-in-law has his daughter show the hero their game "farm" (Ma).[185] In preparation he bathes and puts on skin clothing provided by his wife; she leads him through a hole in the ground down steps to an apartment with four doors of rock crystal, which open to the four directions at the touch of her wand to reveal a beautiful land full of flowers, birds, pollen and various kinds of game (deer, antelope, mountain sheep, elk) (Ma). Here the father-in-law shows him how to make offerings (cigarettes) for each of these animals, and his wife catches a deer by the foot to bring home for meat (Ma).

The night before this expedition his wife has asked his name, which he refuses to divulge until her fourth request (Ma). He tells her both of his names, He Who Teaches Himself and He Who Has Floated, and in turn learns that of his father-in-law, Deer Raiser (Ma).

8. Trials Imposed by Father-in-law (Ma, S&H, Weth)

The remainder of three versions is principally devoted to the hero's successful evasion of trials prepared by his witch father-in-law. (In the Wheelwright story [Wa] there is no malevolent activity on the father-in-law's part; he persuades the hero, despite his initial profession of ignorance, to perform the Water Way ceremony over him and in turn gives the hero more ritual information to teach to his own people. In this story, unlike the other versions, the hero returns to this wife at the conclusion of his further adventures.)

In two of the witch father-in-law versions (Ma, S&H) the old man is married to two women, his wife and his daughter. It is for this daughter that the hero is welcomed as a new son-in-law, whom the jealous father-in-law, however, immediately tries to kill by trickery. The series of trials in both versions includes poisoned food, encounters with bear and snake, and the burnt moccasin incident; the Sapir-Hoijer version adds to these cactus field, mountain lion, and thunder. The hero refuses poisoned food on the advice of his wind monitor (S&H, Weth). Or on each of four days he is warned by wind where the old man has put the poison and each day avoids that portion of the food; the old man is surprised that this trick doesn't work, but his daughter denies having told the secret (Ma). When this trick is unsuccessful, he plots his son-in-law's death while hunting (Ma, S&H). He tries to lead the hero into a box canyon by false deer tracks so that his four pet bears can attack him, but the hero on wind's advice frustrates this plan by staying at the entrance, where he discovers the bears and slays them (Ma). When the father-in-law shows surprise and anger at finding him safe and sorrow over his pet's death, the hero recognizes that he has to deal with a witch, that his father-in-law is jealous of him, because witches practice incest, and that he wants to eat his flesh and use parts of his dead body for witchcraft (Ma). When the hero refuses to skin the game, the old man sends him to get his daughter to help; the old man waylays him in the form of a snake, but warned by wind the hero calls his bluff and makes the old man beg for mercy (Ma). At home he has his wife send her mother to help skin the game, which makes the old man furious because he had wanted his daughter (Ma). Again he is angry when the hero refuses to eat the bear meat (Ma). Next day the old man repeats the treachery while hunting, but this time the hero is victorious over twelve bears (Ma). When they camp on the way home that night, the hero's suspicions are aroused and he exchanges their moccasins before sleeping; during the night the father-in-law takes the moccasins from under his pillow and burns them only to find that they are his own (Ma, S&H). Again the hero gives the wrong message at home and the old man is angry when his wife rather than his daughter comes to bring him another pair of moccasins (Ma, S&H).

In the Sapir-Hoijer version the incident of the burnt moccasins occurs at the beginning of the hunting expedition after the hero has been led to the midst of a field of closely spaced cactuses (S&H). The encounter with a bear follows on the father-in-law's prohibition against venturing in a particular direction (S&H, Weth); the bear, actually the father-in-law transformed, is stopped by running against the hero's planted bow string (S&H). The hero pokes fun at his father-in-law by commenting, "I am not my female clanswoman. One plays pranks with me" (S&H).[186] This incident is repeated with snake (S&H, Weth), mountain lion (S&H), and thunder (S&H), but in each case the father-in-law is unable to kill his new son-in-law (S&H, Weth).

In the Wethrill version the hero disregards further warnings to climb a butte and gathers plants which are gila monster's tobacco. On the way home gila monster is diverted by a conversation with frog about the latter's ugly appearance, and the hero is saved from his anger (Weth).

In the Matthews story disobedience of the father-in-law's instructions not to go east takes the hero to people who tell him of their experience with the father-in-law's evil ways, how he attempts to kill his daughter's suitors out of jealousy because she is also his wife, and how many of their people have been killed on his account (Ma). They rejoice to hear that the hero has killed the bears and give him medicine to counteract his father-in-law's poison and witchcraft (Ma). These people live in conical tents like those of the Plains Indians; they are playing nanzoz when the hero arrives, and he is greeted by a woman who is fairer in color than is usual for the Navaho (Ma). In further disobedience of instructions the hero goes to the other three directions and finds each time a similar reception (Ma). When his father-in-law is finally confronted with this knowledge, he admits his evil ways and asks to be treated with the medicine thus acquired; in so doing the hero performs the first Feather Chant (Ma). He returns to teach this knowledge to his people and then himself departs for Whirling Lake, the destination of his hollow log journey (Ma).

The Sapir-Hoijer version continues with the story of the boy raised by owl. In this case there is no ceremony to cure the father-in-law and her hero leaves his new wife when she becomes pregnant by her father, the offspring to be later thrown away and raised by owl (S&H).

In the Wetherill version the malevolent father-in-law is not specified as a witch. When he sees that the hero "has at last learned to heed a warning," he teaches him the Plume Way ceremony (Weth). The hero returns, is welcomed by his own people and teaches them the ceremony (Weth).

Summary of Wheelwright's "Feather Chant" (Wc)

Wheelwright's informant traces the activities of Deer Raiser, the witch father-in-law of the foregoing versions, back to the pre-emergence times of the general Navaho origin myth. Under the name of He Who Can Change into Anything, he and Coyote are the offenders in the seduction that precipitates the separation of the sexes. They meet the guilty wife at the river where, pretending illness, she is taken each day by her husband, and there is implication that either or both of the seducers practice witchcraft when sticks are thrown down the smokehole at night. During the separation He Who Can Change swims across the river to feed her and she becomes pregnant. Reunion of the sexes is here brought about by the threat of the approaching flood. There follow the familiar events of the emergence, including the placing of heavenly bodies, in which Coyote plays a more prominent role than is usual in the origin myth. He Who Changes is at this time placed in charge of game and renamed One Who Raises Deer. After the birth of war gods and slaying of monsters the events of the chantway legend proper begin.

1. Trip to Sun Father

A boy born to a maiden seeks his sun father. His mother follows his tracks until they disappear and Sun comes to tell her where he has gone. He is given magical help for the hazards of the journey by various persons: from bearers of seeds he gets breath feathers on which he flies over cutting knives; from Fire God a fire stick, which on the advice of wind monitor he uses to burn cutting reeds; from bat, help in descending impassible cliff; from spider a net on which he walks over ice; from frog a rainbow on which he crosses water to meet fierce animals whom he quiets by uttering their names. In similar manner he quiets Sun's door guards — wind, snake, bear, lightning. Jealous of the hero, Sun's wife puts him to sleep, wraps him in four hot cloud coverings, and puts him into perpetual rain. When Sun returns he subjects the hero to tests by lightning and arrows before acknowledging him as his son; then he has his "holy children" make him like Turquoise Girl, his favorite daughter. The hero chooses as gifts a sandpainting of the sun, also "deer and all animals and growth," which have disappeared from the earth. He is returned to his home, where he finds his mother "grown so very old that she did not know him."

2. Corn Planted

After hunting unsuccessfully, the hero meets turkey and goes with him to the place of crossing waters. Turkey directs the making of a raft on which they cross the water and come to a place suitable for farming. Here the turkey shakes seeds from his wings "for the boy's mother to farm."

3. Marriage

The hero and turkey arrive at the home of Deer Raiser, where the hero marries his daughter. He tells of his adventures and is given a new name, He Who Begins to Float.

4. Hunting Adventures

The hero's hunting is now successful, but he kills too many deer and his legs become paralyzed. After each of three ceremonial treatments he still cannot resist killing more game. His wind monitor warns him that this is wrong. Once while hunting he is hidden by mountain sheep people and them found by wind people who are aiding his father-in-law. In the excess of hunting he suddenly realizes that he has turned into an antelope and "gone crazy." He is partially restored by a ceremony.

5. Swallowed by Fish

In this condition he drinks at a pool and is swallowed by a big fish. He kills the fish by cutting his heart and then cuts his way out. Poisoned by the fish, he is unable to walk and his father-in-law cures him with a sandpainting. He returns to his wife, then to his mother, for whom his father-in-law gives a ceremony. Finally, with his ritual knowledge he returns to the place of his birth.

Navaho Wind Way

Haile, 1932c, MS., 176 pp. Navaho Wind Way Ceremony. (H)

Hill and Hill, 1943a, pp. 113-114. Frog Races a Lewd Woman. (H&H)

Wheelwright, 1946b, pp. 1-7. Wind Chant. (Wa)

Wheelwright, 1940, 13 pp. Myth of Sontso (Big Star). (Wb)

Wyman and Bailey, 1946, pp. 215-216, 225. Myth of Navaho Striped Windway. (W&B)

The hero of Haile's Navaho Wind Way legend becomes involved in a series of disastrous events, from which he is restored or extricated by supernatural intervention or, as the story progresses, by his own accumulated power. First he is stolen by snakes and poisoned by flag plants. Five disasters follow his trespassing on forbidden territory: destruction by thunder, seduction by Woman Who Dries People Up; snake transformation; killing of whirlwind boy; and encounter with lightning. The hero then travels about collecting more ceremonial knowledge. The story is connected with that of Plume Way at the point of the hollow log trip (not abstracted here) and concludes with a detailed description of the ceremony held over the hero. One of the principal incidents of the Haile version, seduction by Woman Who Dries People Up, is duplicated in a myth fragment by Hill and Hill, reported as explaining the origin of Mesa Fahada in Caco Canyon.

The events of this story develop the parallel themes of the hero's exposure to dangerous situations and his developing power to cope with them. As in other chantway legends there is variation, or in some adventures uncertainty, in the extent to which the hero is himself responsible for the mishaps thus precipitated. At the opening of the story the hero is chosen by supernaturals for this role, and their function as his protectors is thus established. His first mishap is brought about by his protectors' neglect, through no fault of his own; while they play tag he is stolen by snakes and taken to their subterranean dwelling whence he is rescued by supernaturals. The hero and his family then eat flag plants which prove to be poisonous. Here he seems to be drawn into danger unwittingly but with suspicion, in the manner of presentation of the incident, that this is considered as temptation. Again he is rescued by supernatural cure. In the subsequent five incidents the hero's active part in courting danger grows more explicit; in each case he ventures into forbidden territory wondering why the prohibition. In the first of these adventures his trespassing is combined with an unwitting ritual error (placing his arrows tips downward), and he is shattered by thunder. His next misadventure begins with attendance at a ceremony despite warnings, where he becomes involved with a beautiful maiden who later turns to a ragged, disgusting old woman (Woman Who Dries People Up) and strands him on sky-reaching-rock. The taunt of dove maidens that he has 'valued himself too much" hints that the hero has his own share of responsibility for this disaster. He hunts success-fully in forbidden territory and swallows the colon of the deer he kills, only to find himself transformed by this act into a snake. From this form the supernaturals restore him. Again, in violation of warnings, he hunts unsuccessfully and in anger shoots at and kills a whirlwind. In punishment he is "twisted into the ground" by another whirlwind and has to be restored by his protectors. For the final excursion into forbidden territory, the hero has been fore-armed with magical pro-tection and with this power successfully wards off a lightning attack. After undergoing these adventures he is able to visit a series of super-naturals and obtain ritual information.

Three additional versions of this myth, identified simply as Wind Chant (Wa, Wb) or as Navaho Striped Windway (W&B), present a simi-lar story pattern but omit several of the Haile incidents and add others.[187] These versions begin with the snake transformation and con-tinue with killing of whirlwind boy. They add marriage to snake (Wa, W&B), witch father-in-law (Wa), destruction by thunder (W&B), sky visit (Wa), and teaching of the ceremony to earth people (Wa, Wb). There is variation in the extent to which the heroes of these versions violate taboos consciously. In the complete Wheelwright version (Wa) the hero stumbles into mishaps apparently unintentionally (snake trans-formation, killing of whirlwind boy, snake marriage), except in his suc-cessful disregard of the witch father-in-law warnings. The Wheel-wright Big Star version (Wb) shows him obstinately flouting food taboos to cause his snake transformation and impulsively shooting at whirl-wind boy in anger. Likewise, in Wyman and Bailey's story he shoots the whirlwind in anger and disregards his guardian's warnings against snake marriage and provocation of thunder; the violation of food taboos which result in his snake transformation is here apparently uninten-tional. The usual chantway conclusion of teaching the ceremony to earth people is included in only two versions (Wa, Wb).

In the following abstract the first three episodes are based entirely on Haile's version. Beginning with the fourth episode, material from other versions is added as indicated. The last three episodes are taken from Wheelwright's (Wa) and/or Wyman and Bailey's versions.

1. Stolen by Snakes (H)

First Man and First Woman are told by left-handed wind that earth

will be inhabited by many people; he reads their thoughts when they
wonder how this is to happen and answers that it will become known
at daylight. Next day the jeweled houses of the different colored winds
appear at the four directions. "Woman who encircles the earth" has
four children, in birth order of boy, girl, boy, girl, who visit the homes
of the winds. Talking God jokingly asks these grandchildren to race
with him; the oldest boy is chosen for this by the winds and he becomes
the hero of the legend. The snake and wind people become absorbed
in a game of tag (in which the runner is decided by the direction in
which spittle falls from the center of a hollowed out mound), during
which the boy is stolen. The winds search for him in each direction.
On the advice of yeibichai the winds look in a pool to which the boy's
tracks lead but find only a strange man who scolds them. Big fly notifies thunder people, who strike the water in vain with lightning. In the
course of consultations an unidentified voice suggests that Old Man
from Earth Charcoal Place (apparently another name for Black God)
can help, but he refuses four successive petitions in each of which a
bundle is added to his offering. In another consultation, despite the
drowsiness of appointed doorguards, the unknown voice is identified as
that of bat, who instructs them in the making and presentation of the
proper offering on condition that they not reveal the source of their
information; later he is paid for this service. Black God accepts the
offering suspecting, however, that his doorguard bat has revealed it.
He smokes with the visitor and comes to help after some delay. The
motioning of Black God's cane reveals an opening in the pool and a
ladder leading into the home of the big snakes. Big snake old man
four times refuses his application for return of the hero: "Even great
people are making useless efforts to do this, return away out of here,
you have a strong odor!" Black God intimidates them by setting fire to
the waters with his firedrill, and they plead with him to extinguish it.
The hero is found and returned to his family.

2. Flag Poisoning (H)

The boy is given a little wind monitor in his earfold. He is tested
again by the snakes. Four times flag plants appear near the shore of
the pool and move out to the center, drawing the people out until the
water grows too deep; they want to chew the plant root. The hero finally pulls one up and chews it, and the other people do likewise. They
complain of pains in ankle and interior of body; their voices become
"pulled in" and eyesight blurred, but after each complaint they eat
more of the plant — its root, inner layer and rind, pollen part. The
little wind monitor admonishes them for having done this but advises
that dark wind can help. Bundle offerings are again made in vain on
four successive trials, until big fly tells the proper sacrifice, again for
payment and on condition that the source of their information not be
revealed. Dark wind accepts, is persuaded to come immediately, and
performs a ceremony to counteract the poisoning by applying the flag
plant to the patient in the different forms that had poisoned him.

They move camp and build a new hogan of plants with tips downward. A long and unbearable rain sets in, of he-rain followed by she-rain, and does not stop until the tips of the plants are turned up. "Now it developed that the cause of this was that some people were inhabiting the place, who wished to exclude all others... spider people had their homes there... occupied exclusively in hunting...."

3. Shattered by Thunder (H)[188]

The hero hunts in forbidden territory, wondering about the reason for the prohibition. When a storm gathers he takes shelter under a tall spruce but makes the mistake of placing his arrows with tips down instead of up; his monitor had not warned him of this in time. He is shattered by thunder and his flesh scattered in small pieces. When he does not return, his people worry. At dawn a yeibichai appears pointing to where he met the accident; they find his tracks but no other trace of him. Black ant people are summoned and the singer is prevailed upon to come immediately. Ants collect his body parts and place them on buckskin. He is unable to move until thunder, summoned by big fly sings for him. He is restored to motion by being struck four times by lightning which runs through him in opposite directions. Speech is restored by dark wind and bluebird people, and he returns home.

4. The Woman Who Dries People Up (H, H&H)

The hero wonders why he has been warned not to visit a Female Shooting Way ceremony being held nearby; he sets out for it, this time without the arrows that he usually carries. He finds many beautiful and friendly women at the cooking place, who ask him to sing while they grind. These are bird maidens. They face each other in two lines for the grinding, which is first done with an upward motion. A single kernel is passed through the circuit of both lines, and with each grinding the amount increases. After repeating this four times, grinding is done in the ordinary way with forward and back motion, and great heaps of meal appear at each millstone. They make offerings to the hero until he is covered with the meal. He suggests a test: that each woman will throw a ball of meal into the air; "the ball that rolls to me... with the owner of that ball I shall go home." All the balls break except one, whose owner has spit on it and wrapped a cord about it. When it rolls toward him, she immediately takes him home, giving no chance to escape. He does not yet know that she is Woman Who Dries People Up. (H&H give a different introduction; the hero goes outside during a ceremony in which he is the patient and is grabbed by Woman Who Dries You Up.)

The home of this beautiful maiden is on the "stone which extends into the sky." She unlocks her well furnished house and they enter and sit at the rear. The hero refuses meat four times on the warning of wind monitor, who tells him that she is "one who dries people up" and that if he eats he will have to stay there. She prepares their bed. The hero delays, thinking, "After a while I shall bother her," but she magically puts him to sleep. He awakes next morning to hear noises where she was lying and to find that her hair has become white, her flesh wrinkled, "her inner cheeks she was drawing in and out, her upper row of teeth jutted out of her mouth." When he moves away from her stealthily she asks what he is doing in an apparently ugly mood. He sees the furnishings turned to rags and that the meat hanging on crossbars which she had offered him is dried human flesh, "which surely was unfit to eat." (The Woman Who Dries You Up has taken the hero to a hard rock, where there are all kinds of jewelry, shells, and hides. They go to bed and when he awakes he is frightened to find that she has turned into a bony old woman who snores. During the night the rock has grown up with them. H&H).

He flees from this ugliness in the direction they had come, only to find that there is no means of descent, that the hills are no longer recognizable. He searches in each direction but is warned by wind not to complete the circle or he will always have to stay there. He spends each of three nights at the east, south, and west sides of the rock. During the day she pokes around after him with a stick; "In this way it seems she would dry up the people." After the third night, as he sits with bowed head, hungry and thirsty, he is addressed by two turtle dove maidens who had been among those grinding corn. They taunt him with, "Isn't it true that you used to value yourself very much? It's quite clear now that you are only an ordinary person." He admonishes them for talking thus when he is dying of hunger and thirst. They feed him ritually prepared pollen gruel from an inexhaustible bowl, which they empty with one scoop when he is satisfied, and give him water from a reed. They tell him how big snake can bring him down from the rock; when snake appears next morning he is to place turquoise between his horns, grasp the horns, and close his eyes. When he opens his eyes after this descent he sees the height of the rock from which they have come. (He tries to escape but cannot see ground at the bottom of the rock nor find a way down. The old woman pays no attention to him. The young girls who taunt him are jay and dove; they make fun of him "because the woman he was with ate herself and drank her own urine ..." They feed him meat and water and after four days tell him to climb between the horns of big snake, who will take him down. H&H.)

Warned by his monitor, the hero starts running east; at each of four ridges he looks back to see the "outlines of a slim figure" following. In an open space ahead he sees toad old man, who reads his visitor's thoughts about his appearance — long webbed feet, long legs, no buttocks, small backbone, wide belly, rough skin, bulging eyes, wide mouth. Toad hides him from the pursuing woman in a cornstalk hole and replants the corn. She arrives and, in the face of toad's denial that earth surface people come here, follows her victim's tracks and pulls out the cornstalks in all directions until she finds him. Toad challenges her to race around a mountain; the hero will be the stake. In the form of a maiden she maintains the lead until, near the finish, toad forces her to run in a muddy place where he had urinated on the way out; here she slips, and toad wins. She leaves without a word. The hero pays toad an abalone shell and returns home. His family have discovered the direction in which he has gone by throwing out a cord. (During the pursuit lizard and various frogs cannot help the hero. At his fourth request old man frog hides him in a reed hole. Frog wins the race around the mountain by using wind, cloud, and rain to put the old woman off her course. She is forced to release him, and frog admonishes him never to let anything like this happen again. H&H.)

5. Snake Transformation (H, Wa, W&B) [189]

The hero goes on a hunting expedition alone (Wa, W&B) or with his younger brother (H). This is in defiance of a warning not to trespass, and with the hero wondering what is the reason for the prohibition (H). He pursues a deer which he kills (H, W&B) or finds mysteriously slain (Wa). The deer belongs to big snake, who has used it as decoy (W&B). The hero eats the intestines, which turn into a snake as he swallows them, and by this act he is himself transformed into a snake (H, Wa, W&B). This process is described in detail in the Haile version: As the hero roasts the colon on a tree root, it seems to be alive and wiggling; he eats it and, "When there was exactly three fingers width left of it he sucked his breath in and it ran down into his throat." When toward morning he wakes groaning and twisting, his younger brother reminds him that when he swallowed the colon it seemed to be alive; at daylight the younger brother finds that the hero has turned into a big snake (H). The brother returns to his family in fear and is told that this was why they had been warned not to trespass (H).

It has been specified that the hero lives with his family of mother, father, sister, and brother (Wa, W&B). The family is worried and sad about their son, and Talking God explains to them what has happened (Wa, W&B). They are frightened by their son in snake form (Wa, W&B), who angrily chases his father around a mountain (Wa). Ceremonial help is obtained from wind people: the brother notifies the winds and promises offerings (H); big fly tells the father to apply to wind people with offerings (Wb) or advises the family to get dark wind's help (W&B). The snake attacks those who are trying to save him (Wa, W&B) but is finally grasped and thrown through hoops to be restored to human form (H, Wa, W&B). He complains that he has suffered terribly and that the great snake was cruel to him (Wa). He is treated ceremonially for paralysis (Wa) or loss of voice (W&B). The wind ceremony is held over him (Wa, W&B). The singer, dark wind, pretends to make offerings to snakes but keeps some of the jewels himself (W&B). A series of four ceremonies is necessary before the cure is completed and the ceremony learned; after each ceremony he feels better for a time but again becomes paralyzed, blind, or weak (Wa).

6. Twisted by Wind (H, Wa, W&B)[190]

The hero shoots at a whirlwind, and a human being (H) or little boy (Wa, W&B)[191] falls dead. This happens when he has ventured on forbidden ground, wondering why the prohibition, and has hunted in vain in this beautiful place (H). He is angered by the whirlwind's passing close to him (H) or tumbling him four times (W&B). He is frightened at what he has done and can hear the whirlwind hunting for his son (Wa). He ponders whether this is man or woman, finally decides that it is a man, and extracts his arrow, thinking to himself, "This is really too bad" (H).

In one version no bad consequences result from this action (Wa). In another he does not know how to restore the boy he has shot but sends for dark wind, who gives the proper instructions for restoration (W&B). The hero of Haile's version is punished for this action by being twisted into the ground, leaving only his head showing (H). This version gives details of his restoration as follows (H): The hero's family suspects that he has disobeyed. His brother finds him "a great sight to look at" with his chin yellow, forehead white streaked, face reddened and sparkling with specular iron ore. Talking God appears and indicates by gestures that this is the work of wind. The younger brother applies to dark wind with offerings, and he is prevailed on to come immediately. The five winds pry the hero out with flints, apply pollen with the help of Talking God and House God,[192] place him on buckskin, and take him home. Although he can breathe and walk, his mind and speech have been stolen. The gods perform over him without success. The source of the difficulty is sought in vain by throwing out cotton cords to the four directions. The string does not move when placed successively in front of the winds, the Woman Who Dries People Up (she just chuckles at the emissary and he does not wait to see if she will speak to him but immediately runs away from her), Talking God, House God, small bird people, snake people, spider people, water monster people, thunders and winds. Big fly has acted as messenger in these proceedings. Although discouraged, the people feel that a person should not be abandoned without mind and speech. Finally the cord moves when it is placed before the restless prostituting coyote people. Dark wind enters their home unseen and presents offerings properly before they have time to refuse. He returns with the hero's mind and speech, which are restored to him.

(The Wheelwright version [Wa] interposes further ceremonial details between the conclusion of the snake transformation and the encounter with whirlwind. The hero and his family attend a Mountain Chant at which there is so much magic during the dance of the last night that the spectators grow excited and feel faint, the corral moves, the sky shakes, and the water is stirred; even the bear singer faints and is restored by the hero and his brother. Later he goes with Talking God as patient in a four day ceremony that includes treatment on a bed of spruce boughs over a trench of coals.)

7. Attack by Lightning (H)

The hero ventures a fifth and final time into forbidden territory, as usual wondering what is meant by the prohibition. Four times he hears a voice and recognizes old man horned toad in human form and dressed in flint. Toad specifies his offering and gives him a flint to thrust into his mouth and "blow out with" for magical protection against the "person without mercy" into whose territory he is going. When a storm arises the hero keeps his arrows with point upward. On advice from his monitor, he tells the lightning to "stay high" and at the fourth crash uses the flint which lightning fears. The lightning strikes above his head, missing him, and the storm clears away. The hero returns home, and the winds depart to their new homes in clouds at the four directions.

8. Visits to Supernaturals (H)

The remainder of the Haile version is devoted principally to the hero's travels in search of additional ritual information, equipment, and sandpaintings, and to description of ceremonial procedures. Among the people or places to which the hero and his people travel for more ceremonial knowledge are: spider people; water monster at emergence place; "interior of a pot"; old man toad; snakes; laughing medicine people; bear man and bear people; big wind old man, crazy winds, red and gray winds, wind children, and other wind people; young pinyon and spruce people; rainbow people; thunder people; prostituting coyote; ants; snake people; cactus people. This journey for information takes place both in the sky and on the return to earth, when the various places where the hero had met disaster are visited. The usual pattern of his meetings with these peoples is as follows: the hero sees evidences of strangers but does not meet them until the fourth investigation; he is greeted with the remark that "earth surface people are not allowed"; on advice of his monitor he requests medicines; after receiving the proper offering they either give him the information or refer him to big snake old man, who will make it known to him later.

Some further incidents occur on this journey. The meeting of Flint Way with "down way rite" (Plume Way) is specified when they meet a party of gods preparing a hollow log; the hero participates in the hollow log trip.[193] The meeting with Mountaintop Way is specified at a meeting with bear man. He finds that the "crazy winds," who whirl around in every direction and throw dust on themselves, will not talk to him; his monitor advises him that they do not require a sacrifice; they cause heavy sandstorms; "It is the one which Prostituting Coyote put down." Two groups of wind people roll down a hill on hoops and the hero is able to imitate this action, whereupon they admit that he is surely a holy person; if the hoop had fallen over with him he would have been forced to "remain right there." One group of wind people are doing ugly things; they throw their children into the fire and then restore them by spitting on them; even the women do this. Another group of wind people are doing foolish things, sitting on top of each other's heads.

After these travels the hero again becomes indisposed, and a ceremony is held over him; the details of this ceremony are described.

9. Marriage to Snake (Wa, W&B)

Both the Wheelwright and Wyman and Bailey versions add certain incidents not duplicated in Haile's fuller story. The principal such incident is the hero's marriage to a snake woman (Wa, W&B). He is always getting into trouble by disobeying his guardian dark wind, in this case by his marriage to the snake woman who bears him snake children (W&B). His home is full of little snakes which crawl over him; for this, "He felt disgraceful and sorry for what he had done. So they had to restore him again" (W&B). The difficulties that follow the snake marriage in Wheelwright's version are the hero's trials by the snake father-in-law. His father-in-law plots against him; but the hero not only explores the surrounding country against his wishes but also kills the snakes which his father-in-law sends to kill him (Wa). The hero escapes the angry father-in-law by a horned toad disguise (Wa). Back at home, Talking God tells him that he must take offerings to his snake wife who has borne him twins (Wa).

10. Attack by Thunder (W&B)

Continuing the disobedience of his guardian's instructions, the hero bothers thunder's nest full of eggs. He is destroyed by thunder so that nothing but his bow, arrow, and shoes are left. From this predicament he is restored and returns to his own people for further ceremonial treatment. At the conclusion of this story he departs to the mountains to become a wind god.

11. Sky Visit and Return (Wa)

In the sky the hero visits the homes of the winds. He meets Water Chant people and learns medicine to cure coyote madness. After return to earth, Talking God shows him a pollen painting on skin and he is treated with a ceremony. He is admonished to remember all that he has learned because if forgotten it reverts to the gods. The hero teaches his ceremony to his younger brother. He tells his people that he will be part of the wind and that it will make him angry if they flee from it in fear. He embraces his family and departs in the wind to live with the gods.

Chiricahua Wind Way

Haile, 1932d, MS., 147 pp. Chiricahua Wind Ceremony of the Navaho. Version B. (Hb)

Haile, 1933, MS., 259 pp. Chiricahua Windway Chant. Version A. (Ha)

Chiricahua Wind Way is said to have been adopted from the Chiricahua Apache during the Fort Sumner period, 1864-68. Its story is
briefer than many of the chantway legends and makes use of incidents
which occur also in Navaho Wind Way. In view of the well documented
recency of its adoption, Haile considers it probable that the contamina-
tion proceeds from the Navaho Wind Way legend rather than vice versa.[194]

The story is concerned with a hunter's difficulties as a result of
offending the winds. His first offense of ridiculing wind's fawn meat is
punished by withholding game and by his destruction by cactus in a
fruitless chase after a wind deer; from this disaster he is restored
ritually by the winds. His impulsive shooting of whirlwind boy constitutes his second offense, for which he himself must restore the victim.
In Haile's brief Version B, elements from these two incidents are
woven into a single episode: because of his excess in hunting, the winds
trick the hero into killing a wind deer which he is compelled to restore;
only later does he become ill from these events and require ceremonial
treatment himself. The longer Version A contains the additional incidents of marriage among the snake people and father-in-law trial, partial release of game, and encounter with big dipper on venturing into
forbidden territory. The shooting of whirlwind boy appears in both
versions of Navaho Wind Way, and the hero's marriage among the snake
people occurs in Wheelwright's version of that legend.

In the Chiricahua Wind Way story the hero makes a significant complaint, "Why is it that I suffer these hardships! It appears as though I
were seeking the frightful things that are putting me to a test!" Typically, the motivation for undertaking adventures in the chantway stories
is obscure; it is often left unclear to what extent the hero's tests are
provoked by him or visited upon him. This uncertainty holds true for
the Chiricahua Wind Way; the hero brings down wrath of supernaturals
by his own errors, but how far these are conscious errors is uncertain.
Thus, his offense of shooting a wind deer is engineered by supernaturals. More often the actions which bring him into difficulty seem impetuous or unintentional, as in the ridicule of fawn meat, hunting excess, and shooting of whirlwind boy. His last adventure is provoked,
however, by intentional disregard of a dream warning not to hunt in certain territory.

With increasing boldness the hero also develops ability to protect
himself by ritual power. After marriage to a snake wife he successfully withstands his new father-in-law's lightning attack through a
combination of supernatural aid and his own power. With premonition
of a dream the hero is able to effect release of some game and to hunt
again. While preoccupied with his former bad luck in hunting, he im-
petuously shoots whirlwind boy, but is able, with supernatural help, to
restore the victim and thus avoid further punishment himself.

The following abstract is based on Haile's longer Version A, with supplementary material from his Version B summarized in parentheses at the appropriate places.

1. Attack by Wind

The hero's family consists of mother, father, and sister. He is a good hunter, while his father and sister do the tanning. On the way home from hunting the hero enters the home of wind. He laughs to himself at the condition of the hogan "gray with filth of longstanding" and wonders what is the matter with his host, "Can't he move! What has he hanging there! He ought to know better than that!" His host assumes that his guest has been making fun of the fawn meat he has hanging there, and in retaliation withholds game so that the hero is no longer successful in hunting. Nor can he find even rabbits and field rats; meat hunger torments him.

Wind man and woman release a deer which the hero tracks intently for four days; on each of four attempts to shoot the deer he is puzzled and angry to find that he cannot release the arrow. Still tracking the deer, he follows him in leaping over a series of four cactus plants — sour cactus, heart twister, tree cactus, smooth leafed cactus — after each of which he feels pain successively in his foot, knee, and heart and finally falls to the ground unconscious, with his arms and head dropped backwards, his legs, mouth, and eyes twisted.

That night the family wonders what has happened to their son since he never stays away at night. In the morning big fly reports what has happened, that he was shot to death by a wind deer, and suggests that an old man at the summit of Yucca Mountain can help. The father applies to this old man four times with offerings, each time increasing the number of bundles, but is unsuccessful until big fly explains the proper offering. The old man suspects his doorguard big fly, who disclaims responsibility and protests that he doesn't go anywhere. Four times the father is unable to find the singer's pouch hanging on a tree outside. The old man expresses his scorn, "Clearly, earth surface people are no good! Because they say such things it is small wonder that they go about complaining of suffering," whereupon he goes out and gets a dried-up squirrel skin that the father had overlooked. The old man promises to come later.

The father is instructed not to go on top of a certain hill on his return home, but he disobeys, wondering why the prohibition. He is terrified when tree cactuses gather about him with a rumbling sound, forming a circle and reaching to the sky. Wind from the top of Yucca Mountain twists out a passageway for him to escape and he realizes why this territory was forbidden.

The ceremony for the hero is begun. Winds bring different varieties of cactus which are inserted in the body parts affected and drawn out with the seeds that had been implanted by the attack. With this treatment and with pressing and blowing, he gradually revives until he is well enough to return home, after which the ceremony is repeated with description of the ritual procedures. The hero's story and reasons for the disaster are discussed. It is specified that tree cactus represents the supernatural power of wind and must be treated as a holy thing, also that when wind sounds, "No person must bother us, because there will be meanness in us." Big dipper, angry because he wasn't invited to the ceremony, enters with lightning that strikes everyone in the gathering except the patient and winds. He is pacified by promise of an offering and fully restores the scattered people, with the exception of bear and snake, doorguards who did not make a pollen offering and who stagger off "without getting their full sense."

(Version B. A hunter who has visions lives with his wife and children, a boy and girl. Because he has killed too many deer he becomes "hated by those beyond." A wind deer is sent to entice him; after shooting it, he is informed that he has done a terrible thing, he has killed a man. The winds "resented his wanton slaughter of game and, by punishing him for the death of the wind deer, they sought to check his greed." His attempted escape and the punishment for this act are similar to those in the killing of whirlwind boy in Version A and will be summarized with the account of that incident below. Subsequently, a ceremony is held over the hero which is similar in many details to that recounted here; see concluding incident below. Hb.)

2. Marriage to Snake [195]

Now recovered, the hero again engages in hunting, but only as a pastime, for field rats and rabbits. In his wanderings he comes to the home of snake people, where the women are slim and swaying in their gait; he stays and hunts mice for them. A snake woman gives birth to his children, "similar to a bunch of wool." They play with him when he returns from hunting, crawling along his shoes, garters, and mouth and winding themselves about his waist and head. When he grows tired of them he announces that he is leaving "without any reason in particular" to return home. The eldest child gives his approval saying that he should go if he wishes. On the way he meets his father-in-law and informs him that he is leaving, which he expects will be unpleasant news to him. The father-in-law raises no objection at the time, but in revenge sends a lightning storm hoping to destroy him and prevent his reaching home. He is frightened by the storm and weeps, although he is advised that this is to "remove the former wickedness of the snakes from him." He is told to call himself by his granduncle's name, which his monitor informs him is Holy Young Man. Toad reassures him, and when the storm subsides tells him that the thunders desire a sacrifice. The hero complains, "Why is it that I suffer these hardships! It appears as though I were seeking the frightful things that are putting me to a test!" Thus he survives the storm through outside help and his own acquired holy power. On his return home no hard feelings are to be harbored; it should be pleasant, as though this had never happened.

3. Release of Game

The hero is preoccupied with memories of his former success in hunting. He dreams that he is instructed to present offerings and prayer on a hill top, then to look on the south slope; in the dream someone is singing for him, and on waking he remembers perfectly the two songs thus sung. He carries out the instructions of the dream and finds on the south slope a white streak marking a cave entrance. Deer tracks lead into the cave and it has a strong odor. He enters to find a strange elderly man and wife who control the deer. Although earth surface people are not allowed here, they realize that he has been ordered to come. Their children drive up a herd of deer, one of which is killed, and he enjoys eating the venison. The woman advises him that he must leave quickly, that they value game greatly and will therefore release just sufficient to sustain him. She reminds him too how he is under the control of the wind of Yucca Mountain "who has no mind to release you, because of the incident when you ridiculed him." After this he is able to kill deer again.

4. Killing of Whirlwind Boy

While he is hunting, "the child of a whirlwind picked up at his feet with a swish and ran away." He shoots into the very center of the whirlwind, "because he was still thinking of that other time when the breeze had blown toward the deer and caused it to escape him." Wind's child, a beautiful boy, falls dead. He wonders frantically where he can escape; he finds a spiral hole in a rock into which he goes without being seen, taking food and closing the opening with rocks. Winds find him there and accuse him of having killed their child without cause and order him to restore the child. Four times the hero protests that he is ignorant of the means of restoration and that he "meant no harm at the time." His monitor advises him to seek help from those winds who had sanctified him. Four times they protest that they know no means of restoration, until applying to spotted wind as a last resort he finds the one song needed. The hero restores wind's child, "And the Wind People that had gathered there rushed at him in gladness, brushing him with their hands and licked him with their tongues all over his body telling him how generous he was." (To escape the consequences of killing the wind deer, the hero drills a hole into the face of a solid rock ledge and closes himself in with the round stone cut out. But left handed and spotted winds discover him, accuse him of having killed them, and threaten to kill him unless he can restore them. The hero is told "from somewhere" the correct song and restores the deer. Hb.)

5. Further Hunting Adventures

In another dream his experiences with the winds are reviewed and he is warned not to trespass on a certain hill. For a time he limits his hunting to his immediate surroundings but is only occasionally successful.

He protests to himself that the dream is not important, but when he
ventures on the forbidden hill, male and female big dippers appear and
ask questions about the ceremony that he cannot answer. He is frightened and pleads with them tearfully. Another ceremony is held over
him according to the instructions of big dipper, the procedures of
which are described in detail. During this ceremony taboos on eating
certain parts of the deer are stated — head (will cause nosebleed and
head swelling); kidneys, tail and anus, colon, small intestines, food
pipe (will turn one into snake); heart (will cause bleeding). Bear suffers
a paralytic attack which is finally cured by his making a turquoise
payment, the loss of which he regrets.

(The concluding portion of Version B varies considerably from this;
the ceremony held over him here has many details similar to the first
restoration ceremony in Version A. After restoring the wind deer, the
hero hunts again but becomes ill. Application is made to "two old men
living at Yucca Mountain" in the same manner as for his restoration
after his encounter with the wind deer in Version A. Here the father is
not sent as emissary; the incident of the father's encounter with cactus
on the way home is omitted. The people protest at the delay of the four
wind singers in arriving for the ceremony. Details of the ceremony are
described. In the course of it bear suffers a stroke of paralysis when
he ignores the big snakes' instructions not to lie down; he is restored,
but his gait remains awkward. Coyote, big dipper, and spider complain
at not being invited, and their songs are added. Hb.)

Eagle Way

Newcomb, 1940a, pp. 50-77. Origin Legend of Navajo Eagle Chant. (N)

Wheelwright, 1945, pp. 1-10. Atsah or Eagle Catching Myth. (W)

The story of Eagle Way falls into two loosely connected sections:
1) the wanderings and marriage contest of White Shell Woman and
Turquoise Woman; 2) the marriage and son-in-law testing of the hero,
followed by his victory over stinging insects and his illness from attempting to eat raw meat. From the first to the second part of the
myth, interest shifts from women as central characters to the hero's
exploits, trials, and finally his successful practice of the newly acquired ritual.

The hero meets his first wives when they are fleeing from the monsters, protects them and brings them home with him; they bring corn
as a present from the gods and grind for him. This happy domestic
arrangement is interrupted by the entrance of corn maidens, who win
a marriage test (tossing cornmeal ball) and take the hero to their home.
Here hs is welcomed deceitfully and undergoes witch father-in-law
trials. As in other versions of this episode, he first demonstrates his
own power by giving the new father-in-law a poisonous smoke and

reviving him; he then disregards the father-in-law's warnings of forbidden territory and meets attacks of cannibal eagle, bird monsters, snake, bear, and finally a test of poisoned food. In each of these he is aided by advice from a supernatural monitor. After thus proving his power, he is taught the eagle trapping ceremony by his father-in-law. Again the hero shows his powers by overcoming stinging insects. After these successes, however, the hero falls into difficulty on a hunting trip with animals whose raw food he cannot eat; he breaks their taboos and is banished from their hunting party. He becomes ill, is rescued by supernaturals and returned to his first wives, where he practices the eagle trapping ceremony he has learned.

This story emphasizes the hero's magical powers and his ability to protect himself. At the opening of the story he is represented as a supernatural (identified with Monster Slayer) who is able to protect White Shell and Turquoise Woman, supplement their meager subsistence, and transform property for their use. Throughout the witch father-in-law trials he demonstrates his courage and power, and at their conclusion subdues stinging insects for his wives' people. In the later events of the story the tables are curiously turned; when he violates the taboo on eating raw meat and becomes ill, the supernaturals have to intervene.

The two versions abstracted below are substantially similar. The points at which Wheelwright's version departs from that of Newcomb are indicated in parentheses.[196]

1. Travels of White Shell and Turquoise Woman

White Shell Woman and Turquoise Woman, created from epidermis rubbed from under the breast of Changing Woman, live on a mountain to avoid the monsters until their supply of wild seeds and berries is exhausted. They reconnoiter, the older sister instructing the younger to go to a mountain top to the north, she herself going to the south. Talking God and Hastse Hogan[197] appear to them; Talking God gives each maiden an ear of corn, the "gift of life" which they are never to give away. They journey to the south, living on small game and wild fruits and naming the numerous places through which they pass and the springs at which they camp. A stranger appears; they are too shy to speak to him but offer him food. They eat together, and he advises that berries and plants are plentiful to the south but that they must follow his instructions to avoid the monsters (spouting water which tricks and drowns strangers; big snakes which swallow strangers; a horned monster; twelve destructive antelopes). He reappears four more times during their wanderings, telling them of large game killed by animals which they can use for food and make into carrying bags.

At his fifth appearance the young man offers to take the maidens to his home on top of the mountain to the south, toward which they have been journeying. There they find a beautiful adobe house colored at the four directions and containing a row of twelve metates and manos. The maidens' curiosity finally gets the better of their shyness and they enter. Preparations are made for bathing and dressing the maidens: the young man makes yucca root suds; he produces beautiful clothing and ornaments from a bundle which magically increases in size when the maidens step over it ritually to the accompaniment of his flute playing; he retires to another room while they bathe and dress; finally he provides them with "long hair and eyebrows, bright eyes and smiling mouths." To his inquiries whether it is corn that they have in their bags, they four times answer in the negative because of the god's instructions. He insists that it is corn, that his grandfather had told him, and asks only a kernel from each. After some indecision, in which the younger sister defers to the older, they give him one kernel from each ear. They grind these two kernels on each of the metates in turn, while the young man plays on his flute, and the corn increases magically to fill a basket. This is repeated four times, and they continue grinding corn thus for four nights while the young man hunts by day.

2. Hero's Marriage to Corn Maidens

A distant fire is sighted at night by means of a forked stick, but the young man searches in vain on three successive days for its source. Two maidens enter, similar in appearance to White Shell and Turquoise Woman, and ask if they can grind the corn they have brought. Monster Slayer[198] asks the first two maidens to relinquish the metates, and the newcomers grind all night while he plays the flute. In the morning they depart. Monster Slayer is anxious to see where they go but they disappear, each leaving only one footprint on the path. They return thrice more; they apologize for using the metates but Monster Slayer welcomes them with the words, "We are alone and it is pleasant to have visitors. You are welcome whenever you want to come." Now better acquainted, on their fourth visit they talk and visit with Monster Slayer. At midnight he proposes a grinding contest to see who will marry him, the test being to toss up a ball of cornmeal and have it land without breaking. White Shell and Turquoise Woman fail, but the visiting corn maidens have surreptitiously added egg to the cornmeal, and their balls do not break. (In Wheelwright's version adding of egg is not mentioned; the means of the corn maidens' success is not indicated.) White Shell and Turquoise Woman are sad at Monster Slayer's departure and wonder how they will be able to get food and live. He leaves his bow and arrow with them and promises to return.

3. Reception by Wives' People

The hero accompanies the corn maidens to their hunting camp. The maidens go ahead to see how their new husband will be received by their family. Their maternal grandfather, Cornsmut Man, objects to having an earth person brought in as son-in-law because they "always break our rules." He is angry at the girls, admonishing them,

"Something like this was to be expected considering the way you girls go out at night. Why can't you stay at home?" But the grandmother scolds him for speaking thus to a new son-in-law who may bring needed things, including a supply of tobacco. (In W, Chief of Game plays the same role as Cornsmut Man.) After long argument, they decide that he may live in a new brush shelter at the east side of the camp. Cornsmut Man welcomes the hero, saying that he is glad to see him, that "Earth People are polite and keep all rules and tenets strictly." Wind monitor has reported the original conversation, so that the hero is not deceived by this flattery but offers the old man a deadly mixture of tobacco, which causes him to fall unconscious. At a request from the grand-mother-in-law, transmitted through his wives, the hero restores the old man ritually and gives him a harmless smoke. The wives prepare food which increases magically to furnish enough for the whole family. Monster Slayer hunts, and on successive days a new shelter is built for him at each of the directions. Each time that they move camp the hero and his wives are sent ahead to make ready a shelter for the old people. Impatient for their arrival, and curious as to how the large quantities of meat will be transported, he returns over the trail and observes how the animal helpers transform themselves into game animals for this purpose.

The camping party arrives at the home of the eagle people. Here, the head man, Hair Turning White, objects to the hero's presence in the same manner as did Cornsmut Man, is similarly persuaded by his wife, given the deadly tobacco and restored. (In W he is known as Eagle Chief and is the brother of Chief of Game.) There follows a series of trials and attempts to dispose of the hero, prepared by Cornsmut Man or Hair Turning White. In the first four of these, the hero disobeys certain prohibitions, thus falling into a dangerous situation from which he emerges victorious. Hair Turning White (in W, Chief of Game) warns him successively not to hunt in each of the four directions; how-ever, it is later stipulated that it is Cornsmut Man who controls the monsters and who has prepared the following tests. Disobeying these instructions and taking a roundabout course to the east, the hero finds eaglets which he brings home intending to raise them for arrow feath-ers; he is warned that the cannibal mother eagle will follow with retri-bution; but in returning them to the nest he sings songs that successfully pacify her. Hair Turning White cannot believe that the hero has sur-vived this trial until he sees him still alive. To the south he finds bird monsters, and the same procedure is repeated. To the west he finds a ripe yucca plant but is frightened away by the hiss of a huge rattlesnake coiled in its center; wind advises him that this is "the old man himself," who will be rendered powerless if he thrusts his doubled fist down the snakes's throat; the snake crawls away and the hero brings back the yucca fruit. Hunting for berries to the north, he meets tracking bear; again warned by wind, he kills the bear with a lightning shaft and cuts off his left paw; when he presents the berries to his wives, they go in fear to their grandfather, wanting to move camp to escape the bear who will now find their camp; but they are pacified when the hero shows the bear's paw as trophy. After these four trials Hair Turning White tests him with poisoned food, but each morning wind whispers where the poison is and the hero avoids that part of the food.

Cornsmut Man expresses his surprise, asking what manner of earth person this is who can successfully pass these tests. He accepts the hero into the family, but first he must learn all the songs and prayers of the Eagle Chant. He is shown the ritual catching of eagles, in a pit with live rabbit as bait, and the distribution of feathers to the appropriate gods. Hair Turning White, who is a witch, belittles Cornsmut Man's powers and offers to teach the hero his version of the ceremony and eagle trapping. His method is to stand at the top of a high bluff, place a flat rock on his head on which the birds will light, and pass spruce or different grasses through a hole in his nose. Cornsmut Man warns that this way is witchcraft and that earth people will get diseases and get into bad habits if they use it. The hero elects to continue with Cornsmut man as his teacher, despite Hair Turning White's demonstration of his power by showing the bones of men he has killed in this way. (In W, Eagle Chief's manner of catching eagles is not specified as witchcraft but merely as magic that "is not good for earth dwellers.")

4. War with Stinging Insects

The eagles have been unsuccessful in driving out a swarm of bees from a nearby field. The hero sprinkles medicine to blind them and then kills them with willow whips. On the promise of an old bee woman to be friendly, he leaves some for honey and for their wax, which will take away pain and heal wounds made by eagles' claws.[199]

5. Raw Meat Inedible

Now restless without anything to do, the hero goes hunting with the animal helpers of his wives' people (white and yellow weasels, rattlesnake, mountain lion, spotted lion, lynx, and wolf). At their camp he is fed their usual fare, raw meat. Not wishing to offend them, he eats it but is made sick during the night and vomits, hiding the vomit by burying it in a pile of earth which serves as lynx's pillow. He is left to guard camp while the animals go hunting unsuccessfully on the four following days. Each night they discuss their failure, finally deciding that the hero must be the cause. They call on hornet, fly and ant people to find out how he has broken the rules, and one persistent ant, after four attempts, discovers the vomit. The hero denies that he is at fault, maintaining that this was lynx's sleeping place. Nevertheless he is banished from the hunting party. (W omits the vomiting incident; instead the hero hides the raw meat without eating it.)

6. Return to Earth

Returning to the eagles' village, he finds no one there and becomes ill. An old man returns and advises him to seek a cure to be paid for with his eagle feathers. The hero makes a series of unsuccessful petitions for cure — to water ox, duck, otter, wolf, yellow weasel, white weasel, mountain lion, lynx, bobcat, hawks, eagles, thunders, all of whom do not want to help even though they have medicine. Swallow agrees to do it. Angered at these refusals, his three brothers — Child of the Water, Reared Within the Earth, and Changing Grandchild—come to his aid. They all travel down to earth together, on the way being given medicine and a feather by owl, and bring the hero to the place from which he started. They advise him to return to his first two wives, White Shell and Turquoise Woman.

The last portion of the myth is devoted to performances of the ceremony. Monster Slayer's first wives are glad to see him on his return. They journey to the sacred mountains together. At one camp he plans an eagle trapping ceremony, which the nearby dove poeple will attend. They build a hogan, and dove man sings while it is being enlarged. The holy ones come and praise it. Talking God expresses approval when he learns that the wives still have the corn he had given them, "It is your symbol of fertility and new life." The hero hunts for meat for the guests. In the ceremony he uses a squirrel as decoy in the eagle trap but is advised that a rabbit should be used instead. The holy ones are paid with the appropriate feathers. They travel again, and at a second ceremony a great storm arises when he enters his newmade eagle trapping pit, which is taken as a sign that it has been made in a forbidden place. (In W the second ceremony is likewise unsuccessful but no storm is specified.) At the next attempt the ceremony is successful. The two original ears of corn are decorated to represent an eagle and turned loose. (In W, instead of the two ears of corn, one of the captured birds is blessed and set free with offerings.) They journey to many other places trying to catch eagles, but none of these attempts is successful as were the first ones. Finally the two women depart for the sacred mountains, and Monster Slayer to Shining Water.

Bead Way

Matthews, 1897, pp. 195-208. The Great Shell of Kintyel. (M)

Reichard, 1939, pp. 26-36. Legend of the Bead Chant. (R)

Wheelwright, 1945, pp. 11-16. Yohe (or Bead) Myth. (W)

Hill and Hill, 1943b, pp. 31-36. The Legend of Navajo Eagle-Catching-Way. (H&H)

Kluckhohn, 1941, pp. 7-9. Episode from Eagle Way Chant Legend. (K)

The story of Bead Way tells how Pueblo people trick a poor Navaho
into a feat of obtaining eaglets from a cliff nest with intention of leaving him stranded there; how the Navaho refuses to harm the eaglets and
is himself transported to the eagles' sky home. Here he meets with a
series of accidents when he disobeys instructions not to stray (shot by
bad eagles, storm, captured by spider, coyote transformation, buried
in rock pile, shot by frogs). Subsequently he is able to aid his protectors; with supernatural help he overcomes the eagles' enemies (stinging insects, weeds, rocks) and is rewarded by offer of marriage and
opportunity to learn the ceremony. With his new powers he returns,
bringing ritual knowledge to his people.

This story combines many of the elements already noted for the
chant myths — the hero's subjection to scorn and bad treatment by
Pueblo aliens, his supernatural rescue, further adventures in which he
disregards warnings and has to be rescued or restored and, finally,
successful wielding of his own powers. In these events the hero appears
first as a helpless tool of the Pueblos, a beggar or slave who is forced
or persuaded to carry out their command to enter the eagle's nest (except in one version where he takes the risk voluntarily). Gradually,
through his adventures and supernatural aid, he gains power and pres-
tige. His ultimate triumph is carried into his return to his own people.
Not only does he teach them the ceremonial knowledge he has learned
from the eagles, but the Pueblos who wronged him are in turn tricked
into contributing their valuables for the ceremony, and the hero ascends
with them to the sky.

Four versions of this story, one published just prior to 1900 and the
others almost a half century later, show agreement in the main outlines and repetition in one or another version of many similar details.
A portion of this same story (the war with stinging insects) is reproduced, in a somewhat altered setting, in a myth fragment of the origin
of Eagle Way (K).[200] Three of the versions are given as the origin
legend of Bead Way (M, R, W), a fourth as explanation of ritual used in
pit-trapping eagles and as part of Bead Way (H&H). In the following
abstract, material from all of these versions is summarized event by
event.[201]

1. Pueblos' Eagle Nest Trickery (M, R, W, H&H)

One version (R) begins by pointing out the connection of the hero of
this story with other mythological figures; he is the oldest of two sons
of Bead Woman, who herself is one of five daughters each born from a
body part (chest, side, back, "spirit") of Changing Woman; he is also
indentified with "Holy Man of the Shooting Chant and other chants."
Another states merely that he is a "boy of the first people created" (W).
At the opening of the story the hero is presented as a poor Navaho beggar (M)[202] or as a captive and slave of the Pueblos (R, W) who has been
starved for four nights after capture (W) or who is forced to do hard
work and fed only scraps (R). The pueblos have discovered a nest of

eaglets on an inaccessible rock ledge or cave below an overhanging cliff.[203] They locate it, by sighting through a forked stick the landing place of an eagle, and find that it contains two eaglets (M). They propose to lower the Navaho into the nest in a basket and after he has thrown down the eaglets to leave him stranded there (M, R, H&H). The Navaho is persuaded to attempt this feat on the promise of food (M, W),[204] or simply because as their captive he is forced to do what they wish (R). In one version (H&H) the Navaho is not a captive in the power of the Pueblos but makes his own decision to attempt the feat despite suspicion of their trickery. In this case the Jemez offer a visiting Navaho riches and power (jewelry, horses, and a voice in their affairs, even that he be made head of a neighboring Pueblo) if he will obtain the eaglets. The Navaho at first refuses but then consults his brother, asking him to decide whether he should undertake the feat; he and the brother build a sweathouse in which they discuss the plan; the brother is of the opinion that "even though the Pueblos deceived him, the Navajo would benefit," and would be able to collect his reward. The brothers come together to Jemez where a feast is being prepared for them and warn the Jemez that if they are contemplating trickery, steps will be taken to right the wrong.

In accomplishing this feat the Navaho receives supernatural aid and advice. On the way to the cliff he is given prayersticks and medicine plants by supernaturals as he hangs behind the party that is escorting him (W), or is warned by various medicine people (plants) (R). Wind (M) or the gods whom wind has told of his predicament (R) [205] come to warn him of the Pueblos' trickery, that if he throws down the eaglets they will leave him stranded there. In one case he is dissuaded from throwing down the eaglets when he discovers that they are men (H&H); in another the Pueblo trickery is not made explicit, but he is told that he "will never leave this place" if he throws down the eaglets (W). He refuses to throw them down despite the pleas and promises of the Pueblos. At first they call him by kinship terms in their entreaty (M). On each of the succeeding three days they return, first trying to persuade and to bribe the Navaho and finally threatening, reviling, and shooting at him (M, R, W). They send fire arrows into the nest (M, R).

2. Protected by Eagles (M, R, W, H&H)

Meanwhile, the eaglets recognize him as a friend. They scatter feathers (M, R) or dust from their feathers (W) on the people below, thus causing disease. Where the feathers touch they cause skin irritation like the sting of an ant, which develops into sores as punishment for what they have plotted against the hero and eaglets (R). In the eagle's nest the starving hero doesn't touch the eaglets' food (M, W), although in one case he finds a prairie dog brought by the parent eagles and cooks it on a fire made by rubbing together twigs from the nest (R). He is kept warm by the eaglets' wings (R) or by sleeping between them (M), but in one version he sleeps cold on the edge of the nest because at first

they are afraid of him (W). On their return the parents are grateful for
his treatment of their children (M, R, W, H&H); they feed him cornmeal
and water (M, R, W, H&H), the fact that it is cooked making it suitable
for a human (R). The water is brought in a jointed plant stalk (M, R,
W, H&H); the food is served in an inexhaustible bowl (M, H&H), which
is emptied by one sweep of the eagle's finger (M). In one version the
hero asks for water but the father eagle directs him to eat first (M).[206]

3. Sky Visit (M, R, W, H&H, K)

The hero is transported through the sky hole to the home of the
eagles.[207] This happens after he has stayed in the eagle's nest four
days (M, W, R, H&H). At first the birds (hawks and eagles) who have
gathered for this purpose start to dress him in an eagle garment but
they discard this method of getting him out of the nest (M). The eagles
fly up in a spiral to the sky hole with the hero (W, H&H) supported by
lightning (H&H), sunbeam and rainbow (M), or enclosed in a cloud or in
robes of darkness, dawn and after glow, with a crystal for light and a
reed or horn through which he can breathe (R, W). The birds are not
able to take him through the sky hole because they grow weary (M, H&H)
or because their wings have become wet from the cloud (R). They have
to call on others for help on the final lap—arrow snakes (M); lightning
and arrow snakes paid with eagle feathers (R); racer snakes (W);
lightning, arrow snakes and fringed mouth (H&H). The birds let the
hero drop and he is caught up by the arrow snakes (M, R, H&H). Usually
the arrow snakes are able to complete the trip when the birds fail, but
in one version they too fail and are replaced by fringed mouth, who
places his hat on the hero and takes him "to the sky like wind" (H&H).

In the sky land he finds four pueblos of animals and birds, one at
each of the directions (M, R, W, K). These houses, arranged around a
central plaza with a spring, are all beautiful except that to the north
where live various birds who had not helped the hero (R). He is advised not to visit this pueblo to the north (M, W) where chicken hawk and
other "bad characters" dwell (M), where the largest eagles and buzzards live (W). In their sky home the eagles take off their feather suits
and appear in human form (M, W, H&H), as they had also done in the
eaglets' nest (M, H&H).

Events in the sky home of the birds may be divided into two groups:
a) a series of catastrophes consequent upon the hero's disregard of
warnings; b) his defeat of stinging insects, tumbleweeds, etc. Events
of the first type appear in only two versions (R, W), while the latter are
included in four versions (M, R, W, K).[208]

4. Disobedience of Instructions (R, W)

The hero stays in the eagles' house to the east (R, W). The birds
go hunting each day and the small game they bring back is magically
turned into large game for the hero's food (R). He is given instructions

not to leave the house while they are away (R, W) but to stay inside and cook beans and corn (R). He disobeys these instructions not to wander and on successive days meets with various accidents from which the birds have to rescue him.[209] On the first day he needs water for cook-ing and thoughtlessly goes out to get some from the spring in the cen-tral plaza (R). The people from the house to the north shoot him (R, W). The eagles cure him on their return (R, W). They find him help-less with arrows in his foot, hip, back, and in the back of his head; they fear that Talking God "will never forgive" them if he is harmed and cannot return to earth; their offerings to his attackers, turkey buzzard and black eagle, are not successful until big fly tells the proper offer-ings and until a sandpainting is made (R). After accepting these offer-ings in the proper manner (placing the tobacco on his foot) black eagle protests that big fly must have furnished the information, but big fly denies this (R).

The hero tips over a water jar which he finds when straying, against instructions, to the house at the south; a black cloud escapes and causes rain and angers the eagles, who have to stop it by setting the jar upright (W). In the other version of this incident (R) he is warned specifically not to touch the blue water jars, but he opens them in curiosity and thus causes a hard rain on earth which he cannot stop; frightened at this he runs away, is caught by spider (male) and drawn up to the ceiling in his web. The eagles call on Black God (god of fire) to help rescue him; despite spider's protestations of innocence Black God threatens to burn spider's house. He is deaf to spider's plea for mercy: "Since you are deceiving me, I shall not listen to your plea." When his fire reaches the strings of the web, the hero is released. In the end Black God ac-cepts spider's offerings of prayersticks and hoops and has water sprin-kler stop the fire.

In the next adventure the hero again strays outside; Coyote springs at and touches him, thus turning him into a coyote (R, W). On their return the eagles find that his tracks turn into coyote tracks and at the end of them they find him, scabby and disreputable (R), or fly points out the poor skinny coyote to them (W). He is ritually put through hoops four times until the coyote skin is pushed back and falls off and he fin-ally stands revealed as a human again (R, W).

Again he disregards warnings to leave the house and is buried when he sits on a rock pile trap prepared by swallow (R). The eagles track him and, with the help of hunting people (mountain lion, wolf, lynx, bob-cat, badger), dig out his bones. These are treated ritually, laid on un-wounded deer skin together with feathers and covered with another skin, to restore him to life (R). In place of this adventure the Wheelwright version substitutes an encounter with frogs and toads: he wanders to the river and is shot in the joints by their arrows so that he is lamed and cannot move; again the eagles treat him with hoops to draw out the arrows and restore him (W).

5. War with Stinging Insects (M, R, W, K)

This is the most constant element in the various versions of the sky visit. The eagle warriors go out to unsuccessful battle with stinging insects, weeds, and other enemies (M, R, W, K), in which many of their number are killed or wounded (M, R). The hero follows against their instructions (M, R) or against the warning of spider (K). Three times the eagles scold him for following but he still persists (M). "He wants to go pretty bad. Thinks there is a lot of fun in it" (K). He meets spider, who gives him magical aid and tells him how to overcome the eagles' enemies (M). He comes upon the home of spider woman, a smoke hole in the ground with a ladder leading into it; she is described as a strange looking old woman with a big mouth and uneven protruding teeth that are curved like bear claws;[210] she belittles the strength of the enemies and tells him how to overcome them by spitting the juice of a special plant at them (bees) and by use of her cane (tumbleweeds), gives instructions for saving some of the bees' nests and tumbleweed seeds to take to earth, and asks the hero to get new feathers for her hoops from the eagles who die in battle (M). In another version spider man gives him a feather to travel on and a wand to cure the wounded eagles, tells him how to kill the bees with a rabbit brush, but also gives instructions to leave one pair alive to be sent to earth (W). In a third version spider has merely warned him not to go to battle; it is big fly who tells him how to defeat the enemies (K).

The hero overcomes the enemies of the eagles in one encounter, or on successive days — bees and tumbleweeds (M); bees, tumbleweeds, rocks, grass (R); bees, wasps, swallows, rolling weed (W); yellow wasps, flat rocks, weeds (K). He goes out onto the battlefield after the retreat of the eagles and magically defeats the enemies (M, R, K) according to instructions from spider or big fly (M, K). The bees are defeated by spitting the juice of a special plant to stun them and render their stings harmless (M), by hitting them with the rabbit brush and giving the eagle call (W) or by chewing and using rabbit brush as a whip (K). The tumbleweeds or grass are swept into a pile and burned (M, R, K). A cedar club is used against the rock enemies (K); they are pounded into small pieces (R). He gathers the feathers of the slain birds (M, R), restores the dead or wounded (R, W), and brings spider woman the feathers she has requested (M). He returns to the eagles' home, where they are mourning for their slain relatives (M). He brings them back trophies — two young bumblebees with their feet tied together which he swings around his head, frightening them, but after four repetitions they are no longer frightened by this demonstration (M); or the head wasp, whom he stuns and brings back for the birds to kill, the last big rock and a big weed (K). From each of the encounters he saves some token to be sent to earth people: he leaves one pair of bees alive to send to earth (W); the two young bumblebees brought back as trophies and some tumbleweed seed are sent through the sky hole with the admonition that they are to multiply for earth people but not to become harmful or he will again destroy them (M); the hive and young bees, the tumbleweed and grass seeds, and the pounded rocks for sandpainting[211] are dropped through the sky hole for earth people (explanation of origin of bees and tumbleweed) (R).

6. Marriage to Eagles (M, R, W, H&H, K)

The eagles are grateful (K) and want to reward him (M, R). In gratitude they offer their most precious gift, that he stay with them and marry one of their young girls, but he is advised by wind not to accept this offer until after he has returned to earth if he wishes to see his family again (R). In the other versions this condition is not placed on his marriage among the eagles; he simply marries an eagle as a requirement for being taught Eagle Way (K); they make him a chief and he marries an eagle girl (W); or the chiefs of the four pueblos each promise him two of their beautiful daughters in marriage, and he is attended by his new wives in a beautiful pueblo house where they bathe, feed him, and prepare his bed (M). In the eagles's sky home he learns the ceremony (songs, prayers, offerings, paraphernalia, sandpaintings) which is Bead Way (M, R, W); Eagle Way (K) (here learned before the encounter with stinging insects); or both Bead Way and Eagle-catching-way (H&H), and has it performed over him (W). The hero returns to earth on a sunbeam (K); he is taken to his home by the eagles (H&H), or is dressed in eagle plumage so that he can descend from the sky (M, R, W).

7. Return to Earth (M, R. W, H&H, K)

The hero's family has been mourning for him and are glad to see him (R); the version in which he discussed plans with his brother beforehand stresses his joy at seeing this brother again (H&H). He finds the odors of his own people intolerable and sits outside their lodge until a medicine lodge is built where he may sit by himself (M). He teaches the ceremony to his younger brother (M, R, W, H&H). The brother is taught while the hero is performing the ceremony over Pueblo chiefs who are suffering from infection received when they tried to attack the eagles' nest (R). After teaching the brother, he holds a ceremony over him to initiate him (R, W), and then returns to the sky to live with his eagle wife (R). In the fragmentary version teaching of the ceremony is not specifically stated but may be implied: the hero himself becomes sick because of the killing he has done in the sky;[212] he is cured by an Eagle Way ceremony put up for him by his earth wife's people which he directs with the help of big fly (K).

8. Revenge for Pueblo Trickery (M, R, W, H&H)

The remainder of the story is occupied with revenge taken on the Pueblos for their trickery. Bead Way with a fire dance is held for the

Pueblos by the brother who has just learned it (M, R, W); this ceremony is to cure the disease contracted by contact with the eaglets'
scattered feathers (M). In one version Bead Way is not performed, but
the brothers attend the fire dance of a Mountain Way to which the Jemez
have also been invited (H&H). The hero has remained among earth
people for this ceremony (M, W, H&H) or returns unrecognized from
the sky (R). Revenge is achieved by requiring the Pueblos to contribute
valuables to the ceremony; the hero dances with these jewels in the fire
dance of the last night and ascends to the sky carrying the Pueblo treasure with him. Now, from his experience with the eagles, the hero has
become sleek, well fed, and "molded in beauty in his face and form,"
and the Pueblos do not suspect his identity with the poor beggar they
had left to die (M). With the valuables obtained from the Pueblos the
younger brother intends to pay the hero for teaching him the ceremony,
thus serving the double purpose of payment for the ceremony and revenge for the Pueblos' trickery (R). The Pueblos loan jewels in return
for eagle feathers for an act in the fire dance of the last night (W,
H&H). The Pueblos try to substitute imitation valuables (beads and red
feather bonnet) (R) or to withhold their largest shells (M), but with the
aid of the returned hero or of wind monitor the real jewels are insisted
upon. Whatever the pretence or means of obtaining the Pueblo treasure,
in the dance of the last night the hero ascends to the sky with it (M, R,
W, H&H), despite their laments (M, H&H), entreaties or vain attempts
to pull and shoot him down (R, M). The gods quarrel over the valuables
thus obtained but finally each receives some share (R).

In three versions the ascent with Pueblo valuables is explicitly
phrased as retaliation for their original trickery (M, R, H&H). In a
fourth version (W), this motive is obscured. Here there is no direct
mention of the intention of the Pueblos to leave the hero stranded in the
eagles' nest; the eaglets scatter dust disease over them but the final
ceremony is not specified as cure for the disease thus contracted; after
the hero's ascent with their jewels he throws down in return medicine
herbs for their use. With the evidence of the other three versions, it
may be assumed that retaliation properly underlies the action here as
well.[213]

In two versions (M, R) there appears an interpolated element in
preparation for the fire dance performance of the last night of this ceremony. Invitations are sent out by messenger to surrounding Navahos
to participate in the acts of the last night. These messengers meet
others on a similar mission from another ceremony; they exchange
quivers as token that they have met. In one case they cannot persuade
the other group to come (M), while in the other, both groups agree to
attend the fire dance of the other (R). The refusal to attend is given as
explanation of why the last night of Bead Way now has only a few dances
(M), or it may be specified that henceforth the fire dance is not to be
held as part of Bead Way (R, W), or that Bead Way singers may not be
asked to perform at a fire dance (H&H).

Flint Way

Haile, 1943, 319 pp. Origin Legend of the Navaho Flintway.

   Version A: informant Slim Curly of Crystal, N.M., recorded
                winter 1930-31. (Ha)

   Version B: informant Curly of Parallel Streams clan of Chinlee,
                Ariz., recorded winter 1929-30. (Hb)

Newcomb and Reichard, 1937, pp. 39-40. Myth of Male Shooting Chant.
(N&R)

Reichard, 1939, pp. 68-71. Navajo Medicine Man. (R)

     Two major and independent episodes form the bulk of the Flint Way
legend: a) the destruction of the hero in retaliation for his adultery
with thunder's wife; his subsequent ceremonial restoration by gila
monster, and his successful survival of thunder's further tests; and
b) the trip to the home of buffalo people where the hero is this time
able to withstand the attack of the original husband on his buffalo wives.
Although similar in theme, these two episodes remain separable in the
plot construction.
     In these adventures of the Flint Way hero it is again unclear to what
extent trials are provoked by his own daring and to what extent visited
upon him through no fault of his own. He first meets disaster when he
hunts on forbidden territory and/or commits adultery with thunder's
wife. The extent of his responsibility for the latter act is left unclear;
although he makes advances in asking to accompany the young woman
home, it is not until the next morning that he learns that she is thunder's
wife. On his next hunting expedition he is shattered by thunder. In the
subsequent ritual restoration with help of supernaturals, the hero is
given power to pass thunder's future tests and thus prove his "holiness."
Thus, regardless of the nature of provocation, these trials result in the
hero's accumulation of power to protect himself.
     In a second sexual adventure with buffalo women the hero is able to
withstand the angry husband's attack. Here, too, it is not clear to what
extent he is responsible for his involvement and to what extent he is
drawn into this episode by the woman. Earlier he has spent the night
with an unknown woman, but it is noted specifically that this is not
considered a sexual excess. Later the same woman, in the form of a
buffalo, entices the hunter to her home. On arrival in the buffalo country he is attacked by her offended husband but saves himself by magic
provided by supernaturals, and causes slaughter of the buffalos. Here
again the hero demonstrates his power by reviving the buffalos. After
return he teaches his ceremonial knowledge to his own people.
     The following abstract is based on the complete story given in Haile's
Version A, with elaborations or contradictions from Version B as

indicated. The encounter with buffalo people occurs also in two published versions of the Shooting Way legend (N&R, R), which have been
included in the abstract of this portion of the story.

1. Adultery and Attack by Thunder (Ha, Hb)

In a wandering family of mother, father, older daughter, and two
sons, the older son is an able and careful hunter, never killing game
wantonly. In his travels alone he meets a handsome young woman on
her way for water, who consents to his request to accompny her home.
He finds that she has been making cotton garments and shoes and is
evidently industrious. Only after he has spent the night does he learn
that she is white thunder's wife. On returning home the hero's hunting
is unsuccessful. Starting out on a new hunting expedition he instructs
his family where he will meet them. He ambushes mountain sheep,
draws his bow but is mysteriously unable to shoot until the fourth attempt. The animal he has killed has no left eye and its left horn is
marked by lightning. While he is skinning and cleaning it, a fierce
storm suddenly arises in which the hero is struck by lightning and
"shattered beyond recognition," so that nothing can be seen "but a
stream of blood flowing away." The hero's family waits in vain and
that night his father is worried and sleepless wondering what has happened. Talking God makes his call and appears to inform them by
gestures that their son has been destroyed by white thunder for committing adultery with his wife. Later white thunder also destroys his
own wife; see below. The family is grief stricken. Talking God can
offer no suggestion because he himself fears white thunder. (In Version B the hero is Holy Young Man, oldest son in two sets of twins born
to Sun and white locust woman, who lives with her two elder brothers
and her mother's mother. Here the provocation for his destruction by
thunder is simply that he enters forbidden ground while tracking a
deer.[214] After reporting this news Talking God calls a consultation of
the gods. The hero's family asks for help, protesting that he cannot
be left thus: "A bad situation must eventually arise, if this condition
is allowed to continue!" But the gods cannot help.)

2. Restoration (Ha)

Big fly, who acts as doorguard of gila monster, informs them, on
promise of keeping secret the source of this information, that gila monster knows what to do. Offerings are made to gila monster four times,
with an extra bundle added on each trial. To the family's sorrow, these
offerings are ignored until big fly gives instructions for their proper
preparation and presentation. Although suspecting who has told the
secret of his sacrifice, gila monster accepts and smokes tobacco from
the offering. However, despite being urged to hurry, he takes his time
in coming to the ceremonial gathering. The hero's family weep in
sorrow and apprehension that he cannot restore their son.

Gila monster's procedure is to cut himself up and have the parts scattered, reassembled, and revived ritually as example for the restoration of the hero. First he makes offerings to thunder and other natural phenomena. His parts are scattered and reassembled, including his blood, spread on a fabric; wind goes through them to give breath, sunlight shines to restore the power of winking; his two agate pouches step over the assemblage ritually, and he revives. Likewise the hero's parts are collected, including his blood gathered by ants, nerves replaced by spiders, eyes and ears by Sun, body and head hair by noon and darkness people, face by dawn people, mind by Talking God and pollen boy, his "travelling means" by cornbeetle girl. Thus the hero is restored, but thunder's participation is necessary to enable him to move; he is summoned by an offering, and after a storm and lightning similar to the one in which he was destroyed, the hero arises. Thunder performs ritual procedures and sings. Lastly Sun restores the hero's tears and replaces his eye nerves; wind people cause his nerves and whole interior to move. He is brought home on a stretcher prepared by spider, weaving, and bird people. Songs are sung throughout these ritual procedures.

At home the hero recovers and begins to travel about again, but his father worries about the fact that he is still "frail and pale in color." Gila monster is summoned again and agrees that more ceremonial treatment is necessary, the dark circle of flint and of boughs (different from the ordinary brush corral). Details of the ceremony thus performed by gila monster are given. Gila monster warns the hero that white thunder still holds the same grudge against him, that "he has not forgiven you the adultery committed with his wife." Although he will not come to harm in this way, the hero is urged to prepare himself with medicines because it is not known by what means white thunder may fight him. Some of the songs sung at this time identify the patient's courage with that of Monster Slayer. During the procedures the patient swoons, thus indicating the effectiveness of the ceremony. In one of the acts of the bough circle, the dancing of birds with spruce and pine trees destroys the spectators; while they dance "the flesh of the people who had gathered there appeared as red specks around the center of those spruce trees," and after four rounds of dancing "nothing was left of the former crowd of people inside." (This incident is given as the reason for omitting the bough circle today.) These people are restored by gathering their parts and having gila monster step over them ritually. Saying that perhaps evil things are operating to cause this, gila monster calls for rain; protesting, the birds run for shelter from the rain of flints that results. After conclusion of the ceremony the hero remains for four nights after the spectators have left.

3. White Thunder's Tests and Further Travels

Back with his family the hero again hunts with some success. He spends the night with a beautiful woman whom he finds sitting under a

spruce tree.[215] In his wanderings a messenger comes to him from gila
monster to warn again that white thunder is still plotting against him
and to give him more songs for this. He meets crane and spider people.
The rumbling of white thunder is heard challenging the hero to demonstrate his sacred power. He passes the tests of walking on a cactus-
like line of flints with the help of spider webs and of identifying mountains with the help of wind monitor. White thunder is satisfied that the
hero is holy, no longer holds a grudge, and sends him home. At this
time white thunder also destroys the home of his own wife by lightning.

The hero meets various people in his travels. He sees the crane
people gathering medicine plants which turn into meat. When it is discovered that a crane baby has grass stuck in his throat, the hero is offered six songs from Shooting Way in exchange for curing him, but when
the curing has been effected it is found that Coyote has stolen all but
one of the songs. He complains to the crane people that some of the
songs are missing, and in the enumeration that follows it is discovered
that two sets — one from Flint Way and one from Male Shooting Way —
are alike. On the way home he hears songs of Sun and the singing of
medicine plants. After these events the hero returns home and moves
about with his family; the places to which they travel are enumerated.

4. Trip with Buffalos (Ha, Hb, R, N&R)

One moring the hero's sister sights strange creatures lying at the
lake shore and wakes her brother. He takes bow and arrow and tracks
them, keeping them in sight but unable to reach them or head them off;
they are apparently leading him on. When these creatures, who are
buffalos, come to a moist place they "trample the water out" by stepping on it; when they sniff or bite off plants these turn to medicines.
(The hero at first mistakes his quarry for mountain sheep but discovers
that they are four buffalos — black, white, blue, and yellow [R]. Or,
after a dream of killing four deer he goes hunting without success but
meets four handsome strangers, two men and two women, who reveal
themselves as buffalos when they stop to eat together [N&R].)

At night while the hero sleeps, the buffalos return; two of them bring
their robes, lie down on either side of him, and wake him to ask why he
is following them. One of these is the buffalo woman with whom he
slept previously. She says that they have come for him because "at
that time, you had great plans for me but deceived me." She gives him
her younger sister also as wife because she "did not trust to do it alone,"
and he has intercourse with them both. Next morning he is ill — per-
spiring, dark before his eyes, weak, and unable to rise. The buffalos
cure him with male and female plants that grow up where they urinate.
They feed him from baskets filled with medicine, which turns to meat
and gruel, and sprinkle him with water. (In another version [R] he acquires wives differently; the white and yellow female buffalos are given
to him by the black and blue male buffalos. He has fever, sweating, and
headache because he had not remained continent for four days after the

Shooting Chant held over him, and is cured with herbs that grow where the buffalos lie down and warm the earth.

The hero is provided with a buffalo hide "blown onto him" as means of travel. During the trip he becomes apprehensive, wondering where and why he has come. (The surrounding mountains are forbidden because they are ranges of the buffalo; the hero takes pride in venturing into such tabooed spots, "for he reasoned that he always came back restored and richer in lore for Earth People" [N&R].)

They approach the buffalo home and his reception there appears precarious. His wife points out the four principal buffalos — Abalone Woman (male), Buffalo Woman, Horned Chief, Buffalo Calf — and warns that her husband Abalone Woman is a great one who knows no mercy. After consultation with her people she invites him inside, announcing that "things have become known." The hero has with him for protection "a live one's plume" given him by spider woman. (In version Hb Abalone Woman is the father of the hero's wives; Horned Chief is the husband. The hero waits outside while his wives try to persuade their father to receive their earth surface husband; their mother finally believes their petition and offers to depart, thus instituting the mother-in-law taboo as a means of showing respect [Hb]. When the hero enters his father-in-law admonishes him for the great fault he has committed in taking the wives of such an important person as their chief [Hb]. In Reichard's version the hero has taken the wives of Buffalo Who Never Dies [R]. His new father-in-law is chief of all the buffalo people; the family is angry that he has taken their women [R]. They give him food, however, and his father-in-law asks what means of protection he has and is satisfied when the hero shows his arrows, wands, and sacred soil, saying, "You seem to know how to take care of yourself" [R]. During this conversation he can hear his mother-in-law talking although he has never seen her [R].)[216]

5. Attack by Buffalos (Ha, Hb, N&R)

Abalone Woman is reported as going wild and intending to spare no one; together with the other three chiefs he (Abalone Woman) begins to kill all the buffalos that inhabit the country until blood runs in streams. He then challenges the hero to come up on the mountain; at each of his four charges the hero saves himself with the live one's plume, floating away by means of it and leaving the mountain where he was standing shattered in spray by the buffalo's charge. At the fourth charge the hero shoots Abalone Woman and the other three chiefs are felled by this same shot. (The attack and destruction of buffalo people is reported somewhat differently in other versions. The morning after their arrival the sun rises as a red glare indicating danger; the hero takes his two wives to a mountain top to avoid the anger of Buffalo Who Never Dies and there escapes his four rushing attacks by means of his magic arrows and wands, moving from one mountain to another on a sunbeam [R]. When the hero finally kills him, all of the buffalo people, except his two wives, are also destroyed since he embodies all of their lives; thus indirectly it is the hero who has caused their deaths [R]. In Version Hb also it is the hero himself who kills the buffalo people and Horned Chief. A briefer version of the incident says merely that, because of the hero's venturing into forbidden places, the buffalo people with whom he was staying were attacked and many were killed [N&R].)

6. Restoration of Buffalos. (Ha, R, N&R)

The hero is instrumental in restoring the buffalos. When petitioned for help he directs his father-in-law to extract his arrow from Abalone Woman in a certain manner with song, which revives him. The other buffalos are revived by tapping with foot or hand and then requested to walk to the east single file to see if they have been properly restored. All the people move to the east and back and are found to be fully restored. A single buffalo found out in the valley is likewise revived. (The hero sits with bowed head in remorse for killing the buffalos; his wives embrace him, accusing him of responsibility for their relatives' death and pleading with him to revive them [R]. Telling the women not to look or his powers would fail, he pulls out the four weapons he has shot into Buffalo Who Never Dies, at the same time rubbing his moccasin dust into him and praying; when thus revived the buffalo chief acknowledges the hero's greater power and says he may have the two women [R]. The hero then tells the chief how to restore the other buffalos, which is accomplished with the exception of one whose restoration was spoiled by the fact that one of the wives disobeyed and looked for a moment; this last one is restored ceremonially by turkey buzzards [R]. Or, it is simply stated that when his help was asked, the hero restored the buffalos in return for arrow medicines, and sandpaintings [N&R].)

The whole party resumes its travels toward the east, on the way playing at shooting arrows and restoring each other and singing. Finally they arrive at a stream where the hero has to turn back; he is warned by his monitor that if he crosses he will belong to the buffalos. This is the last time that buffalo people are seen in human form. (Talking God gives him a similar warning, that if he tries to cross he may be devoured by water oxen, that his powers will not be effective on the other side of the stream, and that if he crosses he will not return to his own family [R]. Although the hero "did not heed the warning of most people he met, he listened to Talking God..." [R]. A third version departs from this pattern: The buffalos bring the hero back to his own country; on the way they become unable to proceed and he magically restores their strength with four hoops tied with life feathers [N&R]. A woman gives birth to his child which has a human head and buffalo's body; "after due consideration the Buffalos decided to keep it and by stepping over it, made it all buffalo" [N&R].)

7. Return Home from the Buffalo Country (Ha, Hb)

On his way home the hero becomes lost in darkness. Talking God gives him a hat to make things visible; each time he fans his face with it, light appears and he is able to see again. He comes to a rock cliff with no passageway down; he descends by climbing down a tree. At the foot of this cliff Talking God appears and requests his hat.

At home again the hero still feels indisposed and wishes another ceremony, for which gila monster is summoned. The details of this and a subsequent ceremony are recounted, together with instructions for the preparation of equipment and medicines. On a final journey the hero meets Holy Young Man of Shooting Way; they address each other as older and younger brother and exchange information about their respective ceremonies. (It is specified that certain medicine and equipment are similar in both chants and may be used interchangeably [Hb].) The hero performs the ceremony over three of his younger brothers,[217] at the same time teaching it to them. (Or he teaches it to his younger brother and sister and departs to the shore of Wide River [Hb].)

Ghostway Ritual of Male Shooting Way

Haile, 1950, pp. 1-288. Legend of the Ghostway Ritual in the Male Branch of Shootingway.

The story of the ghostway ritual of Shooting Way is principally concerned with evasion of witchcraft or restoration from its effects. In general ghostway rituals, which exist for several other chants, are directed at removing the "ugly conditions" created by the use of witchcraft; they are concerned with native as contrasted with Enemy Way, which is also conducted according to ghostway ritual but which is concerned with ghosts of aliens.[218]

This story is a continuation of the Shooting Way narrative following the episode of the buffalo journey.[219] Holy Young Man is the hero and he is aided by his brother Holy Boy. The myth is brief and contains three episodes: the hero's successful evasion of attacks by his witch father-in-law; his transformation by Coyote; and his bewitchment by Coyote. The first two episodes are familiar, but the third does not appear elsewhere in this series of myths.

The setting and trials of the witch father-in-law episode are similar to those which follow the hero's hollow log trip in Plume Way, although they are here reported in greater detail. The hero explores to the four directions in defiance of his new father-in-law's warnings; he is attacked by bear, snake, and thunder and tricked on hunting expeditions. The father-in-law is said to practice incest with his daughter, but she aids the hero by warnings and by furnishing the secret of her father's name which is used to combat his evil power. Although the popular Navaho term for witchcraft is not used, the father-in-law's activity is described

as a "stealthy attempt at control of the course of events by foul means,"
which is identified as witchery.[220] Following the hero's marriage Coyote
transforms him in order to steal his wife,[221] but his actions arouse the
wife's suspicions. The hero's brother searches for him and obtains the
help of supernaturals to restore him by being passed ceremonially
through hoops. But there is still ill will between Coyote and the hero,
who is annoyed when he hears that Coyote wishes to assume a name
similar to his own. Angered by the hero's threats, Coyote twice directs
witchcraft against him. This is first combatted with the help of birds
who shoot tree arrows into Coyote's anus, but later a ceremony is required to kill the "former ghost of coyote" and restore the hero.

The following abstract is summarized from the free translation of
Haile's text recording. Details of ceremonial procedure have been
omitted from the abstract.

1. Father-in-law Trials

The hero (Holy Man) travels with his group (his brother and two sisters) to pinnacle-that-reaches-the-sky. Three times he sights a distant
fire at night "prompted by a desire to learn whose fire it was and what
people might be living there." He seeks in vain until the fourth time
when he finds a snake. The "informant at his earfolds" tells him that
this is a home, whose entrance is through the snake's mouth, and gives
him the proper words to enter safely through the endless snake guards.
Within he finds an old man, his wife, and a beautiful young woman who
is working at a "designed robe." The old man admonishes that "earth
surface man is not allowed here," but the hero is nevertheless greeted
as son-in-law and the old man sends his wife away. "Socalled sex
jealousy" immediately enters the old man's mind "because his daughter
is also his wife."

The hero refuses the tobacco of his host, whom he now addresses as
granduncle rather than father-in-law, and smokes his own. The old man
asks four times for some of his tobacco and when given it falls unconscious. The young woman runs to tell her mother, who offers a snake
garment in return for his restoration. This procedure is repeated three
more times until he has won bow and arrows and a total of four garments,
and the old man is finally able to smoke without harm. The old man
tries to substitute his pouch with poisoned tobacco, but the hero is
warned of the trickery by his informant.

That night the hero sleeps with the young woman, but to her father's
questioning the next morning she answers that he did not bother her.
She warns the hero of her father's trickery, that he uses snake, bear,
thunder, and wind transformations, and tells him the secret of his name.
The hero sets out to the east in violation of the father-in-law's instructions. He quiets the doorguards — snakes, bat, and rabbit — by gifts of the
garments and arrows won from the old man. On this expedition he
climbs a mountain where he finds yucca fruit and meets a snake. His
informant warns that this is the old man and instructs him to feel

around in the snake's mouth and call his name to render him powerless.
On his return home he finds the old man, who admonishes him for disobeying instructions. He claims that he saw only the yucca fruit which
he has brought back.

A similar procedure is repeated three more times. The hero spends
each night with the young woman without having intercourse. He is
warned not to go to the west, south, and north but disobeys. To the west
he finds choke cherries and meets the old man in the guise of a bear,
whom he turns away again by calling his name and putting a hand in his
mouth. On his return the hero protests that it is folly to forbid a place
"where ripe things are plentiful." To the south the old man tracks deer
with him. His pride is hurt when the hero kills four bucks, and he summons a thunder storm which is dissipated by the hero's offerings. To
the north the old man hunts mountain sheep with him, and tries to trap
him in a box canyon to be killed by a white bear. His informant warns
him not to carry the venison in the hide nor to take the lead on the way
home or he will become crippled. On each of these three mornings the
hero has been offered poisoned food which he is warned to avoid. At
home the old man now admits that the hero is more powerful. On the
fifth night, at the conclusion of these trials, the hero has intercourse
with the young woman and is now a son-in-law.

2. Coyote Transformation

The hero visits his brother and sisters and promises to return to
them after hunting. He does not tell them of his marriage. Meanwhile
Coyote wants to steal the hero's wife. When he returns to his wife, he
is told that Coyote has inquired after him. His angry response, "What
a fool of a coyote is talking anyway," provokes Coyote, who overtakes
him while hunting and transforms him by blowing his hide onto him.
He is unsuccessful at hunting with the hero's equipment, and this
arouses the wife's suspicions, together with his careless treatment of the
stalking outfit, his ravenous eating, and disregard of etiquette. He inquires what is being made in the other room and asks the women to
bring him some of it.[222] She cannot spend the night with him because of
the strong odor of coyote urine and returns to her mother.

The hero's younger brother, Holy Boy, is worried when he does not
return in four nights. He tracks him to the new wife's home and, mis-
taking him for the hero because of his similarity in appearance, the
mother-in-law runs into the rear room. The brother finds evidences of
the coyote transformation. With the help of supernaturals — wind, big
fly, Sun, moon, winds, ye-killer, "who draws a (flint) knife," Monster
Slayer, and Born for Water — the hero is passed through hoops and the
coyote skin thus stripped off. Thunders, winds, and cornbeetle restore
his speech, mind, and motion. In his anger the hero wants to kill Coyote
but is dissuaded for fear of his witchery. Instead he blows the skin back
onto Coyote, whereupon his own garments drop off. Both the hero and
his garments have to be cleansed of the coyote odor by bathing.[223]

3. Bewitched by Coyote

The hero is still preoccupied with the harm Coyote has done him. Talking God reports that Coyote wants to be called "holy young man" because he is ashamed of his own name, "roamer." The hero protests, "Does this roamer consider himself fit to have the same name as I have? Does he threaten to rob me of my name?" The hero threatens to "shoot him up" on sight but is warned by Talking God not to make trouble because Coyote is directed by First Man and First Woman and is powerful. On returning home he complains that Coyote has "protecting interference." Calling God similarly advises against bothering Coyote, but the hero is still "somewhat sorry about it." Talking God gives him two songs to pacify him.

Coyote, exasperated at the hero's threats, directs witchery at him. Informed by big fly of this witchery, the hero applies to kingbird and chickadee people for help. They make arrows by pulling up spruce and pine trees, which Coyote ridicules. Angered by this, they shoot these arrows at him ritually. The arrows pursue Coyote, turning to follow him in his flight, and enter his anus. Because the people are afraid that Coyote will bear ill will and witch them, he is restored and promises not to ridicule arrows again.

Nevertheless, Coyote again bewitches the hero, prompted by First Man and First Woman, presumably for the sake of having his songs and sacrifices included in the ceremony. The hero's "former thinking power was much weakened, everything seemed to be beyond him." The former ghost of Coyote has gone into his interior; he cannot sleep, everything smells of coyote urine to him, and he vomits continually. Again with the help of numerous supernaturals the cause of the trouble is finally diagnosed, and the ritual performed over him is described in detail. The hero's father-in-law participates in this ritual, but big fly warns that he still holds a grudge against the hero because he has not been able to practice incest with his daughter since the marriage. Two of the officiating supernaturals argue about the order of songs, and it is explained, "Accordingly too people at present engage in arguments." Monster Slayer and Born for Water have been forgotten in the invitations, but their anger is pacified when they are invited and assigned their part in the ritual. In the course of the ceremony the former ghost of Coyote which has become the hero's own ghost is killed and the patient recovers.

Enemy Way

Haile, 1938a, pp. 141-217. "Enemy Way Legend" and "The Group Dance." (Ha)

Haile, 1932b (MS.), pp. 1-17. Beauty Way. (Hb)

Curtis, 1907, pp. 106-111. "Legend of the Happiness Chant." (C)

Wheelwright, 1951, pp. 1-16. Myth of Mountain Chant. (Wa)

Wheelwright, 1951, pp. 17-22. Myth of Beauty Chant. (Wb)

The Enemy Way story, as it is presented in these five versions, clearly illustrates the branching interconnections among Navaho legends. In Haile's published version the Enemy Way story follows upon a portion of the generalized Navaho origin myth, the exploits of the war gods in ridding the world of monsters (titled here Monster Way). The conclusion of Enemy Way proper, as given by Haile, leads into the stories of two sisters whose attempts to evade their snake and bear husbands introduce respectively the legends of Beauty Way and Mountaintop Way.

The principal episodes of Enemy Way legend are: trickery of witch father-in-law is demonstrated in raids on Pueblos, in one of which the hero's people are destroyed; frog and turtle escape after a raid on Pueblos; snake and bear old men win suitor test of obtaining jeweled scalps in Pueblo raid as well as subsequent tests of skill, but are not awarded the promised maidens; in the form of handsome young men snake and bear trick maidens into marriage but turn to old men in the morning.

In Navaho ceremonial classification, Enemy Way is a rite rather than a chant.[224] Its story, too, differs from the usual chantway pattern of a hero who successfully weathers trials and thereby gains ritual knowledge. The hero of Enemy Way becomes embroiled in raids upon Pueblo neighbors, and the interest shifts to the action of these raids and to other actors, to the old men and the sisters who take part in the continuation of this story in Beauty and Mountaintop Way. In the two major episodes the hero remains defeated, as it were. In contests with his new witch father-in-law he is temporarily successful, but by trickery the father-in-law involves him in a raid on Taos in which all of his relatives are killed. In the second episode the hero avenges himself by a second successful raid on Taos, but at the same time he is tricked by two old men in the suitor contest he has set for his two nieces. These unacceptable suitors win the Taos jeweled scalps and subsequent tests of skill, but they finally have to resort to magic to seduce the two maidens. This part of the story ends with the girls' flight both from their husbands, now returned to the form of disgusting old men, and from the anger of their own people at their marriage choice.

Running through this story is the theme of successful war against Pueblos. The raids with the witch father-in-law are successful except as he wishes to mortify his son-in-law. The Navahos come off best in their retaliatory raid, even though the hero's suitor test misfires. In an interpolated episode, which in one version sets off the series of mutual raids between Navahos and Pueblos, turtle and frog magically escape with Taos jeweled scalps. But these very successes constitute an excess, and it is for the dangers emanating from the great slaughter that the Enemy Way rite is instituted.

The first episode, recounting how the hero is worsted and his people slain through the scheming of his witch father-in-law, appears only in

Haile's story of Enemy Way proper. Two versions of Beauty Way (Hb, Wb) take up the story with the successful raid of frog and turtle, while the others (Wb, C) begin with the suitor test and raid on Pueblos for jeweled scalps.

1. Tricked by Father-in-law (Ha)

A man of the corn people visits a family of the rock crystal people and is immediately greeted as son-in-law. He marries the daughter because she is very pretty. He finds, however, that she is also married to her father, who becomes jealous of both young people ("he was just as jealous of one as he was of the other") and follows them everywhere, even when they go to urinate or defecate. By use of his medicine bundle the visitor tries to keep his wife away from her father.

The father-in-law proposes raids on Taos in which the son-in-law is humiliated by his own failure to obtain a prisoner. Together at dawn they ambush a Taos boy at a watering place; the old man tells his son-in-law to grab him, but as he tries to do this he realizes that the old man already has the boy by the arm. The hero becomes puzzled and worried about how this happened. They repeat the expedition in a few days, this time catching a girl, and the old man taunts his son-in-law for being slow. "You certainly must be just about dead." The hero asks his wife how the old man does this. She knows his witch ways, says that "he really is no good," and points out how he watches their excrement. She proposes a trick to exchange the medicine bundles of the two men (that of her father contains parts of a fetus); the hero is to suggest a sweat-bath, and while they are inside she will steal her father's medicine bundle. The exchange is effected, and on the next expedition the tables are turned; the hero catches a Taos boy in similar manner and taunts his father-in-law.

The old man is grieved; his lips were parched and turned dark. He suspects his son-in-law's trickery and, while acting friendly toward the young people, plots to do him more harm. "No harm that I can do him is too great." Before starting out on another raid he suggests that they lay out their medicines side by side; each deprecates his own poor medicine bundle. By sleight of hand the father-in-law exchanges them again while laughing and commenting that they are just alike and that their powers must be equal. The old man now proposes a bigger raid for goods as well as captives, and invites his son-in-law's numerous relatives, the corn people, to participate. This is agreeable to the hero, who believes that he still has the powerful medicine bundle. The party is unwittingly surrounded on a neck of rock and all are slain except for a few who hide in trees and survive even after the trees are tossed off the rock. The hero worries over the fact that all of his young relatives have been killed.

2. Suitor Test (Ha, Hb, C, Wa, Wb)

In Haile's complete version (Ha) revenge for the defeat at Taos provides the somewhat tenuous linkage of the preceding episode with the suitor test of obtaining the jeweled scalps from Taos. Corn Man, hero of the previous story, has two nieces (his younger sisters' daughters) whom he has raised and for whom he shows great affection; he refuses requests for them in marriage, setting as trial for their suitors to "square matters for all of his relatives who have been killed." First scolder comes to learn why they have been refused in marriage and to get specification of the suitor test. At first Corn Man is impatient with him as a meddler and tries to send him away; finally he specifies the test — obtaining the turquoise and white bead scalps of two non-sunlight-struck Taos maidens. News of the test is not believed at first by Monster Slayer and Born for Water because of first scolder's reputation for untruths. When it is later confirmed by turtle dove man, Monster Slayer orders preparatory war ritual which is repeated four times — offerings, gesture dance, enemy songs — and the date is set for the raid three days later.

In other versions the suitor test is the same but details of the story vary. Taos is chosen for the raid simply as a traditional enemy, or the motive for the raid on Taos is again revenge, but here for the killing of bird children in the mutual raids following the escape of toad and turtle (Hb); see 3. below. The birds appeal unsuccessfully for help in avenging their children's deaths (enumeration of thirty-four places to which they apply in vain); toad and turtle admit to being the cause of the raids but claim "what can two of us do"; finally Monster Slayer and Born for Water take pity on the birds and organize a war party (Hb). Here the fact that the two maidens have been promised to the taker of the jeweled scalps is mentioned only incidentally in the description of the subsequent raid (Hb).

3. Escape of Frog (Toad) and Turtle (Ha, Hb, Wa, Wb)

This episode appears in four versions of the attack on the Pueblo (Ha, Hb, Wa, Wb). It precedes the story of the main attack (Ha, Hb, Wa) or constitutes this attack (Wb). The scalps which they obtain are, however, not the object of the suitor test. Frog and turtle kill the enemy (Ha) or their young women (Hb, Wa, Wb). They have hidden in the "walled up water supply" which is drawn off to reveal them (Hb). When discovered by the enemy they are subjected to trials: heated pit (Hb), chopping (Ha, Hb, Wa, Wb), fire in pit (Ha, Hb, Wa, Wb), boiling pot (Ha, Hb, Wa), and tossing from cliff (Ha, Hb, Wa, Wb). They escape unharmed; in each case one or the other is able magically to avert destruction and protect them both. When put into heated pit or fire pit, turtle is mortally afraid but frog urinates, forming a pool of water or steam into which they can retreat (Ha, Hb, Wa, Wb). When put into a pot in the fire or attacked with an ax, frog is afraid, but turtle breaks the pot with his shell (Ha, Hb, Wa) or the blows glance off of his shell, under which frog has taken cover (Ha, Hb, Wa, Wb), and injure only the attackers (Ha, Wa, Hb). When the attempt is made to toss them off the cliff, the person holding them falls instead and they slip out of his hand (Hb). The Taos people realize that these are "not the ordinary kind" of people (Hb). They are finally thrown into the river and swim away, displaying the scalps they have taken (Ha, Hb, Wa, Wb), to the anguish and weeping of their attackers (Hb, Wa, Wb).

In one version this incident begins the mutual raids which result in Monster Slayer's war party (Hb); see above. In another, turtle dove brings the report of this raid on Taos to Monster Slayer, who hears it with pleasure, apparently as warrant for the successful conduct of such a raid, and who welcomes the news that they did not take the jeweled scalps (Ha). It is reported that on the way to the attack and on the return they used a different form of speech, called "altered mention" (Ha).

4. Raid on Pueblo (Ha, Hb, C, Wa, Wb)

Three preliminary attacks are unsuccessful (Wa). The raiding party is led by Monster Slayer (Ha, Hb), or the war gods join the party (Wa). They camp four nights on the way (Ha, Hb, C) and proceed with the proper prayers and rituals, among which are talking only in "altered mention" language, offerings, the "talking out" of the enemy in prayer, and drawing of line over which they may not pass (Ha). The party is joined by bear and snake (Wa), two old men who are variously described as "extremely old men, apparently choking with cough" (Ha), "about ready to die with old age" (Hb), or old white-haired brothers of an alien tribe (C). Despite warnings that they will only get killed, they persist and are allowed to remain (C). Or, the leader receives them with annoyance and anger; their coughing interferes with the holiness of the ritual; they are scolded and told to depart but reappear at each evening camp; they are allowed to stay when they tell the leader that they don't want to participate in a running fight but merely to witness it from some elevation (Ha).

They are joined also by flint people, who camp nearby with much noise, shouting and chasing each other around the fire (Ha, Hb, Wa). Monster Slayer is angry at this interference with his ritual (Ha); it is feared that the noise will warn the enemy of their presence, and messages are sent for them to quiet down, but to no avail (Ha, Hb, Wa). When Monster Slayer threatens to attack, they challenge him in flint, sunray, and rainbow clothes, armed with lightning and hail; now realizing that they are the hard flint boys, he speaks mildly to them and apologizes, and they continue their noise without restraint until daylight (Ha). Or, the invincible Monster Slayer is afraid and "pleads in apology" when the hard flint boys challenge him in response to his scolding (Hb). The war party is pacified when an old woman (ground squirrel woman [Hb] or Mountain Goddess [Wa]) tells him that their noise does no harm because they are invisible and inaudible, that they are here to help. Hard flint woman (Ha), or Mountain Goddess (Wa), secures corn and melons from the enemy's fields. Ground squirrel woman proposes to go ahead and cook bread and corn for their travel, assuring Monster Slayer that she too is invisible to the enemy so that he need not fear that this will spoil their surprise attack (Hb).

As they prepare to attack, Talking God appears to dissuade them, saying that he stands for everything peaceful (Hb), that Taos is a source of nice offerings for him — plumes, jewels, cornmeal, pollen (Hb, Ha). Monster Slayer, however, cannot be dissuaded (Ha, Hb). He is able to pass the test of identifying representations on Talking God's prayer-stick, whereupon Talking God can no longer oppose the attack (Ha, Hb), but departs dejected (Ha).

In one version a magically powerful monster, the "so-called bone-less enemy," must be circumvented (Hb). "... if he were able to look just once among them their limbs would be paralyzed," and they would be killed without being able to defend themselves. The following ruse is proposed for Monster Slayer: "Pretend to be out of your mind! In that way some of your men will hold your limbs apart and start running with you. This will cause them to run out from yonder with the boneless enemy. Thus, before it has taken a look among you, it can be killed." This ruse is successful, and the boneless enemy is clubbed to death.

The attack proceeds, and they fight even in the village (Ha). Two of Sun's children are killed, and Sun rises red and trembling until the perfect shell discs in which they were dressed are recovered for him (Ha). After the fighting, which has continued all day (C), the attackers withdraw, but without the jeweled scalps (Ha, Hb), so it is believed, until it is discovered that the two disreputable old men have captured them (Ha, Hb, C, Wa). It is preposterous that they should win the maidens, and more suitor tests of skill are held on the return trip: precision arrow shooting (through center of yucca plant, through hole in rock, at black mark or yucca blade hung in bark of tree), or distance shooting (over pinnacle or rim of high cliff [Ha, Hb, C, Wa, Wb]), racing (C), thrusting hand into hole in rock (Hb, C), and shinny game (Wb). Although all of these tests are won by the two old men, no attention is paid to them; they are not awarded the maidens (Ha, Hb, C, Wa, Wb).

5. Seduction by Snake and Bear (Ha, Hb, C, Wa, Wb)

Back at home ritual is performed for the warriors who took part in the raid (Hb, Wa, Wb), to "club the death ghost of enemy into the ground" (Ha), and during the dance or sway-singing the maidens are told to choose whom they wish (as husband) (Ha, C). Meanwhile, the two old men are camped at a distance and smoke a sweet smelling tobacco (Ha, Hb, C, Wa, Wb), a magical mixture of plants "which rob one of his mind" (Hb), or make one speak without knowing what one says (Wa). They smoke "with apparent resolution, blowing forth cloud after cloud of filmy whiteness...," and as they do this they grow youthful in appearance, their tattered clothes become fine (C). After dancing,

the maidens go for a drink (Ha, Wa). The maidens are enticed by the
sweet smell of this smoke (Ha, Hb, C, Wa, Wb). The older sister urges
that they follow it, while the reluctant younger sister in vain protests,
"Don't do it, my older sister, is everything safe that smells?" (Hb).
Thus they are led to the men's campfire where they find them as handsome or beautifully dressed young strangers (Ha, Hb, C, Wa, Wb),
wearing jewelry (Wa). They realize that the men are aliens, "but a
moment's hesitation gave them assurance, for surely, they thought, such
finely dressed, handsome men could mean no harm" (C). The maidens
ask to smoke too (Ha, Hb, Wa, Wb); at first their presence and request
are ignored (Ha, Hb). The young men pretend not to notice them and
tell each other stories (Hb); they ask the girls why they go about like
this, don't they know "that men had a great love for you." The girls
admit to being drawn by the sweet smell; when they ask for a smoke the
men deprecate their own tobacco (Ha) or dispute four times, each asking
the other to prepare it (Hb). In one version when asked about the deli-
cious smelling tobacco, the men immediately invite the maidens to
marry them and to come with them to their country rich in jewels and
crops, where they will always live in abundance (C). The girls spend
the night with these strangers (Ha, Hb, C, Wa, Wb). The older sister
goes to the side of bear man, the younger to snake man (Hb, Wb); both
are given a smoke, after which they lose consciousness (Wa, Wb), or
"their minds were not the same as before" (Hb). Each lies behind her
man, strapped to him with a rainbow (bear man) (Hb) or a snake (snake)
(Hb, Wb). (Of the latter it is said that "he bothers people across their
loins by that which he had used in strapping her to himself" [Hb].)

The girls wake in the morning to find a bear (Hb) and snake (Hb, Wa)
guarding the entrance; their husbands have turned to shrivelled, disgusting old men (Ha, Hb, C, Wa, Wb). The girls want to escape, but
their people have now turned on them in anger for disobeying the plans
made for them (Hb, C, Wa, Wb) and want to beat them to death for their
marriage choice (Hb, C, Wa). When they try to carry this out, the girls
are borne off on magic baskets (Wa) or on the "live one's plume" and
"pulp of flag" given them by their husbands (Ha). With return home thus
blocked, the girls flee (Hb, Wa, Wb). Their husbands track them by
smoking and following the direction in which the smoke blows (Ha, Hb,
C). Their disillusionment and flight conclude the story of Enemy Way;
the further account of their pursuit and adventures with their husbands'
people constitute the Beauty and Mountaintop Way legends.

6. Purification Ceremony (Ha)

The remainder of Enemy Way legend is concerned with the origin
and explanation of ritual details of the ceremony. The corn people who
undertook the raid on Taos, as well as other water and mountain people,
are now degenerate, weak and sick. Consultations are held with Young
Man of Jarring Mountain, his wife and mother-in-law, and also with
spider; they say this is because of the killing of monsters and other

enemies and leaving them to rot on the ground, but the cure is not known. Big fly suggests that they consult Black God for proper remedies. After four unsuccessful presentations of the medicine bundle, big fly tells them the proper preparation and presentation of the offering. Although Black God suspects who has told his secret (disclaimed by big fly), he is constrained to answer and undertakes the ritual. He explains that the ghosts of the monsters are preparing to do greater evil. Ghosts have swarmed from the slaughter at Taos which was not in the plan and this has accelerated the evil; they will try to persuade people not to observe the proper taboos, and he warns against giving in to this. The ceremony will be a means of self defense in the future. The subsequent actions of Black God in directing the ceremony form the warrant for its present day conduct.

VIII. REFERENCES

Notes

[1] Boas, 1916a and 1935.

[2] E.g., Ehrlich, 1937; Cole, 1915; Radin, 1926 and 1933; Wittfogel and Goldfrank, 1943; Spencer, 1947. For a summary statement of the approach of these studies, see Spencer, 1947, pp. 7-11.

[3] Malinowski, 1926; Radcliffe-Brown, 1915.

[4] Benedict, 1935 and 1946.

[5] The conception of value used here was partially developed in seminar discussions held in the summer of 1949 at the inception of the Values Study ("Memorandum on Values," Comparative Study of Values, 8 pp. mimeo.). It was based initially in large part on the analysis contained in T. Parsons, "The Role of Ideas in Social Action" (1949, pp. 151-166), and its final formulation utilizes the framework, presented in C. Kluckhohn, "Values and Value-Orientations in the Theory of Action" (1951).

[6] Kluckhohn, 1951, p. 395.

[7] Kluckhohn, 1951, pp. 409-410. He points out the similarities and differences between this notion and that of cultural orientations developed by F. Kluckhohn, 1950.

[8] The character of the Navaho life view has been described by Kluckhohn (1949), Kluckhohn and Leighton (1946), and Reichard (1950) in more comprehensive terms and in greater detail than is possible on the basis of mythological data. In the area of value-orientations the mythological analysis is seen as supplementing these general formulations and is on all essential points consistent with them.

[9] A convenient survey of psychological approaches to mythological material is contained in Lindgren, 1933. More recent surveys and critiques are provided by Hallowell, 1947, and LaBarre, 1948.

[10] Boas, 1916a, p. 881.

[11] Boas, 1914. See his discussion of the role of imagination and wish fulfilment in myth formation in "Mythology and Folk Tales of the North American Indian" (1914, p. 489) and in "The Development of Folk Tales and Myths" (1916b, p. 405), both articles reprinted in *Race, Language and Culture*.

[12] See Murray, 1938, pp. 109-110, for discussion of the relation of needs to cathected objects and the images of these objects.

[13] Benedict, 1935.

[14] Although not specifically directed to values, Benedict's analysis of themes in Zuni mythology (Benedict, 1935, Introduction) demonstrates the possibilities of such an approach. Analogous thematic analyses of literary and dramatic productions, from a psychological viewpoint and without attempt at cultural controls, are found in Wolfenstein and Leites, 1950, in White, 1947, and in the type of thematic apperception analyses of fiction represented by Rosenzweig, 1943.

219

[15]See Waterman, 1914.

[16]Kluckhohn, 1951, pp. 403-405. The other operational indices which he suggests — differential effort expended and action in "choice" situations — did not lend themselves to the type of content examination undertaken here, although their use is implicit in the thematic analysis.

[17]See Thompson, 1938. The Aarne-Thompson classifications of tale types and motifs are designed for geographical and historical analysis.

[18]See Murray, 1938.

[19]Murdock, et al, 1950.

[20]Convenient summaries of Navaho ceremonialism are contained in Kluckhohn and Leighton, 1946, pp. 139-158, and in Wyman, 1950, pp. 349-351. For more detailed discussion of ceremonial principles and classification, see such works as Reichard, 1950; Wyman and Kluckhohn, 1938; and Haile, 1942.

[21]See Spencer, 1947, for bibliography of versions of the general origin myth.

[22]The Department of Anthropology, University of Chicago, kindly made microfilms of these manuscripts available.

[23]Reference is made to the notes on and portions of these manuscripts as they appear in Wyman, 1952. Other manuscripts in the possession of Haile, Hill, Reichard, Wheelwright, and Wyman were not consulted (see Wyman, 1952, for record of these mss.). The published versions plus the Haile and Wetherill manuscript collections were considered to furnish a sufficiently substantial and representative collection of the myths.

[24]The Enemy Way story is properly a rite myth, although it forms the beginning of two chantway myths which branch off from it. The origin myth of Night Way contains two distinct stories, "The Visionary" and "The Stricken Twins," which will be referred to separately in the mythological analysis.

[25]Kluckhohn and Leighton, 1946, pp. 155-156; Wyman, 1950, p. 350.

[26]Wyman, 1950, pp. 350-351.

[27]See Hill, 1935; Morgan, 1931; Sapir and Hoijer, 1942, pp. 73-77; and Wyman, 1936a and 1936b. The chantway myth is said to be similar to that of the origin of divinitory rites.

[28]A fragment which tells of the meeting of Navaho and white dogs is published in Hill and Hill, 1943a.

[29]There are said to be manuscripts of this myth in the possession of Haile, Reichard, and Wyman.

[30]Haile and Wheelwright have manuscripts.

[31]Manuscript in possession of Reichard.

[32]Lincoln (1935, p. 219) refers to a myth of this ceremony presumably recorded by Armer which is not the same story as that of Matthews.

[33]Manuscript in possession of Wheelwright.

[34]Wyman and Bailey, 1943, p. 6. See also Haile, 1942, and Wheelwright, 1949, for the mythological background of Upward-reaching-way.

[35]Wyman and Kluckhohn, 1938.

[36]This index was checked against the summary of mythological materials made by Wyman in connection with his analysis of the sandpaintings in the Wetherill collection (Wyman, 1952). Citations of manuscript materials not used here come principally from his notes. The chart presented here adds a few references to fragmentary data not included in his index.

[37]Reichard, 1950. Two forms of Navaho aesthetic expression which are closely related to the ritual system have recently been analyzed in investigations of the Values Study. Mills (1953) examines the relation of visual arts, including ceremonial drypaintings, to Navaho cultural premises, and McAllester (1954) uses music and attitudes toward music as an avenue for exploring cultural values.

[38]Kluckhohn, 1949.

[39]Kluckhohn and Leighton, 1946, pp. 136-138.

[40]Róheim, 1950a and 1950b, pp. 319-360. The outlines of the present analysis had taken shape and the following discussion of themes had been completed substantially in its present form before Róheim's more extended discussion of some of the same mythological material was consulted (Róheim, 1950b). Although the present analysis differs in the phrasing of its problem and in terminology, its findings are congruent with the general tenor of his analysis.

[41]See Raglan (1936, pp. 178-209) for the type hero in Eastern Mediterranean myth; also Klapp (1949, pp. 17-25) for discussion of the general attributes of the folk hero.

[42]Lowie's classic study of the test-theme in North American myth (Lowie, 1908), although theoretically oriented toward refuting Ehrenreich's naturalistic interpretations, gives a distributional analysis of some of these elements.

[43]See, for example, Farrand, 1915; Reichard, 1921; Lowie, 1942.

[44]In these references the two stories of Night Way will be distinguished as "Visionary" and "Twins."

[45]Here and in subsequent pages, initials following the chantway name indicate the authorship of the particular version in question. For the key to initials, see the introductions to each of the chantway abstracts in VII.

[46]The evil father-in-law is a popular episode in northwestern North America. See Lowie, 1908.

[47]Kluckhohn and Leighton, 1946, p. 132; Reichard, 1950, p. 80.

[48]See Reichard's description of symptoms connected with anxiety and nervousness (1950, pp. 91-92).

[49]Kluckhohn, 1944, pp. 60-62.

[50]Wyman and Kluckhohn, 1938; Kluckhohn and Leighton, 1946, pp. 132, 147, 155; Reichard, 1950, p. 82.

[51]Reichard, 1950, pp. xxviii, 49; Wyman, 1950, pp. 341-346; Kluckhohn and Leighton, 1946, p. 224.

[52]Kluckhohn and Leighton, 1946, p. 224; Reichard, 1944b. It may be

noted that whereas the form of illness tends toward hysterical manifestations, control over it, in myth and in practice, is maintained by ritual that in psychological terms is par excellence an obsessive-compulsive technique.

[53] In Thematic Apperception Test stories obtained from a series of Navaho veterans, Kaplan and Vogt found considerable emphasis on nurturant older male figures (Kaplan, personal communication; see also the analysis of personality data in the case histories in Vogt, 1951, especially p. 80 where the need for succorance or support from the father is noted). Since these subjects were contemporary, acculturated Navahos, a direct correspondence between the mythological picture and their personality dynamics cannot be assumed. However, the search for nurturant male figures in personal fantasy is congruent with the fantasy elements in the chantway hero's similar search for supernatural help. (An analysis of the Rorschach responses of Navaho veterans is contained in Kaplan, 1954.)

[54] Kluckhohn and Leighton, 1946, pp. 163, 178.

[55] Kluckhohn and Leighton, 1946, pp. 50, 57-62, 136-138.

[56] Kluckhohn and Leighton, 1946, pp. 57, 176.

[57] Other versions are: Matthews, 1885; Sapir and Hoijer, 1942, p. 37 ff.; and Róheim, 1950b, p. 325. In both of the latter references the incident appears as part of the story of the boy raised by owl.

[58] If myths are taken as group fantasy expressions, their most direct relationship is to the personality forms of the persons whose fantasy they represent. Although Navaho child training practices and the concomitant child development trends have been analyzed (Kluckhohn, 1947) and the treatment of various sectors of Navaho culture has provided valuable insight into psychological aspects of Navaho life (Kluckhohn and Leighton, 1946; Kluckhohn, 1944; Róheim, 1950b), no complete analysis of the adult personality picture is available as reference point for interpretation of the mythological data. The following analysis of the psychological significance of the self-assertion theme and its connection with the other value areas discussed is, therefore, advanced as a tentative interpretation. It is hoped that such hypotheses may prove useful in the further systematic delineation of Navaho personality trends.

[59] Leighton and Leighton, 1942.

[60] Throughout this analysis we are taking the principal action of the chantway stories as representing the position of the Navaho male. The few instances in which female characters play the central role show expectable differences. Instead of trial by a witch father-in-law we have seen how the woman is punished by her own family for an unacceptable marriage choice.

[61] Cf. Reichard, 1950, p. xxxi.

[62] Leighton and Kluckhohn, 1947, pp. 56-60.

[63] Reichard, 1950, p. xxix. Vogt (1951, p. 131) notes that a frequent theme in the Thematic Apperception Test stories given by his series of Navaho veterans is that of "asocial aggression and acquisition followed by social disapproval, punishment and subsequent reform of the hero."

[64] Kluckhohn and Leighton, 1946, p. 170; Reichard, 1950, pp. xxv-xxvii.

[65] Waterman, 1914.

[66]Wetherill's mythological fragments (Wyman, 1952) show greater emphasis on rainmaking and fertility than the other collections utilized here.

[67]Cf. Haeberlin, 1916.

[68]Passing reference is also made to some well-known taboos or ritual practices without explanation of their origin or the penalty for infraction, e.g., taboos on eating certain parts of deer, on sleeping in an arroyo or lying with head close to a tree (Big Star); prohibition on sexual relations for four days after a ceremony (Flint, Shooting Ra) and on talking during the sweathouse ritual (Twins); use of a special warpath language and the interference of noise with preparatory war ritual (Enemy Ha).

[69]Haile (1932b) notes that "leaving a wife" is meant, although he indicates that the sense is not clear.

[70]Kluckhohn and Leighton (1946, p. 137) note that the relation of patient and singer has elements of a kinship relationship which would preclude sexual contact. See also Kluckhohn, 1939, pp. 57-58.

[71]As a focus for repressed sexual wishes, defenses against which are evidenced in witchcraft stories involving brother and sister relationships. See Kluckhohn, 1944, pp. 58-60.

[72]Similar shaping is done by the hero's half-sisters in the trip to his sun father in Plume Way (Plume Wc) and in the portion of the general Navaho origin myth dealing with the war gods. For versions of the latter incident, see Spencer, 1947, pp. 45-47.

[73]Newcomb, 1940b.

[74]Cf. Kluckhohn and Leighton, 1946, pp. 66-67; see also Spencer (1947, p. 102) for other references to magical use of names.

[75]This differential treatment of agriculture and hunting may have significance for the time level represented by these myths. The action of the stories seems to refer principally to an earlier time before the Navaho had acquired agriculture. Cf. Spencer, 1947, pp. 26-30.

[76]Kluckhohn, 1942; Malinowski, 1925; Homans, 1941.

[77]Cf. Radcliffe-Brown's definition of "Social Sanction" in the *Encyclopedia of the Social Sciences* (1934): "A sanction is a reaction on the part of a society or of a considerable number of its members to a mode of behavior which is thereby approved (positive sanctions) or disapproved (negative sanctions)." His formulation and classification will be used as a framework for the following discussion of sanctions.

[78]Kluckhohn, 1951, pp. 393-404.

[79]Radcliffe-Brown (1934) distinguishes retaliation from revenge in that the former is socially approved, controlled, and limited.

[80]See note 75.

[81]The English name given to this chantway reflects in its connotations two elements that figure in the myth — sexual excess and payment for sexual rights. See note 160.

[82]The evidence marshaled by Hobson (1954) from a number of field workers indicates that the Navaho have an "uncommon degree of anxiety" about poverty

and that ridicule operates as a sanction against this condition. His material also shows the need for property to gain sexual access to women.

[83]Gambling is also among the faults of the irresponsible hero in Wetherill's version of Big Star Way (see introduction to abstract of Big Star Way).

[84]Other Navaho myths not in the chantway series show alien gamblers as powerful figures who are finally defeated. See Matthews, 1889; 1897, pp. 82-87; Goddard, 1933, pp. 140-146; Wetherill and Cummings, 1922; and Chapin, 1940.

[85]Hobson (1954) sees the fear of losing wealth as the source of negative sanctions imposed on gambling rather than any disapproval of games as such.

[86]Dyk, 1938.

[87]Benedict, 1935.

[88]Census data on the Ramah Navaho community, on file with the Comparative Study of Values, Harvard University.

[89]Kluckhohn and Leighton, 1946, p. 137.

[90]Kluckhohn, personal communication.

[91]An unusual variation on parental desertion in time of stress or danger occurs in a popularized version of Mountaintop Way (C). A father hands over the sister heroines to the Utes to stop their raids; it later develops that the father has magic power to recall his daughters and he claims that his intention in sending them was to have them steal the Ute "treasure" for him.

[92]In analogous situations Zuni stories take opportunity to elaborate a favorite theme of shaming parents for their desertion. Benedict, 1935.

[93]Except in the sun's testing of hero brothers (Shooting). The role of the sun as a punishing father figure, particularly in the origin myth of the twin war gods, is discussed by Roheim, 1950b. The origin myth of hero twins who travel to their sun father for powers and are tested by him or by other powerful male figures is widespread in the Southwest and occurs in Pueblo and Apache myth.

[94]Kluckhohn, 1944, pp. 15, 58.

[95]In this version there are no father and mother, but the trials are engineered by the wife's grandfather and her grandmother plays the role of mother.

[96]Leighton and Kluckhohn, 1947, p. 45.

[97]Kluckhohn and Leighton, 1946, pp. 58, 136, 176.

[98]Haile, 1931b, MS., Intro.

[99]Spencer, 1947, pp. 45-47.

[100]Kluckhohn and Leighton, 1946, p. 58; Leighton and Kluckhohn, 1947, pp. 99-101.

[101]Reichard, 1928, pp. 56-57, 87; Kluckhohn and Leighton, 1946, pp. 58-59; Leighton and Kluckhohn, 1947, pp. 79, 101-102.

[102]In one case she is the daughter of a younger sister (Enemy). In the other, relationship through the sister is not specified but this seems to be a legitimate assumption since she lives with the hero in the presumably matrilocal family group (Plume).

[103] One version of this story has the hero offer his own sister for the suitor test (Enemy C).

[104] Reichard (1950, p. xxvii) sees the cooperative arrangements of Navaho society as related to the "fight against loneliness." Mills in his analysis of art (1953) and McAllester in his analysis of music (1954) find preoccupation with loneliness in their Navaho materials.

[105] Astrov, 1950.

[106] This theme also appears in autobiographies. See personality data in the case histories in Vogt, 1951.

[107] Kluckhohn and Leighton, 1946, p. 178.

[108] Kluckhohn and Leighton, 1946, pp. 220, 225.

[109] See p. 52 for the distinction between retaliation and revenge.

[110] Reichard (1950, pp. 63-64, 70-71) classifies certain supernaturals as "undependable" or mean (e.g., First Man and First Woman) and others as "unpersuadable" or evil (the monsters).

[111] Kluckhohn and Leighton (1946, p. 220) note that the Navaho word most often translated into English as "mean" is sometimes rendered "he gets mad pretty easy."

[112] Haile (1950, p. xvii) notes that Coyote often figures as "the scapegoat for contemporary behavior and its condemnation," and that Navaho thought "ironically enough believes that, what is contemptible in coyote's behavior cannot fail to impress youth."

[113] Haile, 1950, p. xvi.

[114] Haile (1950, pp. xii-xiii) describes the big snake father-in-law's malevolent activity as "stealthy attempt at control of the course of events by foul means" and thus identifies it as witchery or witch power, although the popular Navaho term for witchery is not used.

[115] See Kluckhohn, 1944, pp. 15, 18, for a discussion of these "symptoms" of witchcraft.

[116] A witchcraft activity; see Kluckhohn, 1944, p. 15.

[117] Kluckhohn and Leighton, 1946, p. 136.

[118] Kluckhohn, 1944, pp. 21-24.

[119] It should be noted that the love magic is directed principally toward Pueblo women. Cf. Kluckhohn, 1944, p. 24.

[120] Kluckhohn and Leighton, 1946, p. 225.

[121] See Kluckhohn, 1944, pp. 9-13, 21-24.

[122] Kluckhohn, 1949, pp. 360-364.

[123] Kluckhohn and Leighton, 1946, p. 219. Kluckhohn (1949, pp. 366-367, 372) discusses the traditionalistic and situational character of Navaho morality and the fact that deceit may be considered proper in some situations. The fact that patterned deceit, mistrust and hypocrisy have been identified as noteworthy characteristics among some Northern Athabascan groups may indicate an historical depth to the phenomena under consideration here. Cf. Osgood, 1933, p. 73; 1936, p. 131; and Honigman, 1946, p. 72, and 1949.

[124] Malinowski, 1926; Radcliffe-Brown, 1922.

[125] Cf. Parsons' analysis of the position of the adolescent in American culture (Parsons, 1950).

[126] Benedict (1935, v. 1, p. xxi) points out the fact that Zuni tales differ from most North American Indian mythology in the absence of accounts of warfare, supernatural encounters, and acquisition of power. Benedict's MSS. of Zuni ceremonial myths, consulted through the kindness of Margaret Mead, did not reveal any similarities with the Navaho ceremonial myths. The father-in-law tests seem to be absent from Zuni and other Pueblo mythology.

[127] Benedict, 1935, v. 1, pp. xvii, xxv-xxvii. It may be noted that the Navaho chantway myths appear to be remarkably controlled by comparison with the bizarre imagery and unrestrained violence characteristic of the Zuni tales. Milgroom (1948) finds abundant expression of hostility and aggression in the Zuni myths.

[128] Cf. for example, the Tanaina, Osgood, 1937. While there is considerable mythological material from the Northern Athabaskans, including such early records as those of Petitot and Jetté, its geographical derivation seems to be scattered. Although this material has not been systematically investigated in connection with the present study, there appears to be some similarity in minor motifs, such as the hollow log trip (see, for example, Jetté, 1908, Tale 7).

[129] Lowie, 1908.

[130] To avoid the use of phonetic characters, Navaho names have been given in translation, or, in some cases, a non-technical transcription has been chosen from those that appear in the English rendering of the stories. The forms used for proper names vary widely in the mythological sources, but for the purposes of these abstracts the attempt has been made to establish as much uniformity as possible. Capitalization has been used for the names of central characters, for the more important supernaturals, and where it contributes to clarity in identifying lesser characters.

[131] See Flint Way and Navaho Wind Way legends for similar destruction and a more detailed account of the subsequent ritual restoration.

[132] There is some variation in the names of characters in the two versions, e.g., winter and dark thunders vs. white and black thunders; Rainboy vs. Moisture Boy; frog vs. toad, etc.

[133] Matthews and Haile formerly gave the translation "Hogan God" or "House God." More recently Haile (1951, pp. 39-40) has substituted the translation "Calling God."

[134] Reichard notes that a part of this incident was omitted as "too dirty" to tell to women. Cf. her discussion of the association of Begochidi with insects (1950, p. 387).

[135] Ritual details of the two versions will not be compared; only differences in the story action are noted.

[136] Reichard notes that crying may have been the origin of his song.

[137] Reichard notes that part of the story is omitted here because the informant had forgotten it.

[138]The butterfly seduction appears also in a story of the Rain Chant referred to by the Coolidges (1930, p. 86). Details are not given but this apparently combines elements from the Great Gambler story of the general Navaho origin myth with the butterfly seduction of the above recordings of Water and Prostitution Ways. Here the wives of the Rain God are seduced by the Great Gambler of Pueblo Bonito but later recovered by their own husband. Wyman (1942, pp. 23-26) summarizes a myth of Water Way in the Wetherill collection which, however, gives only episodes from the emergence story, namely, progression through the underworlds, separation of the sexes, Coyote's theft of the water monster's baby, the great flood and great drought.

[139]See discussion of the role of women in Prostitution Way, from which come most of the episodes in which women thus figure.

[140]Both the butterfly seduction and contest with Gambler seem to be drawn from Prostitution Way, where details of these episodes are summarized.

[141]Since his mother is identified as belonging to the Kisahni clan, it is not clear whether the Pueblos are aliens or whether the hero should be considered one of them.

[142]See note 133.

[143]Wheelwright notes that the informant Big Moustache did not know the accompanying ceremony and that other informants say that his version includes parts of the Feather Chant (Wheelwright, 1946a, p. 55). As noted below, some of the material here occurs also in Prostitution Way.

[144]Kisahni is here given as a clan; elsewhere in the story it seems to refer to Pueblos.

[145]Kluckhohn and Wyman (1940, pp. 45-46, 156-157) give fragments of the legend for the Female Branch of Shooting Way.

[146]Reichard, 1939, p. 37.

[147]Haile's prayerstick cutting text of this myth (1947, pp. 77, 83) makes only brief reference to events other than ritual procedures, i.e., that the hero has been shattered and restored by thunder and later that he becomes ill again from violation of food restrictions following a ceremony. Wyman (1952, p. 33) lists three manuscript versions of Shooting Way, one his own, one belonging to Haile and one to Reichard, none of which have been utilized for this abstract.

[148]These two are said to be counterparts of Slayer of Alien Gods and Child of the Water respectively.

[149]These events are described in Ra and Rb but merely referred to in N&R. Places where the Rb and N&R accounts are fuller are indicated in parentheses.

[150]See note 149.

[151]Lincoln (1935, pp. 215-216) quotes brief passages from what is apparently the Wheelwright manuscript on which this summary is based. Wyman (1952, p. 39) lists Reichard's manuscript version of Big Star Way, which has not been used here. Wyman (1952, pp. 40-44) gives also Wetherill's origin myth for Big Star Way. This is an entirely different story, which, like several mythological fragments in this collection, emphasizes rain making. The wayward hero gambles and refuses to work, ridicules the ceremonies for rain, and commits the sacrilege of stealing ceremonial offerings. His spirit of

revolt spreads among the people and drought follows. The hero is banished
with threat of death if he returns. Wandering cold and hungry, he recon-
siders his actions and decides to pray and make offerings of the stolen
jewels. Drought is dispelled by rain. Taken to the sky, he is admonished for
causing his people suffering and learns the Big Star ceremony, which he returns to teach to his people.

[152]Wheelwright indicates that the older brother hero of the second portion
becomes a practitioner of the "Wind ceremony." It has seemed preferable,
however, to deal with these fragments here rather than to incorporate them
in the abstract of Navaho Wind Way.

[153]See abstracts of Enemy Way and Beauty Way legends for references to
this younger sister's adventures.

[154]Haile in giving some of the mythological background of the fire dance
(1946, pp. 1-57 passim) refers to various events in this story — a witch shooting and restoration in which the heroine's brothers find her attackers and
have her restored by withdrawal of the arrows from her body; mother bear's
bouncing of bear cubs as though to teach them to dance; meeting with a brother
of Changing Bear Maiden, who performs trench firing for the heroine's ach-
ing body; reputedly lazy boy's success as runner for fire dance and his later
races for Navaho against aliens (see similar incidents in Matthews and
Coolidge versions); return of sisters to their family in fear because of former
threats to kill them, their welcome and teaching of the ceremonials to a
younger brother before departure to live with the holy people. Lincoln (1935,
p. 219) refers to a myth of this ceremony presumably recorded by Armer
which is said to differ from Matthews' story. Wyman (1952, pp. 51, 55-56)
gives two fragments from Wetherill's mythological notes for Mountaintop
Way, both of which concern a girl's ritual contacts with bears. In the first of
these a bear singer cures the girl and teaches her people how to cure bear
sickness. In the second, a poor girl wandering in search of food follows a
rainbow, out of curiosity and hopes that she will find people; for four nights
she sleeps in the empty homes of bear people; about to give up her search,
she is captured by a rainbow rope and taken to learn the ceremony, which
she is instructed to teach to her people.

[155]Wyman (1952, p. 56) comments on the heroine of Wetherill's fragments
from Mountaintop Way: "This myth is unusual in that the main character who
learns the ceremonial from the supernaturals is a girl. Female singers
seem to be as scarce in Navaho mythology as they are in real life."

[156]See introduction to Beauty Way for a different account of both sisters'
adventures, in which they marry and live happily among bear and snake
people (Curtis, 1907, p. 111).

[157]The incidents here summarized occur in other Navaho stories which
are not specifically identified as chantway myths: raised by owl and guided
by poker in Sapir and Hoijer (1942, pp. 25-73); hero becomes dangerous to
his people and has to flee in Matthews' story of the origin of Utes (1885, pp.
27-74). The incident of the boy raised by owl occurs also in a fragment of
the legend for Female Shooting Holy Way in Kluckhohn and Wyman (1940, pp.
156-157).

[158]Hill, (1938) p. 123, gives a mythological account of the introduction of
hunting in the Stalking Way, which was first taught to the people of Begochidi
and further demonstrated by "the game god."

[159]Note that the aliens concerned here are Apaches, Utes, etc., rather than Pueblos.

[160]The Kluckhohn version indicates that the chant name Prostitution Way refers specifically to this payment for wives, although it may be noted that here it is in the sense of payment for legitimate sexual rights. Reichard (1947) criticizes use of the term "Prostitution" as too narrow in its connotations for the data comprehended by the ceremony; it is directed toward success in love, trading or gambling, and it is also used for curing the effects of sexual excess with one's own wife.

[161]The concluding portion of one version of the Water Way story (Wa) may more properly be considered as part of Prostitution Way since it duplicates many of these details — rejection of hero and his mother by Pueblos, his learning of love and hunting magic and the ability to transform property by chewing and blowing, and his marriage to the chief's daughters now that the Pueblos admire him for his riches.

[162]This duplication of events is explained in one version of Water Way (Hb) as the conjunction of the two ceremonies: "As for what is taking place now, it will be called the meeting line for a short distance of the Water Way and Prostitute Way. . . On this side the Water Way line will be stringing along..., on the other the Prostitute Way's blessing (rite) line will (string) along...."

[163]For the contests in games and racing with White Butterfly there are parallels in other Navaho tales about the Great Gambler. Cf. Wetherill and Cummings, 1922; Chapin, 1940; Matthews, 1889a and 1897, pp. 82-87. These stories of the Great Gambler appear as isolated stories or as part of the general origin myth rather than as chantway legends.

[164]The Haile manuscript version deals with these events in somewhat greater detail. Here, however, the flirtation with Pueblo women occurs before the hero has acquired magical powers and, rather than being successful, is a source of ridicule.

[165]Of the relationship between Moth Way and Prostitution Way, Father Berard says: "The two ceremonies are intimately connected with one another in defining the limitations of sexual intercourse. Promiscuous intercourse is never sanctioned between relatives, a law which, as Moth Way shows, cannot be transgressed with impunity. While, therefore, nothing of these limitations is emphasized in the account of the Prostituting Way, these limitations are set forth in the Moth Way and must be interpreted by the general practice of Navaho society, specifically by the reserve which clan relatives exercise toward one another." Haile, 1931a and b, MS., Introd.

[166]This mad action is likened to drunkenness, the only reference found in these chantway myths to liquor and its effects.

[167]Haile notes that the word for moth is also the term for insanity "which follows marriage between close blood relatives" and for the ceremony which cures this condition. Haile, pp. 118-119.

[168]He does this also to hunters when they are about to shoot game, thus making them miss it, and to women and men when they urinate or when they are about to have intercourse. For this practice he moves about in haze or mirage. His name is explained as meaning "the bego who touches." Haile

(1931b, MS., pp. 94-96, 117) notes that he can discover no meaning for "bego."
Hill (1938, p. 99) and Reichard (1950, p. 389) give similar accounts of Begochidi and his activities.

[169] The Coolidges (1930, p. 148) refer to a story apparently similar to the
one abstracted here. Although identified as the legend for Beauty Way, the
Curtis version (Curtis, 1907, p. 111, "Legend of the Happiness Chant")
furnishes merely a simplified summary of this portion of the story and does
not distinguish between the adventures of the two sisters in originating their
respective ceremonies. The sisters are overtaken by snake and bear and
follow them to their home in the west, where they find that their husbands
already have wives and children; the sisters, therefore, marry the eldest
sons of these families, live happily in their new homes, where they learn the
ceremonies of the snake and bear people and teach them to their younger
brother who comes to visit. Wyman(1952, pp. 62-78) gives five mythological
excerpts from Wetherill's notes for Beauty Way, none of which are similar to
the events abstracted here. Three brief fragments tell, respectively, of
getting snake medicine from the Hopi, rescue of little black beetle who has
been eaten by frog, and quarrel of earth and heavens. The longer excerpts
have the flavor of moral tales. One tells how irresponsible and lazy people
are prevailed upon to give offerings and pray for rain and are thus released
from drought. The other also concerns rainmaking, but it bears more similarity to the chantway pattern. A brother and sister disobey their parents and
run away to the lakeside to play. They are taken by lightnings to learn a
ceremony and are told that since they have disobeyed their people they must
"now do something for them." On their return with curing powers they send
their parents to form rain clouds; "Thenceforth the Navajos and their children prayed to them to form the clouds and make it rain, which they do if the
children have not been wicked."

[170] According to the Coolidges (1930, pp. 147, 187) the story of the Stricken
Twins is the origin legend for Big God Way, a chantway closely allied to Night
Way. This story has a Zuni counterpart, and it may be noted that certain
aberrant features in the Navaho story indicate a possible alien source, although the details have been worked out in typical Navaho manner.

[171] One version departs from this pattern (C). The hero is described as a
wayward, roving gambler who offends by staking his brother's property in
gambling.

[172] The Coolidges also give a brief version (1930, pp. 189-190) which is
similar in essentials to those abstracted here. Matthews' classical description of Night Way is of the Rock Center Branch (Wyman and Kluckhohn, 1938,
p. 26). He also gives an origin myth for some of the songs of Night Way
(Matthews, 1907, pp. 25-30) in which the hero successfully braves the gods
with a song and offerings and acquires the ritual and equipment that he desires. Wyman (1952, p. 83-86) gives three mythological fragments from
Wetherill's notes for Night Way, all of which refer to events of the emergence.

[173] In the Coolidges' version only one of the two birds is killed but there is
a similar expression of righteous indignation by the gods: "Those fellows
were always eating what other people had killed. I am glad that one of them
got killed." (Coolidges, 1930, p. 189.)

[174] In Mb this does not happen until after the hero has returned from his
visit with the holy ones.

[175] Stevenson's summary version can be dropped from consideration at this point since he gives no details of the visit with supernaturals.

[176] See note 133.

[177] Matthews points out the similarity of this affliction and ritual technique for its cure with those that figure in another myth of Night Way, "The Stricken Twins."

[178] It should be noted that in these versions it was originally specified that the hero was the next to youngest of the group of brothers, whereas in two others he was the youngest (W, S&H).

[179] Hill (1938, p. 54) gives a mythological account of the origin of agriculture in which the people are instructed by Changing Woman.

[180] In Goddard's version the witch father-in-law incidents are omitted but the hero acquires game power from the supernaturals. Hill (1938, p. 100) gives an abstract of a hollow log story that purports to explain hunting ritual. As in the Plume Way legends, the hero is assisted by a pet turkey and supernaturals. At the end of his journey he meets a girl and a man; in disregard of the man's warnings not to travel to the four directions, he learns hunting rituals which he returns to teach to his people.

[181] Wyman (1952, pp. 91-94) gives two additional mythological fragments for Plume Way from Wetherill's notes. In one of these, buffalos give rituals and medicines in exchange for jet horns; in the other spider gives medicine to the gods.

[182] In Wa it is specified that this is where the Water Way legend joins those of Plume and Night Ways. Haile's version of Navaho Wind Way (see below) also makes reference to a hollow log trip as the point where this story joins that of Plume Way. The Navaho Wind Way version of the hollow log trip introduces no new elements and did not seem full enough to warrant inclusion in this abstract. Supernaturals prepare the log for the hero and send turkey to help guide it; the log arrives at a place without exit where ritual information is exchanged with the inhabitants.

[183] In Hill's abstract (1938, p. 100) the hero is turned out by his three elder brothers for gambling away all his property.

[184] See note 133.

[185] It should be noted that the Goddard version of the hollow log is entitled "Game Story." Here, in addition to corn famine, the game animals have vanished in the hero's absence. After his return with corn, Talking God and other supernaturals show him images of the game animals together with instructions for killing and cooking them and the proper songs. The hero is then able to hunt successfully, and it is implied that he thus restores game power to his people. Cf. Hill's origin myth of hunting ritual noted above.

[186] Hoijer notes that the meaning is not clear here.

[187] See abstract of Big Star Way for the narrative of Wheelwright's second version (Wb). Wyman and Kluckhohn (1938, p. 13, no. 30) give two fragments of the Wind Chant myth: snake transformation and restoration by being passed through hoops; poisoned by cactus.

[188] Cf. similar incidents in Hail, Water and Flint Way legends, where except for Haile's Version B of Flint Way the provocation is different.

[189] For summary of these events in Wb, see Big Star Way.

[190] For summary of these events in Wb, see Big Star Way.

[191] In W&B this incident is added to the main story by another informant; Wyman and Bailey, 1946, p. 225.

[192] See note 133.

[193] For summary of this version of the hollow log incident, see note 182 of Plume Way legend.

[194] Kluckhohn and Wyman (1940, pp. 140-141) discuss the recent origin of this chantway and its popularity in the Ramah-Atarque area.

[195] Cf. the incident of marriage to snake in Wheelwright's version of the Navaho Wind Way legend.

[196] A fragment of the Eagle Way legend given by Kluckhohn (1941, pp. 9-10) bears no resemblance to these versions. Sky Yellow Tail and Sky White Tail come up from the water and address each other as brother. They travel on lightning and rainbow to a winged rock and enter to find a man and woman similar to themselves, who claim to be their father and maternal grandmother. The rock is borne east by thunder and finally resettles as Shiprock. The brothers are sung over and the rock is designated as their home. The father instructs them about the future inhabitants of the earth and how earth people are to care for and make offerings to this rock.

[197] See note 133.

[198] At this point the mysterious young man is thus identified and is referred to by this name throughout the remainder of the story.

[199] Cf. defeat of stinging insects in legend for Bead Way and Big Star Way.

[200] A ritual closely associated with Bead Way, both of which constitute a subgroup of Holy Way ritual (Wyman and Kluckhohn, 1938, pp. 6, 29).

[201] In describing the Eagle Nest sandpainting the Coolidges (1930, pp. 233-234) refer to a few mythological details, none differing from the versions here discussed except as indicated in notes to the abstract. Two brief variants of the Bead Way story have been published. In Pepper's fragmentary account (1905, pp. 6-7), the hero is taken captive in war and kept by the Pueblos in a circular, roofless room from which he is taken to the sky by eagles and snakes. Wyman (1952, pp. 105-106) gives a story collected by Wetherill which omits the eagles' nest incident. This story opens with a ceremonial cure after which the hero "... would no longer listen to his parents when they talked to him and went wandering around dirty and ragged." When he visits the Hopi in this condition, they treat him kindly, feed and clean him, and dress him in jewels. On a rainbow he escapes with their valuables through the sky opening despite their efforts to draw him down. These jewels he gives to eagle and star people who teach him the Bead Way ceremony. On his return he recompenses the Hopi with the snake song and marries two of their women.

[202] The Coolidges refer to the Navaho beggar as Picks Up Scraps (1930, p. 233); in M he is called He Who Picks Up (like a bird); and in R his name is Scavenger.

REFERENCES

[203] The Pueblos are variously identified as: Kintyel (Broad House in Chaco Canyon) and Kindotliz (Blue House) (M); White House and Blue House (R); Kintyel and Kin-Doklish (Aztec and Pueblo Bonito) (W); and Jemez (H&H).

[204] In the fullest version of the myth (M), the Navaho beggar accepts the task with these words: "I lead but a poor life at best. Existence is not sweet to a man who always hungers. It would be pleasant to eat such food (feast that has been given him as an inducement) for the rest of my days, and some time or other I must die. I shall do as you wish."

[205] In the Coolidges' reference to this myth (1933, p. 233) messenger fly, butterfly and rock wren in turn warn the hero of the Pueblos' trickery.

[206] The sandpainting described by the Coolidges (1930, pp. 233-234) shows on the eagles' breasts the buckskin pouches with "pinole" and the "Yellow Cup...a magic cruse which never became empty," from which they fed "the starving boy."

[207] The fragment recorded by Kluckhohn does not include the preceding incidents of the eagle's nest and Pueblo trickery. Instead it is introduced as follows: A man goes around killing eaglets in their nests (repeated four times); a big eagle comes to ask him why he does this; he is angry and takes the man up through the sky hole.

[208] Hill and Hill omit the events in the sky. Their version summarizes the sky visit with the statement that here the hero learns Bead Way and Eagle-catching-way; see below.

[209] The order of these events differs in the two versions. Here they will be treated as they occur in R. W's version recounts them in the following order: coyote transformation; tipping over of water jars; shooting by frogs and toads; shooting by people from northern pueblo.

[210] "Her teeth were not set in her head evenly and regularly, like those of an Indian; they protruded from her mouth, were set at a distance from one another, and were curved like the claws of a bear" (M).

[211] The Coolidges (1930, pp. 223-224, 233) refer to the hero of this story as "the Navajo Beggar, who is credited with inventing sandpainting." The paintings he was shown in the sky were done on buckskin, but he was given instructions that on earth they should be made of ground up rocks.

[212] "The life of each one of the four enemies (the chiefs) had gone into evil spirits and bothered him." Note that in this fragment there has been no trickery by the Pueblos; the hero was taken to the sky because of his excess in killing eaglets.

[213] The fifth version (K) is a fragment and deals only with the war against stinging insects; it does not include the original Pueblo trickery nor revenge for it.

[214] See Navaho Wind Way legend for similar provocation and subsequent restoration.

[215] Later it becomes known that she is a buffalo woman; see below. Haile notes that this is not considered sexual excess.

[216] Reichard indicates that this is an interpolated remark typical of Navaho joking.

[217]The informant notes that this is inconsistent with the family composition stated at the outset of the story.

[218]Haile, 1951, pp. vii–viii.

[219]Haile, 1951, p. 6, n. 13.

[220]Haile, 1951, pp. xii–xiii.

[221]Kluckhohn and Wyman (1940, p. 157) give a fragment of the legend for female Shooting Evil Way in which Coyote steals the wife of First Man and transforms him into a coyote.

[222]Father Berard notes that this inquiry is highly improper and shows Coyote's utter disregard for conventionalities. The presentation of the incident is cited as an example of Navaho humor.

[223]The songs and prayers used here emphasize the hero's return to "people of his relationship."

[224]The myth is included in the present analysis because of its close connection with certain chantway myths and because of the availability of recordings of high quality. It should be noted that the story abstracted here appears also as a preliminary but integral part of the myths of Beauty and Mountaintop Ways. Wheelwright (1951, p. 16) notes that her story for Mountaintop Way explains the procedure of the "Squaw Dance," a popular term for Enemy Way rites.

BIBLIOGRAPHY

Astrov, Margot
    1950.   The concept of motion as the psychological Leitmotif of Navaho life and literature. *Journal of American Folklore,* Vol. 63, pp. 45-56.

Benedict, Ruth
    1935.   Zuni mythology. *Columbia University Contributions to Anthropology,* Vol. 21. 2 vols.
    1946.   The chrysanthemum and the sword. Boston.

Boas, Franz
    1914.   Mythology and folk-tales of the North American Indians. *Journal of American Folklore,* Vol. 27, pp. 374-410.
    1916a.   Tsimshian mythology. *Bureau of American Ethnology, Thirty-first Annual Report,* pp. 29-1037.
    1916b.   The development of folk-tales and myths. *Scientific Monthly,* Vol. 3, pp. 335-343.
    1935.   Kwakiutl culture as reflected in mythology. *American Folklore Society, Memoirs,* Vol. 28.

Chapin, Gretchen
    1940.   A Navaho myth from the Chaco Canyon. *New Mexico Anthropologist,* Vol. 5, pp. 63-67.

Cole, Fay Cooper
    1915.   Traditions of the Tinguian; a study in Philippine folklore. *Field Museum of Natural History, Anthropological Series,* Vol. 14, No. 1.

Coolidge, Dane, and Coolidge, Mary R.
    1930.   The Navaho Indians. Boston.

Curtis, Edward S.
    1907.   The North American Indian. Vol. 1. Seattle.

Dyk, Walter
    1938.   Son of Old Man Hat, a Navajo autobiography. New York.

Ehrlich, Clara
    1937.   Tribal culture in Crow mythology. *Journal of American Folklore,* Vol. 50, pp. 307-408.

Farrand, L.
    1915.   Shasta and Athapascan myths from Oregon (ed., L. J. Frachtenberg). *Journal of American Folklore,* Vol. 28, pp. 207-242.

Goddard, Pliny E.
    1933.   Navajo texts. *American Museum of Natural History, Anthropological Papers,* Vol. 34, Pt. 1.

Haeberlin, H. K.
    1916.   The idea of fertilization in the culture of the Pueblo Indians. *American Anthropological Association, Memoirs,* Vol. 3, No. 1.

Haile, Berard
    1931a.   Prostituting Way. Manuscript. 94 pp.
    1931b.   Moth Way. Manuscript. 10 p. (1931a and b are contained in one manuscript with notes.)
    1932a.   Ceremony in the Water Way. Manuscript. 110 pp.

1932b.   Beauty Way. Manuscript. 91 pp.

1932c.   Navaho Wind Way Ceremony. Manuscript. 176 pp.

1932d.   Chiricahua Wind Ceremony of the Navaho. Manuscript. 147 pp.

1933.   Chiricahua Windway Chant. Manuscript. 259 pp.

1938a.   Origin legend of the Navaho Enemy Way. *Yale University Publications in Anthropology,* No. 17.

1938b.   Navaho chantways and ceremonials. *American Anthropologist,* Vol. 40, pp. 639-652.

1942.   Navaho Upward-Reaching Way and Emergence Place. *American Anthropologist,* Vol. 44, pp. 407-420.

1943.   Origin legend of the Navaho Flintway. Chicago.

1946.   The Navaho Fire Dance or Corral Dance. St. Michaels, Arizona.

1947.   Prayer stick cutting in a five night Navaho ceremonial of the Male Branch of Shootingway. Chicago.

1950.   Legend of the Ghostway Ritual in the Male Branch of Shootingway and Suckingway, its legend and practice. St. Michaels, Arizona.

1951.   A stem vocabulary of the Navaho language, English-Navaho. St. Michaels, Arizona.

Hallowell, A. I.

1947.   Myth, culture and personality. *American Anthropologist,* Vol. 49, pp. 544-556.

Hill, W. W.

1935.   The Hand Trembling Ceremony of the Navaho. *El Palacio,* Vol. 38, pp. 65-68.

1938   The agricultural and hunting methods of the Navaho Indians. *Yale University Publications in Anthropology,* No. 18.

Hill, W. W., and Hill, Dorothy W.

1943a.   Two Navajo myths. *New Mexico Anthropologist,* Vols. 6-7, pp. 111-114.

1943b.   The legend of Navajo Eagle-Catching-Way. *New Mexico Anthropologist,* Vols. 6-7, pp. 31-36.

Hobson, R.

1954.   Navaho acquisitive values. *Peabody Museum of Harvard University, Papers,* Vol. 42, No. 3.

Homans, G. C.

1941.   Anxiety and ritual: the theories of Malinowski and Radcliffe-Brown. *American Anthropologist,* Vol. 43, pp. 164-172.

Honigman, John J.

1946.   Ethnography and acculturation of the Fort Nelson Slave. *Yale University Publications in Anthropology,* No. 33.

1949.   Culture and ethos of Kaska society. *Yale University Publications in Anthropology,* No. 40.

Jetté, Rev. J.

1908.   On Ten'a folklore. *Journal of the Royal Anthropological Institute,* Vol. 38, pp. 298-367.

Kaplan, B.

1954.   A study of Rorschach responses in four cultures. *Peabody Museum of Harvard University, Papers,* Vol. 42, No. 3.

Klapp, Orrin E.

1949.   The folk hero. *Journal of American Folklore,* Vol. 62, pp. 17-25.

Kluckhohn, Clyde

1939.   Some personal and social aspects of Navaho ceremonial practice. *Harvard Theological Review,* Vol. 32, pp. 57-82.

1941.   Notes on Navajo Eagle Way. *New Mexico Anthropologist*, Vol. 5,
        pp. 6-14.
1942.   Myths and rituals. *Harvard Theological Review*, Vol. 35, pp.
        45-79.
1944.   Navaho witchcraft. *Peabody Museum of Harvard University,
        Papers*, Vol. 22, No. 2.
1947.   Some aspects of Navaho infancy and early childhood. *Psycho-
        analysis and the Social Sciences* (ed., Geza Roheim), Vol. 1,
        pp. 37-86.
1949.   The philosophy of the Navaho Indians. *Ideological Differences
        and World Order* (ed., F. S.C. Northrup), pp. 356-384.
1951.   Values and value orientations in the theory of action. *Toward
        a General Theory of Action* (eds., Talcott Parsons and Edward
        Shils), pp. 388-433.
Kluckhohn, Clyde, and Leighton, Dorothea
1946.   The Navaho. Cambridge, Mass.
Kluckhohn, Clyde, and Wyman, Leland C.
1940.   An introduction to Navaho Chant practice. *American Anthro-
        pological Association, Memoirs*, No. 53.
Kluckhohn, F.
1950.   Dominant and substitute profiles of cultural orientations: their
        significance for the analysis of social stratification. *Social
        Forces*, Vol. 28, pp. 376-393.
LaBarre, Weston
1948.   Folklore and psychology. *Journal of American Folklore*, Vol.
        61, pp. 382-390.
Leighton, Alexander H. and Leighton, Dorothea
1942.   Some types of uneasiness and fear in a Navaho Indian community.
        American Anthropologist, Vol. 44, pp. 194-210.
Leighton, Dorothea, and Kluckhohn, Clyde
1947.   Children of the People. Cambridge, Mass.
Lincoln, Jackson S.
1935.   The dream in primitive cultures. London.
Lindgren, E. J.
1933.   The collection and analysis of folklore. *The Study of Society*
        (eds., F. C. Bartlett, et al.), pp. 328-378.
Lowie, Robert H.
1908.   The test-theme in North American mythology. *Journal of
        American Folklore*, Vol. 21, pp. 97-148.
1942.   Studies of Plains Indian folklore. *University of California
        Publications in American Archaeology and Ethnology*, Vol. 40,
        No. 1, pp. 1-28.
Malinowski, Bronislaw
1925.   Magic, science and religion. *Science, Religion and Reality*
        (ed., J. Needham). (Reprinted in *Magic, Science and Religion*,
        1948, pp. 1-71.)
1926.   Myth in primitive psychology. London.
Matthews, Washington
1885.   The origin of the Utes, a Navajo myth. *American Antiquarian*,
        Vol. 7, pp. 271-274.
1887.   The Mountain Chant. *Bureau of American Ethnology, Fifth
        Annual Report*, pp. 379-467.

1889.   Noquoilpi, the gambler: a Navajo myth. *Journal of American Folklore*, Vol. 2, pp. 89-94.
1897.   Navaho legends. *American Folklore Society, Memoirs*, No. 5.
1902.   The Night Chant. *American Museum of Natural History, Memoirs*, Vol. 6. (Anthropology, Vol. 5).
1907.   Navaho myths, prayers and songs. *University of California Publications in American Archaeology and Ethnology*, Vol. 5. pp. 21-63.
McAllester, D. P.
1954.   Enemy Way music: a study of social and esthetic values as seen in Navaho music. *Peabody Museum of Harvard University, Papers*, Vol. 41, No. 3.
Milgroom, Berenice M.
1948.   The reflection of Zuni personality in Zuni mythology. Manuscript, 87 pp.; B.A. Honor's Thesis, Department of Social Relations, Harvard University.
Mills, G.
1953.   Navaho art and culture: a study of the relations among cultural premises, art styles, and art values. Manuscript. 462 pp. and appendices.
Morgan, William
1931.   Navaho treatment of sickness: diagnosticians. *American Anthropologist*, Vol. 33, pp. 390-402.
Murdock, George P., et al.
1950.   Outline of cultural materials. *Behavior Science Outlines*, Vol. 1.
Murray, Henry A.
1938.   Explorations in Personality. New York.
Newcomb, Franc J.
1940a. Origin legend of the Navjo Eagle Chant. *Journal of American Folklore*, Vol. 53, pp. 50-77.
1940b. Navajo omens and taboos. Santa Fe.
Newcomb, Franc J., and Reichard, Gladys A.
1937.   Sandpaintings of the Navajo Shooting Chant. New York.
Osgood, Cornelius
1933.   The ethnography of the Great Bear Lake Indians. *National Museum of Canada, Annual Report for 1931*, pp. 31-97.
1936.   Contributions to the ethnography of the Kutchin. *Yale University Publications in Anthropology*, No. 14.
1937.   The ethnography of the Tanaina. *Yale University Publications in Anthropology*, No. 16.
Parsons, Talcott
1949.   Essays in sociological theory, pure and applied. Glencoe, Illinois.
1950.   Psychoanalysis and the social structure. *Psychoanalytic Quarterly*, Vol. 19, pp. 371-384.
Pepper, George H.
1905.   An unusual Navajo medicine ceremony. Reprinted from the *Southern Workman* (Hampton Institute, Va.), pp. 1-10.
1908.   Ah-Jih-Lee-Hah-Neh. *Journal of American Folklore*, Vol. 21, pp. 178-183.
Radcliffe-Brown, A. R.
1922.   The Andaman Islanders. Cambridge
1934.   Sanction, Social. *Encyclopedia of the Social Sciences*, Vol. 13, pp. 531-534.

Radin, Paul
  1926.   Literary aspects of Winnebago mythology. *Journal of American Folklore*, Vol. 39, pp. 18-52.
  1933.   Method and theory of ethnology. New York.
Raglan, Lord
  1936.   The hero: a study in tradition, myth, and drama. London.
Reichard, Gladys A.
  1921.   Literary types and dissemination of myths. *Journal of American Folklore*, Vol. 34, pp. 269-307.
  1928.   Social life of the Navajo Indians. *Columbia University Contributions to Anthropology*, Vol. 7.
  1934.   Spider Woman; a story of Navajo weavers and chanters. New York.
  1939.   Navaho medicine man. New York.
  1944a.   The story of the Navajo Hail Chant. New York.
  1944b.   Prayer: the compulsive word. *American Ethnological Society, Monographs*, Vol. 7.
  1947.   Review of Kluckhohn, "Navaho Witchcraft." *Journal of American Folklore*, Vol. 60, pp. 90-92.
  1950.   Navaho religion: a study of symbolism. 2 vols. New York.
Roheim, Geza
  1950a.   The Oedipus complex, magic and culture. *Psychoanalysis and the Social Sciences* (ed., Geza Roheim), Vol. 2, pp. 173-228.
  1950b.   Psychoanalysis and anthropology. New York.
Sapir, Edward, and Hoijer, Harry
  1942.   Navaho texts, Iowa City.
Spencer, Katherine
  1947.   Reflection of social life in the Navaho origin myth. *University of New Mexico Publications in Anthropology*, No. 3.
Stevenson, James
  1891.   Ceremonial of Hasjelti Dailjis and mythical sand painting of the Navajo Indians. *Bureau of American Ethnology, Eighth Annual Report*, pp. 229-285.
Thompson, Stith
  1938.   The purpose and importance of an index of types and motifs. *Folk-liv*, No. 1, pp. 103-108.
Vogt, E. Z.
  1951.   Navaho Veterans: a study of changing values. *Peabody Museum of Harvard University, Papers*, Vol. 41, No. 1.
Waterman, T. T.
  1914.   The explanatory element in the folk-tales of the North American Indians. *Journal of American Folklore*, Vol. 27, pp. 1-54.
Wetherill, Louisa W.
  1952.   See Wyman, 1952.
Wetherill, Louisa W., and Cummings, Byron
  1922.   A Navaho folk tale of Pueblo Bonito. *American Archaeology*, Vol. 14, pp. 132-136.
Wheelwright, Mary C.
  1938.   Tleji or Yehbechai myth. *The House of Navajo Religion, Bulletin*, No. 1.
  1940.   Myth of Sontso (Big Star). *Museum of Navajo Ceremonial Art, Bulletin*, No. 2.

1945. Atsah or Eagle Catching Myth and Yohe or Bead Myth. *Museum of Navajo Ceremonial Art, Bulletin,* No. 3.

1946a. Hail Chant and Water Chant. *Navajo Religion Series,* Vol. 2.

1946b. Nilth Chiji Bakaji (Wind Chant) and Feather Chant. *Museum of Navajo Ceremonial Art, Bulletin,* No. 4.

1949. Emergence myth according to the Hanelthnayhe or Upward-Reaching Rite. *Navajo Religion Series,* Vol. 3.

1951. Myth of Mountain Chant and myth of Beauty Chant. *Museum of Navajo Ceremonial Art, Bulletin,* No. 5.

White, Ralph K.
1947. Black Boy: a value analysis. *Journal of Abnormal and Social Psychology,* Vol. 42, pp. 440-461.

Wittfogel, Karl A., and Goldfrank, Esther S.
1943. Some aspects of Pueblo mythology and society. *Journal of American Folklore,* Vol. 56, pp. 17-30.

Wolfenstein, Martha, and Leites, Nathan
1950. Movies: a psychological study. Glencoe, Illinois.

Wyman, Leland C.
1936a. Origin legends of Navaho divinatory rites. *Journal of American Folklore,* Vol. 49, pp. 134-142.

1936b. Navaho diagnosticians. *American Anthropologist,* Vol. 38, pp. 236-246.

1950. The religion of the Navaho Indians. *Forgotten Religions* (ed., Virgilius Ferm), pp. 341-361.

1952. The sandpaintings of the Kayenta Navaho: an analysis of the Louisa Wade Wetherill collection. *University of New Mexico Publications in Anthropology,* No. 7.

Wyman, Leland C., and Bailey, Flora
1943. Navaho Upward-Reaching Way: objective behavior, rationale, and sanction. *University of New Mexico Bulletin, Anthropological Series,* Vol. 4, No. 2.

1946. Navaho Striped Windway, an Injury-Way Chant. *Southwestern Journal of Anthropology,* Vol. 2, pp. 213-238.

Wyman, Leland C., and Kluckhohn, Clyde
1938. Navaho classification of their song ceremonials. *American Anthropological Association, Memoirs,* No. 50.